The Hoosier Mama

BOOK OF PIE

The Hoosier Mama

BOOK OF PIE
♥ DELUXE RECIPES ♥

By **PAULA HANEY**

with
ALLISON SCOTT

Printed in China.

Photo credits:
Dedication page and pages 14, 23, 37, 39, 40 (strawberry pie), 61, 68, 140, 180, 192, 196, 210, 214, 260, 278, 285, 290 (filling, forming, and crimping hand pies), 350, 351, 352 by Fourfried.com/Daniel & Marc Klutznick
Pages 8, 48, 122, 128, 248 by Rob Warner
Page 13 by Brian M. Heiser
Pages 17, 26, 27, 30, 31, 33, 35, 40, 43, 88, 89, 90, 168, 173 by Debbie Carlos
Pages 54, 56, 73, 158, 184, 212, 220, 236, 243, 274, 286, 290 (Allie and Avery Leavitt) by Brad Snyder
Pages 58, 110, 175, 188 by Dan Zemans
Pages 106 and 329 by Steve & Anne Truppe of trü studio

Design by DesignScout.

Library of Congress Cataloging-in-Publication Data

Haney, Paula.
   The Hoosier Mama book of pie : recipes, techniques, and wisdom from the Hoosier Mama Pie Co. / Paula Haney, with Allison Scott.
      pages cm
   Includes bibliographical references and index.
   ISBN 978-1-57284-143-7 (hardcover) -- ISBN 978-1-57284-719-4 (ebook)
1. Pies. 2. Hoosier Mama Pie Company (Chicago, Ill.) 3. Cooking--Indiana. I. Scott, Allison. II. Title.
TX773.H256 2013
641.59772--dc23
                              2013008711

10 9 8 7 6 5 4   14 15 16 17 18

Midway is an imprint of Agate Publishing. Agate books are available in bulk at discount prices.
For more information, go to agatepublishing.com.

FOR CRAIG, DASHIELL, AND ESME,
MY MOST ENTHUSIASTIC PIE TASTERS.

CONTENTS

WELCOME TO THE HOOSIER MAMA PIE COMPANY

When I unlocked the door there was already a line. It was March 14th, 2009, opening day at the Hoosier Mama Pie Company's new shop in the Ukrainian Village neighborhood of Chicago. After months of worrying if a bakery devoted to just one product could cover the rent, I had a new fear: Did I make enough pie?!

In two hours I had my answer: No way! We closed the shop, baked like crazy, and reopened. In an hour, the racks were empty again. Turns out I wasn't the only one craving a good slice of pie.

It had started out as a joke. My husband Craig and I made up a fictitious pie shop while I was the pastry chef at Trio, a fine dining restaurant just outside of Chicago. I was lucky enough to be working there when the owner brought in an unknown chef from California named Grant Achatz. For those who don't already know, Chef Achatz quickly set about reinventing American dining as we know it, earning Michelin stars and opening two acclaimed restaurants along the way. It was my small task to make desserts that kept up with his super-creative, boundary-pushing food. It was exhilarating and exhausting and on my days off, I went looking for the comfort of pie. Disappointed with what we found, Craig and I wondered what it would be like to open our own shop.

We wanted a place where you could sit down and have a slice of pie and a cup of coffee. Some-place where you could go to talk about the play you just saw, or read a book. But we also wanted it to be a place where pie was taken seriously. We would approach pie the same way I approached fine-dining desserts. We would use the best ingredients I could find, the best techniques I could learn, and no pie would make it onto the menu without multiple rounds of testing and tasting. The menu would change daily to reflect the best we could offer on any particular day.

At the end of that first day, my assistant Anne and I went home thrilled, but exhausted. I found out later that we both awoke in the middle of the night thinking the same thing, "Oh no, we have to do this again tomorrow!"

We quickly hired a dishwasher and two pie slingers to work the counter. Luckily, all three did a great job with little guidance while Anne and I interviewed baker after baker. The idea of a shop devoted to just pie was a new one, or, more precisely, an old one that had been forgotten, and it took a while to find good cooks who wanted to make the same unglamorous dessert day in and day out.

This wasn't always the case. In 1909, according to an article in the *Chicago Daily Tribune*, there were some 2,000 bakers making pies day and night for the growing city. In that year alone, according to the article, Chicago's 200,000 residents ate an astounding 70,000 pies a day.

In the early days of the 20th century, Chicago enjoyed at least a half-dozen pie companies, each with horse-drawn "pie wagons" that delivered to workmen's cottages and businessmen's clubs alike. In a 1911 advertisement in the *Chicago Loxias*, a local Ukrainian newspaper, the Case pie company boasted they could produce 14 pies a minute in their new "clean and sanitary" bakery. Sadly, by the late '80s most of the old pie bakeries were gone, and most pie was bought from the freezer case at the grocery store.

By 2009, the mention of a shop devoted to just pie brought blank stares. "You're going to make cupcakes, too, right?" was a frequent response. Several concerned and well-meaning chefs I knew offered to share some good cake recipes.

Why did pie fall from favor? Lives changed dramatically in the 20th-century United States. According to *The First Measured Century,* in 1900, most people lived in the country and made their living from farming. But just 40 years later, close to 60 percent of Americans lived in cities. City dwellers had access to restaurants and supermarkets. They didn't need to make a pie to use up the extra apples they had harvested or the green tomatoes that were left on the vine in the fall. They simply bought what they needed, when they needed it. Pie held on for a "citified" generation or two as mothers and later grandmothers cooked traditional recipes for their families, but folks soon forgot how great pie tastes at the end of a meal.

Because it no longer served a utilitarian purpose, pie became "old-fashioned." People wanted to try the "modern," sophisticated foods they saw in magazines or tasted on trips to Europe, as travel abroad was becoming faster and cheaper. While Americans strove for a new, more cosmopolitan lifestyle, pie became less and less popular.

Another factor is that making pie is a pain in the ass. You have to make the dough, peel the fruit, rest the dough, assemble the pie, and then bake it for an hour or more. As more and more women worked outside the home, fewer and fewer had time to spend an afternoon in the kitchen making a pie. In the professional kitchen, I know from experience that a single pie order can throw off the rhythm of an entire bakery. I can make 100 cupcakes in the time it takes to make a single apple pie. I knew that in order to be successful, I needed a bakery that ran on "pie time."

What do I mean by pie time? Well, at Hoosier Mama the mornings start with making dough, and then loading it into the cooler to rest while the pastry cream production begins. By late morning, the dough is pulled out of the cooler for rolling and to make room for chilling the completed pastry creams. Some of the dough gets rolled, crimped, and put in the freezer to set; some gets rolled into "doubles" for fruit pies. By early afternoon, the crimped shells are pulled from the freezer for blind baking, just in time to make room for the assembled fruit pies. Pie sets the rhythm of the kitchen and leaves little time for cakes or cookies.

We started out small, renting time and space in a shared-use commercial kitchen to test our plan. We sold pies at local farmers' markets and wholesale to coffee houses. We met some great farmers and started buying most of our produce directly from them. We baked seasonally, except for apple pie, which we offer year-round because, well, it's apple pie. It's bad enough turning down all the requests for cherry pie in December!

After much searching and many, many unreturned calls to leasing agents and realtors, we finally found a spot on Craigslist we thought might work. It was a hot-dog-stand-turned-egg-roll-shop in a 100-plus-year-old building on the edge of some trendy neighborhoods. We rudely cajoled friends and family into service. They painted the walls, laid the floor, and babysat our one-year-old twins. We moved into the kitchen three days before Thanksgiving (a bad idea!) and opened the pie shop four months later.

The place is tiny—55 feet long with a mere 8½ feet of storefront. There are eight seats in the "dining room." A vintage dresser-turned-front-counter marks the line between customer and kitchen. To our delight, one food writer dubbed it "comically small."

The kitchen holds one double-stacked convection oven, a 30-quart mixer, two freezers, three coolers, and a stainless steel prep table. The most important piece of equipment—the six-foot butcher block table where we make the pie dough and roll out pie shells—sits just inside the back door.

Despite the shop's challenging dimensions, by our fourth birthday, in 2013, we'd made more than 100,000 pies, all by hand. In that time, our customers have generously shared their own pie memories and even a few family recipes with us. It's obvious that pie holds a special place in our hearts, and while we have found that nearly everyone still loves a good piece of pie, fewer and fewer people feel confident making their own.

In the first half of the 20th century, pie knowledge was taken for granted. Pie recipes in cookbooks of the day often said things like, "make a pie crust in the usual manner," and gave only the barest instructions for pie fillings. Sadly, as Americans began to follow new food trends, and to look abroad for more sophisticated fare, pie making was forgotten. Lately, to my chagrin, pie itself has been dubbed a "trend," and even "the new cupcake." But I suggest that pie is too elemental to be trendy. Trends fade, but simple, seasonal food made from good ingredients should not.

We wrote this book to share what we have learned with everyone else out there who wants to make good pie—so that pie knowledge can once again be taken for granted but never again forgotten.

HOW TO USE THIS BOOK

Some folks like to use traditional cups and tablespoons when they are baking; others wouldn't think of following a recipe that wasn't measured out in grams. We've written all of the recipes in this book both ways: gram measurements appear in the right-hand column of the ingredients lists, while all other measurements are on the left. Simply choose the version you like best and read the ingredients from top to bottom. Occasionally an ingredient, like nutmeg, is too light to weigh. If no weight is listed in the gram column, use the volume measurement for that ingredient instead.

Whichever version you choose, be sure to read the recipe all the way through at least once before you start. No one wants to find out they are missing a crucial ingredient an hour before their guests arrive.

The baking times and temperatures in this book are for standard conventional ovens—the kind found in most home kitchens. If you have a convection oven, decrease the oven temperature by 50 degrees and decrease the cooking time by about 20 percent. Consider buying an oven thermometer. They cost a few dollars in most grocery stores and could save you some headaches. It is not unusual for even new high-end ovens to be off by 25 to 50 degrees.

Please keep in mind that all baking times are approximate. Ovens vary widely and all kinds of things, from the temperature of the ingredients you use to the weather, can affect baking times. All the recipes include a test besides time to determine if a pie is done. When in doubt, follow your nose! Most pies are the most aromatic right before they are done.

If you are new to pie baking, chess pies are a great place to start. They are some of the best pies around and no one needs to know how easy they are to make!

Most of all, have fun with these recipes and proceed with confidence. Historians tell us humans have been baking pies for two thousand years. If all of those folks can bake a pie, so can you!

LESSONS FROM THE ROLLING TABLE
The making, rolling, and handling of pie dough

I don't want to frighten anyone here, but making good pie dough is hard. It takes time and patience, and will almost certainly go awry on your first attempt or two. Ignore the seasoned pie maker who tells you dismissively that pie crust is easy. It may be easy for them—easy like driving a stick shift is easy after you've lurched and stalled around town for two weeks! Also ignore anyone who claims you need to possess "cold hands," "pie genes," or any other pie-making voodoo. All it really takes is practice. The good news is that just a little effort can make a great pie maker out of anyone who appreciates great pie.

I once took a summer off between jobs and devoted it entirely to making pie dough. Despite years of making pies at Christmas and Thanksgiving, and years in professional kitchens, I was only a so-so dough maker. Sometimes my pie crusts were so dry I could barely roll them out. Other times they were so

Pie maker Erica Taylor

wet that I had to scrape them off the kitchen counter with a metal spatula. Sometimes I resorted to store-bought pie crusts.

I felt like a fraud. Sure, I could make "fancy desserts" in a four-star restaurant, but what would my farm-raised aunts—women who began Sunday dinner preparations by strangling a chicken—say if they knew I couldn't make a decent pie crust?

It took most of the summer but I finally devised a recipe I was happy with. I wanted a crust that was flavorful, flaky, and worked with a range of sweet and savory fillings. I tested different flours, sweeteners, fats, and several kinds of salt. I read every old cookbook I could find. In the end, not surprisingly, it was the simplest ingredients and oldest techniques that worked best.

INGREDIENTS

FLOUR

At the pie shop, we use unbleached all-purpose flour from Heartland Mills, which is in Mariethal, Kansas. It fits the bill for us because it is both local and organic. We're also fans of King Arthur's Organic line and Ceresota, which is also sold as Heckers on the East Coast (Heckers and Ceresota are not organic). Really, any basic all-purpose flour should work so feel free to use your favorite brand, or experiment with a local mill if you are lucky enough to have one nearby. Just skip any flour that has been chemically bleached. The food additives used to bleach US flour were banned in Europe in the '90s due to health concerns. While there is no proof that bleached flour is harmful, it is unnecessary for pie dough. Flour's natural yellow-beige color is perfect for pie, so why add extra chemicals?

BUTTER

I was six years old when I tasted butter for the first time. I was in a chain restaurant in the mall near my house in Indianapolis. It was the '70s, and the restaurant had high-backed wicker chairs and mismatched art on the walls. I thought it was outrageously cool.

Our server, wearing a floor-length quilted skirt, left a basket of bread and butter on the table. I spread some butter on a piece of bread and took a bite, expecting the bland and oily margarine we ate at home. (Those were the days when we thought margarine was good for us.) Instead, the butter was sweet and creamy. It melted away in my mouth. My eyes opened wide. "What is this?" I asked. I finished off that basket of bread and one more before my mom made me stop. I convinced her to buy a pound of butter on the way home.

Actually, Mom didn't take much convincing. She grew up on a small family farm where they milked their own cows and churned their own butter to make money. Since they sold everything they made, they did not get to eat the butter themselves and so it became a special luxury.

For that reason, they almost never used butter in their pie crusts. They used lard from the hogs they raised or, later, vegetable shortening, which was cheaper and easier than rendering lard (or churning butter, for that matter).

A lot of folks think you have to use a vegetable shortening, like Crisco, to get a flaky crust. While vegetable shortening pretty much guarantees a flaky

CRISCO

Candle maker William Proctor and his brother-in-law, a soap maker named James Gamble, invented Crisco in 1907, but not as a food.

Both men needed large amounts of lard to manufacture their products. In the 1890s, a meatpacking monopoly kept the price of lard high. Searching for an alternative, they bought eight cottonseed mills in Mississippi and hired German Chemist E.C. Kayser to hydrogenate the cottonseed oil. The result was a fluffy, white, tasteless, and odorless fat that stayed solid at room temperature.

The invention was a success, but by then electric lights were replacing candles, and the two men went looking for a new market. If the new substance replaced lard in candles and soap, why not use it for cooking as well? In June of 1911, Crisco (The name is a mashup of "crystallized cottonseed") was launched.

Proctor and Gamble printed a cookbook in which all 615 recipes called for Crisco, and gave it away to housewives they lauded as "progressive" and "modern" for using their product. They held focus groups over tea, marketed specifically to Jewish households using kosher packaging, and, with rather tortured logic, told women their children would have good characters and their men would accomplish "big things" because Crisco promoted good digestion.

It was the first time a company set out to create demand for a product nobody knew they wanted, and it worked like a dream: in 2001, Proctor and Gamble sold Crisco, along with Jif peanut butter, to J.M. Smucker's for $813 million in stock.

crust, the result is flavorless and leaves a pasty aftertaste. Once you learn the technique for a flaky all-butter pie crust, it's no problem to make a flaky and flavorful crust every time. To me, it still tastes like a luxury.

My All-Butter Pie Dough (p. 24) calls for unsalted butter. Read the butter packaging very carefully to make sure you buy the right product. Until a few years ago, all unsalted butter was labeled simply "sweet cream," and salted butter was labeled "salted." Some brands still follow this convention. Others, however, dropped the "sweet cream" altogether and switched to "salted" and "unsalted" for clarity. To add to the confusion, some brands have very recently started labeling both salted and unsalted butter as "sweet cream," presumably because it sounds so delicious! So, now it is possible to buy salted or unsalted "sweet cream" butter. When all else fails, check the list of ingredients, but do not substitute. The amount of salt in salted butter varies widely from manufacturer to manufacturer, so substituting it for unsalted butter and then omitting any additional salt in the recipe almost never works!

VINEGAR

At the pie shop, we use red wine vinegar. I like the bright, earthy flavor, and the intense color leaves little doubt that you remembered to add it to your dough water! Apple cider vinegar and distilled white vinegar work fine too. Do not use balsamic.

SUGAR AND SALT

I like to add both salt and sugar to my pie dough, which some folks find odd—every time we publish the pie dough recipe we get calls and e-mails that question the decision.

Salty and sweet are essential flavors, whether you are cooking or baking. The best sweet pastry will taste flat and dull without just a hint of salt to stand up to the sweetness, and a savory dish may need a bit of sweetness to fully bring out all the savory flavors. If you taste raw pie dough on its own, it will seem slightly salty. I think the saltiness is a perfect foil to the sweetness of our dessert pies and the richness of our savory pies. A little sugar in the pie dough will melt and caramelize in the oven, helping the dough brown.

In the end, though, the choice is yours. The dough will still turn out without the sugar and you can cut back on the salt if the dough is too salty for your taste. All of our recipes are meant merely to be guides. Nothing would make us happier at Hoosier Mama than to know our recipes inspired you to write your own.

PIE WASH

Before we bake any of our sweet double-crust or chess pies, we like to brush the dough (see the photo on p. 89) with equal parts whole milk and cream, a mixture we've christened "Pie Wash." Before settling on Pie Wash, I experimented with all kinds of glazes and washes, from whole eggs to straight cream. I baked off a few "naked" pies for comparison. The egg wash made the pie super shiny and evenly brown, but looked too finished or "prissy" for my taste—and it made the crust too crunchy. The naked pie looked too amateur. The heavy cream browned nicely, but the large amount of butterfat made the crust too soft. Pie Wash gets it just right. There is enough butterfat in the mixture to make the outer layer of the crust tender, but not enough to compromise the flakiness. It gives a slight shine and bakes to a nice golden brown. It's also great for sticking pie dough cutouts and sugar to the top of the pies.

Simply mix equal parts whole milk and cream in a small bowl or liquid measuring cup. Give it a good stir or the cream will float on top of the mixture.

CRUST DUST

At the pie shop, we use lots of different techniques to keep our double-crust fruit pies from getting soggy bottom crusts. One of my favorites showed up in several vintage cookbooks I turned to for research. Mix equal parts all-purpose flour and granulated sugar, then lightly dust it across the bottom of the pie shell before adding the fruit filling (see the photo on p. 88). The flour thickens the

MEASURING SALT

All of the recipes in this book call for kosher salt. It doesn't have the bitterness of iodized table salt and it's great for bringing out the flavor in food without being overbearing.

Measuring kosher salt, however, can be tricky. Table salt is made up of fine grains that pack together tightly, while kosher has larger flakes that leave lots of empty space between. In fact, a teaspoon of table salt may contain up to twice as much salt as a teaspoon of kosher salt. To make matters more confusing, different brands of kosher salt have flakes of different shapes and sizes.

Your best bet is to measure salt by weight, preferably in grams since recipes often call for small amounts of salt. All salt is interchangeable by weight, so six grams of table salt (about a teaspoon) equals six grams of any brand of kosher salt. In case you don't have a scale handy, here are some general equivalents:

1T Morton's kosher salt = 1¹⁷⁄₂₀T Diamond Crystal kosher salt

---

1T table salt = 2¼T Diamond Crystal kosher salt or 1¼T Morton's kosher salt

---

I wrote the recipes in this book using Diamond Crystal kosher salt, for no other reason than it was the brand used in my first professional kitchen. All the volume measurements are accurate for that brand only—feel free to use any brand you like, and when in doubt, don't forget to taste!

fruit juices before they can seep into the crust, and the sugar keeps the flour from clumping. At the shop we call it "Crust Dust" and keep a one-quart container of it ready at all times. It turns up in most of our fruit pie recipes, so you might want to do the same. Crust Dust can be stored indefinitely in an airtight container at room temperature.

TRADITIONAL ALL-BUTTER PIE CRUST
TECHNIQUE

There are two things you must do to make a great and flaky all-butter pie crust and one thing you must not do.

First, you must mix the flour and butter so that small pieces of butter get coated in flour. This creates small pockets of butter in the dough. When you roll the dough, these pockets are flattened and stretched, creating thin sheets of butter surrounded by flour. When the dough is baked, the butter melts, leaving empty spaces between sheets of dough. Steam from both the moisture in the melting butter and the water in the dough separates the sheets and creates flakes.

Second, you must limit the growth of long gluten chains in the dough. Gluten is the protein in wheat flour that forms long stretchy strands when it

Perfect, flaky crust

is mixed with water. Some of these strands are essential; your dough would break apart without them. However, too many strands make the dough tough and hard to work with. To counteract this, we add a little vinegar to the cold water before mixing it into the pie dough. The acid in the vinegar helps cut the gluten strands down to a manageable size.

Third, you must not overwork the pie dough. Working the pie dough twists and tangles the gluten chains, making the dough tough and elastic. Perfectly fine pie dough can be ruined by overworking. This is also why we let the dough rest after kneading and rolling. Resting allows the gluten strands to relax, and makes the dough easier to roll and less likely to shrink in the pie tin. Be forewarned that no amount of resting will fix dough that has already been overworked.

All-Butter Pie Dough

This is the most important recipe at the pie shop. It is the secret to ninety percent of the pies we make, both sweet and savory. New bakers aren't considered full members of the pie team until they master it.

Ingredients

Makes one double-crust pie
or two single-crust pies

1¾ sticks	**unsalted butter, divided**	196g
1 Tablespoon	**red wine vinegar**	12g
½ cup (119mL)	**cold water**	118g
2¼ cups	**all-purpose flour**	333g
2¼ teaspoons	**kosher salt**	6.5g
½ Tablespoon	**granulated sugar**	6.5g

Once the dough is rested, it can be stored in the refrigerator for up to 3 days, or frozen for up to 1 week.

PIE TINS

At the pie shop we use disposable aluminum pie tins, a practical necessity I'm still not completely happy with. I prefer basic, old-fashioned, tinned-steel pie plates, but the returnable pie tin program we had early on failed spectacularly, as we ran through all our tinned steel pans in two weeks with only a handful of returns. I like the pans because they are relatively inexpensive (if you are not stocking a pie company!), transfer heat well, and produce a nicely browned bottom crust. Look for pans with generous rims to support a nice deep crimp. I haven't had much luck with nonstick versions; I usually end up scratching the finish.

We lightly coat our pie tins with canola-based cooking spray and dust them with flour, much like you would grease and flour a cake pan. Pie slices lift out easier, cleanup's faster, and some pies, like custards or chess pies, can be lifted out of the tins whole and transferred to prettier plates for serving.

1   Cut the butter into ½-inch (13-mm) cubes. Freeze 5 tablespoons (70g) for 20 minutes or overnight; chill the remaining 1⅛ sticks in the refrigerator until ready to use.

2   Stir the red wine vinegar into the cold water and set aside.

3   Combine the flour, salt, and sugar in the bowl of a food processor and pulse 5 or 6 times to combine.

4   Add the chilled butter and mix for 25 to 30 seconds, until the mixture resembles coarse meal.

5   Add the frozen butter and pulse 15 to 20 times, until the butter is in pea-sized pieces.

6   Add 6 tablespoons of the vinegar water and pulse 6 times. The dough should start to look crumbly. Test the dough by squeezing a small amount in the palm of your hand. If it easily holds together, it is done. If not, add ½ tablespoon of the vinegar water and pulse 3 more times. Repeat this process as needed until the dough holds together.

7   Transfer the dough to a lightly floured work surface and knead together until smooth; dough should never come together in the food processor.

8   Divide the dough into 2 equal parts and roll each into a ball. Flatten the balls slightly and wrap separately in plastic wrap. Let the dough rest in the refrigerator until ready to use, at least 20 minutes but preferably overnight.

THYME DOUGH VARIATION

We use thyme dough for our Chicken Pot Pie (p. 262), because thyme and chicken taste great together. The flecks of thyme make an attractive crust and with so many different pies at the shop, it helps us tell them apart! Simply take ¾ teaspoon (about 4 sprigs or .75g) of fresh thyme, remove and discard the stems, and roughly chop the leaves. Add it to the food processor along with the other dry ingredients in step 3. You can also try mixing in another herb like sage, or a spice like freshly ground black pepper.

Top, left to right: Cubed butter; cutting the butter into the dry ingredients.
Middle, left to right: The dough after adding the chilled butter;
the dough after adding the frozen butter.
Bottom, left to right: Water and red wine vinegar; dough that is too dry.

Top, left to right: Dough that is too wet; dough that is just right!
Middle, left to right: Kneading the dough together.
Bottom, left to right: Kneading the dough; a ball of smooth, kneaded dough.

THIS IS HOW WE ROLL!

The trick to rolling pie dough quickly and easily is making sure it is both properly rested and at the perfect temperature before you roll it out. Dough that is too cold will crack. Dough that is too warm will stick to your rolling pin and tear. The sooner you admit that the dough is in charge and plan your schedule accordingly, the happier you will be!

For best results, the dough should be slightly cooler than room temperature. Try taking the dough out of the refrigerator 30 to 45 minutes before you plan to roll it out. The dough is ready when you can press the heel of your hand halfway into the dough by applying medium pressure. It should still feel slightly cool to the touch. Be prepared to spend some time moving the dough in and out of the refrigerator until you get it just right. Just be careful not to let the dough get so warm that the butter starts to melt, ruining your carefully constructed butter pockets. I know it hurts to start over, but if you lose the butter pockets you can't get them back. If the surface of the dough looks shiny or feels oily, it's time to start over with new dough.

Just like people, dough responds best if it is well rested! If at all possible, let the dough rest overnight before rolling it out, at least for your first few batches. That way, the gluten will be relaxed and the dough won't spring back as you try to shape it.

Rolled dough rounds can be stored in the refrigerator for up to 6 hours uncovered. A dough round that has been pressed into a pie tin can be stored loosely wrapped in plastic wrap, or tied up in a plastic bag, for up to 3 days. If you are storing multiple pie shells, be sure to place a sheet of parchment or wax paper between them to prevent them from sticking together. Scrap dough can be wrapped in plastic wrap and stored in the refrigerator for 2 days, or frozen for up to 1 week.

ROLLING STEPS

1 Liberally dust your rolling surface with flour and keep a container of flour nearby.

2 Place a ball of dough on the rolling surface and flatten it halfway with the heel of your hand.

3 Rub a handful of flour over your rolling pin and pound the dough until it is half as thick as when you started. Don't be timid; it takes more aggression than you think! Pounding the dough flattens it without working the gluten very much and softens it up for the finish rolling you are about to do.

4 Rub more flour over the rolling pin and, working out from the center; make long passes over the dough. Rotate the dough 1 to 2 inches (2.5–5cm) after each pass, to make sure it isn't sticking to the table and to help form an even circle. If the dough starts to stick, lift up one corner and scatter more flour underneath. Rub flour on the rolling pin as needed to keep it from sticking to the dough.

5 Keep rolling until the dough is ¹⁄₁₆ to ⅛ inch (1.5–3mm) thick and is a sufficient size to cut out a circle with a 14-inch (35-cm) diameter (16 inches or 40cm for a lattice-topped pie).

6 Cut a 14-inch (35-cm) circle out of the dough. At the pie shop, we use a series of commercial pizza pans as guides. At home, a pot lid, plate, or bowl works just as well. Place your guide in the middle of the dough and gently cut around it with a bench scraper or paring knife. (Just be careful not to press so hard that you cut your countertops!)

7 Lightly coat a 9-inch (22.5-cm) pie tin with cooking spray and dust with flour. Rotate the tin to coat the side. Turn the tin over and tap out any excess flour.

8 Pick the dough circle up firmly by the edges and center onto the prepared pie tin. Tap the pie tin on the counter several times until the dough settles into it. Gently press the dough into the corners of the pie tin with your fingertips.

9 If you are making a single-crust pie (p. 32) or a lattice-topped pie (p. 42), proceed to the appropriate crimping and finishing instructions. If you are making a double-crust pie, set the pie tin aside while you roll another 14-inch (35-cm) dough round for the top crust. Proceed according to the individual pie recipe before crimping and finishing.

10 Gather up any leftover dough and knead it into a ball to use for Pie Crust Cookies (p. 309), or to help make shingles and lattice. Scrap dough will need to rest for at least 20 minutes before it can be rolled out again.

Top left: To roll the dough, start by pressing with your hands.

Top right: Pound flat with a rolling pin.

Bottom left: Roll from the center in one sweeping pass.

Bottom right: Rotate 1 to 2 inches after each roll.

Top left: Roll until the dough is the right size and thickness for your pie.

Top right: Center the guide.

Bottom left: Cut around the guide to form a round.

Bottom right: Press the dough into the pie tin to make a pie shell.

A pie is defined by its crust. Now that you know how to make pie dough, it is time to talk about what kind of pie you will make: a single-crust, double-crust, lattice-top, or shingle-top pie.

SINGLE-CRUST PIES

A single-crust pie is just that: a pie with a single crust lining the bottom of the pie tin and no dough on top of the filling. They are typically used for open-faced fruit pies, shingle-top pies, crumble-top pies, creams, custards, and quiches.

After you have rolled out and pressed your single dough round into a pie tin, you'll need to finish it with a crimp, or decorative edge. Pretty and functional, the crimp adds height to help contain the pie filling.

TRADITIONAL CRIMP

1 Gently roll the edges of the pie dough under, with your thumb and index finger resting the rolled edge on the rim of the tin. Be careful not to pull the dough up out of the pie tin as you go. This will cause the shell to sink back into the tin as it bakes and leave you with a too-short pie crust.

2 Once the edge is rolled under, work your way back around the pie tin, pinching the rolled edge up with your thumb while pressing the dough into the tin with your fingertips.

3 Grab the edge of the pie shell with the thumb and index finger of each hand, about an inch (2.5cm) apart. Bring your right hand toward you and to the left as you push your left hand away from you and to the right. Place your left hand ½ inch (13mm) to the right of the first crimp and repeat the process until you have worked your way around the pie shell.

4 Place your index finger behind each crimp and squeeze the point on the outside of the pie shell with your thumb and index finger. Because our pie dough is all butter, and butter softens and melts so quickly in the oven, it is important to start with as sharp and well-defined a crimp as possible.

5 Place the crimped pie shell in the refrigerator to rest for at least 20 minutes, then transfer to the freezer for 20 minutes to overnight.

The crimped pie dough can be stored in the freezer, uncovered for 3 days. Gently wrap in plastic wrap or tie up in a plastic bag to store frozen for up to 1 week.

Top left: Roll the edges of the pie dough under.
Top right: Bring your right hand toward you and to the left as you push your left hand away from you and to the right.
Bottom left: Place your index finger behind the crimp and squeeze the point on the outside of the pie shell.
Bottom right: Napkin folds.

BLIND BAKING

Blind baking is a funny-sounding term that simply means baking a pie shell prior to filling it. Though it has been a part of kitchen-speak for centuries, no one has any idea where the term came from. Lately, "pre-baking" has taken its place in contemporary recipes, and while it is certainly more descriptive, at Hoosier Mama we prefer the traditional term. Use "blind baking" confidently in a sentence and you get automatic membership in the secret society of pie makers!

Blind baking is used for pies like Chocolate Cream (p. 141), where the filling is not cooked in the pie shell, and for quiches and some custards, where the shell needs to bake longer than the filling. We also blind bake the shells for pies like Pumpkin (p. 149) or Hoosier Sugar Cream (p. 171), where the pie filling bakes for up to an hour in the pie shell. We find it keeps the bottom crust from getting soggy.

In blind baking, pie shells are lined with parchment paper and filled with weights to keep air pockets from forming as the shells bake. You can buy ceramic weights or stainless steel "pie chains" at specialty cooking stores, but dried pinto beans are inexpensive and work just as well. At the shop, we line the shells with 13x5-inch (32.5x12.5-cm) coffee filters instead of parchment paper; they fit the 9-inch (22.5-cm) crimps perfectly and let air flow through to the bottom crust. Don't use foil or wax paper; foil blocks airflow, resulting in a tough, dense bottom crust, and the coating on wax paper will burn and smoke in a hot oven.

1   Preheat the oven to 400°F (200°C).

2   Place a frozen, crimped pie shell on a baking sheet. Line the inside of the shell with parchment paper or a coffee filter. Fill with uncooked beans until the beans are even with the top edge of the crimp. Press down on the beans to make sure they spread to the edges of the shell.

3   Bake for 20 minutes, rotating 180 degrees halfway through. The outer edge of the crimp should be dry and golden brown.

4   Remove the shell from the oven and carefully remove the parchment paper/coffee filter full of beans. If the paper sticks to the pie, bake it for 3 more minutes and try again. Once the parchment paper or coffee filter is removed, prick the bottom of the shell all over with a fork. Bake for 3 more minutes, until the interior of the shell is dry and light golden brown.

We use large coffee filters filled with dried pinto beans to blind bake.

NAPKIN FOLD

Napkin-fold pie shells are pretty and quick. They work best for single-crust pies that don't require blind-baked pie crusts. We use this style on all our chess pies; we adopted the technique after seeing and tasting some wonderful chess pies at Dangerously Delicious Pies in Baltimore, Maryland, which is definitely worth a pie road trip!

1 Grab the edge of the pie dough between the thumb and index finger of your right hand. Be careful not to pull the dough up out of the pie tin as you work.

2 Gently fold a ½- to 1-inch (13mm–2.5cm) section of dough over so it points toward the center of the pie shell. Place your left thumb on top of the first fold.

3 Grab a second ½- to 1-inch (13mm–2.5cm) piece of pie dough between your thumb and index finger, next to the first fold, and gently fold it over like the first piece. Repeat this process all the way around the pie. The more folds you make, the rounder your pie shell will be, but large folds look appealingly rustic.

4 When you are finished with the folds, tap the pie tin against the counter several times. If the pie dough falls down into the pie tin, or unfolds and falls off the rim of the pie tin, unfold that section of dough and make adjustments. If the pie shell holds its shape, gently press the folds down onto the rim of the pie tin.

5 Place the finished napkin-fold pie shell in the refrigerator to rest for at least 20 minutes before use. Well-rested shells hold their shape the best.

Napkin-fold pie shells can be stored in the refrigerator, uncovered, for up to 2 days, or wrapped and frozen for 1 week.

SHINGLE TOP

A shingle-top pie has overlapping, or shingled, dough cutouts directly on top of the pie filling. This makes a beautiful pie, but be forewarned: it is very time-consuming. We chose this top for our Pear Pie (p. 98) because pear desserts are typically slow sellers (to the frustration of pastry chefs everywhere), and we reasoned that we could afford to spend extra time on the few we do make. Turns out our customers love it as much as we do, and every pear season we cut thousands of 2-inch (5-cm) fluted circles for shingling.

1 Roll 1 ball of dough according to the rolling instructions (p. 29). Punch out dough circles approximately 2 inches (5cm) in diameter. Reroll the scrap dough to make more shingles (you will need about 30 to top a pie).

2 Brush the top of the pie shell's crimp with Pie Wash (p. 21).

3 Place the first circle, or cutout, on the pie so that ⅛ to ¼ of an inch (3–6mm) extends past the crimp. Place the second circle on the pie so it overlaps the first circle by ⅛ to ¼ of an inch (3–6mm). Continue layering the cutouts in concentric circles until the pie is covered.

4 Finish according to the recipe instructions.

DOUBLE-CRUST PIES

A double-crust pie has both a top crust and a bottom crust. The two crusts are then sealed together around the pie filling. From medieval times all the way until colonial America, these crusts were referred to as "coffins" or "coffyns." Not surprisingly, this term eventually fell out of favor and "double crust" took its place.

Though we make more than thirty sweet and savory double-crust pie varieties at the shop, each one looks different. Sometimes the difference is out of necessity; a blueberry pie, for example, is too juicy for a full double crust. It needs a lattice top so the fruit juices can bubble up through the open spaces without swamping the top crust. Peach pies also need room for fruit juices to simmer, but the delicate fruit can scorch when left exposed in an open-weave lattice top. So, for peach, we either make a tighter lattice, or we use small cookie cutters to cut decorative holes in the top crust that let the peach juices bubble up but still leave most of the fruit protected.

Sometimes the difference is intentional. It would be a shame to hide the wonderful color of a cherry pie under a full double crust, so we finish it with an open-weave lattice that lets the deep red fruit shine through.

For pies like apple and apple-quince, or strawberry and strawberry-rhubarb, which could easily look identical, we use different cookie cutters to cut shapes out of scrap dough, which we then appliqué to the top of the pies. Simply brush the top of the pie with Pie Wash and place the shapes wherever you like.

This was a fine idea in the beginning and it makes for a very pretty pie. However, it's become a running joke in the pie shop, as we struggle to keep oak leaves (apple pie), willow leaves (apple, honey, and currant pie), red oak leaves (apple-quince pie), and a slew of other leaf, flower, geometric, and even barnyard animal (for savory pies!) shapes straight.

TRADITIONAL DOUBLE-CRUST CRIMP

1   Start with a pie shell full of filling. Gently smooth the top of the filling with a spatula. The filling doesn't have to be perfectly flat, but any pointy pieces of fruit that stick up may tear the top crust. If the pie base and top have been stored in the refrigerator, let them warm up enough to be pliable before you begin.

2   If you are cutting decorative shapes out of the top crust, do it now. Try to keep the cutouts toward the center of the top crust. Otherwise, they will get pulled into the crimp and stretched out of shape.

3   Center the top pie dough round over the pie. Line up the edges of the top and bottom crust and gently roll them under with your thumb and index finger. Work your way back around the pie, pinching the rolled edge up. Make sure the edge is resting on the rim of the pie tin.

4   Grab the edge of the pie shell with the thumb and index finger of each hand, about 1 inch (2.5cm) apart. Bring your right hand toward you and to the left as you push your left hand away from you and to the right.

5   Place your left hand ½ inch (13mm) to the right of the first crimp and repeat the process until you have worked your way around the pie shell. Place your index finger behind each crimp and squeeze the point on the outside of the pie shell with your thumb and index finger.

6   Vent the pie, then finish according to the recipe instructions.

Long before the shop opens, Janice Allen makes dough and bakes off the day's fruit pies.

Top left: To crimp a double-crust pie, roll the bottom
crust and top crust edges together and under.
Top right: Pinch up the edges.
Bottom left: Form the crimps.
Bottom right: Dough cutouts on a strawberry pie.

FORK CRIMP

A fork crimp is an easy and nicely rustic way to finish a double-crust or lattice-topped pie. It works best with pies whose filling doesn't mound up out of the pie shell—in other words, pies where the filling keeps a generally flat profile. We use it for cherry, funeral, and mincemeat pies, as well as any other pies for which a tall crimp might make the pie look scrawny. It is also nice if you want to cut back a little on the amount of crust. We use it a lot on savory pies so the fillings can have top billing. It doesn't work well for extra-juicy pies like blueberry or peach, where the fruit can spill over the low edge as it bakes.

1 Perform steps 1 through 3 of the traditional double-crust crimp instructions. Once the pie dough is rolled under, run your hand around the outside or the pie, pressing any dough that spills over the edge back onto the pie tin.

2 Hold the fork perpendicular against the side of the pie tin and rock the tines of the fork down onto the edge of the pie. This helps keep the edge of the pie even with the edge of the pie tin. You can make your fork marks side by side as you work your way around the pie, or leave a bit of space in between crimps. Make sure you press hard enough to seal the two layers of dough together.

3 Vent the pie, then finish according to the recipe instructions.

Feel free to experiment with other utensils, like the tip of a spoon, a Popsicle stick, or the decorative handle of Grandma's silver that might make an interesting design.

VENTS

If you are not cutting decorative shapes in the top of the pie you will need another way to let the steam escape as the pie bakes. Three or four simple slits in the top crust will do the trick, although pie bakers have used the vents as decoration for centuries, coming up with all kinds of pretty patterns. Feel free to get creative! At the pie shop we use the vents as guides to easily slice the pies into six pieces later.

CHEATER'S LATTICE TOP

Lattice-topped pies are some of the prettiest pies in the pie case. Weaving lattice is time-consuming if you are making more than one or two pies, and nearly impossible when the temperature in the pie shop hits 80 and 90 degrees. Years ago, an assistant at Trio taught me her mother's trick for fast and lovely lattice. She doesn't weave strips of dough, but simply alternates them across the top of the pie. Most people won't notice the difference—and if they do, you can point out how cool the slightly asymmetrical lines look.

1   Roll 1 ball of dough between ⅛ and ¼ of an inch (3–6mm) thick. Using a fluted pastry wheel or pizza cutter, cut strips of dough that are ½- to ¾-inch (13–19mm) wide by about 1 foot (30cm) long. It's OK if you end up with some shorter pieces; you can use those at the top or bottom of the pie. You will need 10 strips per pie for an open lattice and 12 to 14 for a tighter lattice.

2   Place a 16-inch (40-mm) round of pie dough in a prepared 9-inch (22.5-cm) pie tin. Fill according to the recipe you are following. Smooth the top with a spatula.

3   Take the shortest strip of lattice and place it vertically down the left-hand edge of the pie. Place a second piece of lattice horizontally across the top edge of the pie, overlapping the first lattice strip in the upper left-hand corner of the pie. Continue alternating vertical and horizontal lattice strips until the pie is covered. Trim the ends of the lattice strips so they are even with the edge of the bottom pie crust.

4   Take 1 lattice strip and the edge of the bottom pie crust between your thumb and index finger and gently roll the dough under, until it rests on the rim of the pie tin. Be careful not to pull the dough up out of the pie tin, as this will make your pie sink down too low.

5   Work your way around the pie until all of the lattice is rolled under. Finish with a traditional or fork crimp (p. 41).

6   Finish the pie according to the recipe instructions.

PREP NOTE   *For an extra-fancy pie, decorate the lattice with pastry cutouts.*

Top left: Cut lattice with a fluted pastry wheel.

Top right: Alternate vertical and horizontal lattice strips.

Bottom left: Finishing a lattice-top pie.

Bottom right: Floury hands keep the dough from sticking.

CRUMB SHELLS

Crumb-shell pies are the shortest distance between you and pie. The simplest versions are a mixture of melted butter, sugar, and cookie or graham cracker crumbs. The shells freeze well and are great to keep on hand in case pie cravings strike.

At the pie shop, we've developed specific shells for specific pies, but feel free to mix and match them.

THE HOOSIER MAMA CRUMB SHELL METHOD

1 Lightly brush a 9-inch (22.5-cm) pie tin with melted butter.

2 Place the crumb mixture in the pie tin and press it firmly into an even layer across the bottom and up the side of the pie tin.

3 Place a second 9-inch (22.5-cm) disposable aluminum pie tin directly on top of the crumb mixture. Press firmly on the bottom of the pie tin, working your way out from the center so that you smooth the crumbs from the center of the pie tin toward the side.

4 Work your way around the tin, starting where the bottom of the tin meets the side and working your way up. Some of the crumb mixture will be pushed up over the edge of the first tin. Press it back down around the top of the disposable pie tin. This will form a rim.

5 Remove the second pie tin and fill in any bare or thin spots. Use the second pie tin to tamp down your patches.

6 Place the finished shell on a baking sheet and bake at 350°F (180°C) for 6 minutes. Do not overbake. Allow the shell to cool slightly before filling.

The unbaked pie shell can be stored in the freezer, tightly wrapped, for up to 2 weeks, or in the refrigerator for up to 3 days. The baked shell can be stored at room temperature for up to 2 days—do not refrigerate. We've found that crumb shells freeze best if they are unbaked. Shells that are baked and then frozen end up hard and crumbly.

Gingersnap Crumb Crust

You can use homemade or store-bought gingersnaps

to make this shell. If you are using homemade, be sure to let them dry out a bit before grinding them into crumbs.

Ingredients

Makes one 9-inch (22.5-cm) pie shell

1 cup	**gingersnap cookie crumbs**	150g
2 Tablespoons	**granulated sugar**	25g
3 Tablespoons	**unsalted butter, melted**	42g

1. In a medium bowl, combine the dry ingredients (gingersnap crumbs and sugar).

2. Pour in the melted butter.

3. Rub the butter into the crumbs with your fingers, until the mixture holds together when a small amount is squeezed in the palm of your hand.

4. Finish as directed in the crumb-shell instructions (p. 44).

 **PREP NOTE** *You can make gingersnap crumbs without a food processor by placing the cookies in a freezer bag and then crushing with a rolling pin.*

VARIATIONS

Follow the steps on page 45, using the ingredients as listed for each shell type.

GRAHAM CRACKER CRUMB CRUST

1 cup	**graham cracker crumbs (about 8 graham crackers)**	132g
2 Tablespoons	**granulated sugar**	26g
3 Tablespoons	**unsalted butter, melted**	42g

GRAHAM–PECAN CRUMB CRUST

1 cup plus 2 Tablespoons	**graham cracker crumbs (about 8 graham crackers)**	148g
¾ cup	**chopped toasted pecans (sidebar p. 105)**	94g
2 Tablespoons	**dark brown sugar**	30g
2 Tablespoons	**all-purpose flour**	18g
¼ teaspoon	**ground nutmeg**	1g
Pinch	**kosher salt**	
7 Tablespoons	**unsalted butter, melted**	98g

GRAHAM, PEANUT, AND PRETZEL CRUMB CRUST

1 cup plus 2 Tablespoons	**graham cracker crumbs (about 8 graham crackers)**	148g
¾ cup	**roughly ground pretzels**	30g
¼ cup	**roughly ground salted dry roasted peanuts**	30g
2 Tablespoons	**dark brown sugar**	30g
2 Tablespoons	**all-purpose flour**	18g
Pinch	**kosher salt**	
9 Tablespoons	**unsalted butter, melted**	126g

CHOCOLATE WAFER CRUMB CRUST

2 cups	**Chocolate Wafer crumbs (recipe p. 304)**	380g
2 Tablespoons	**granulated sugar**	25g
2 Tablespoons	**cocoa powder**	12g
2 Tablespoons	**all-purpose flour**	18g
3 Tablespoons	**unsalted butter, melted**	42g

Additional Dough Recipes

PEPPERY CORNMEAL DOUGH

We use this dough for our Chicken Tomatillo Pie (p. 244). Roll it out as you would the All-Butter Pie Dough, but keep it a little thicker—about ¼ thick (6mm) instead of ¹⁄₁₆ to ⅛ inch (1.5–3mm).

Ingredients

Makes enough dough for one double-crust pie

2 sticks	**very cold unsalted butter**	224g
1 Tablespoon	**red wine vinegar**	12g
7 Tablespoons (103.5mL)	**cold water**	108g
2 cups	**all-purpose flour**	296g
1 cup	**yellow cornmeal**	170g
1½ teaspoons	**kosher salt**	4.5g
1 teaspoon	**granulated sugar**	5.5g
½ teaspoon	**freshly ground white pepper**	1.5g
¼–½ teaspoon	**sweet paprika**	1.5g

1 Cut the butter into ½-inch (13-mm) cubes.

2 Stir the red wine vinegar into the cold water and set aside.

3 Combine the flour, cornmeal, salt, sugar, and white pepper in the bowl of a food processor and pulse a few times to combine.

4 Add the butter and pulse 8 to 10 times, until ingredients start to look sandy.

5 Add the vinegar water and pulse an additional 4 to 5 times, or until the ingredients just start to come together.

6 Turn the dough out onto a lightly floured surface. Sprinkle with the sweet paprika and gently knead the dough together; dough should never come together in the food processor.

7 Divide the dough into 2 equal balls and wrap separately in plastic wrap. Let the dough rest in the refrigerator until ready to use, at least 20 minutes.

HONEY CORNMEAL DOUGH VARIATION

We use this dough for our Ham and Bean Pie (p. 271). Follow the instructions on page 47, omitting the white pepper and paprika and adding ¼ cup (80g) of honey to the food processor along with the butter in step 4.

Once the dough is rested, it can be stored in the refrigerator for 1 day. Do not freeze.

Once rolled out, the dough should be used immediately; do not chill, as it is prone to drying out and crumbling. Cornmeal crusts work best with a fork crimp (p. 41).

FRITO CRUMB CRUST

This is the crust for our Frito–Chili Pie (p. 253). A couple of single-serving (2-ounce) bags of corn chips can make the crumb shells, with some left over for garnish. If, like us, you cannot resist snacking, go for the big bag at the supermarket.

 *Ingredients*

Makes four 6-inch (15-cm) shells

1 Tablespoon	**red wine vinegar**	12g		½ teaspoon	**granulated sugar**	2.75g
½ cup (119mL)	**cold water**	118g		¼ teaspoon	**freshly ground black pepper**	.5g
3 ounces	**Fritos® corn chips, divided**	85g		1 stick	**cold unsalted butter, cut into cubes**	112g
1 cup	**all-purpose flour**	148g		1 ounce	**shredded sharp Cheddar cheese**	28g
¾ cup	**yellow cornmeal**	103g				
1 Tablespoon	**kosher salt**	9g				

1 Stir the red wine vinegar into the cold water and set aside.

2 Place 2 ounces (57g) of the corn chips in the bowl of a food processor. Pulse until the corn chips form uniform, small crumbs, about 30 seconds. This should make approximately ½ cup of crumbs.

3 Add the flour, cornmeal, salt, sugar, and black pepper and pulse 2 to 3 more times to bring the ingredients together.

4 Add the cubed butter and continue to pulse just until sandy, about 20 to 30 seconds.

5 Break up 1 ounce (28g) of the corn chips with your fingers, slightly smashing the chips into smaller pieces. Add the slightly smashed corn chips and shredded cheese to the food processor and pulse 2 to 3 times.

6 Add ¼ cup (59mL) of vinegar water and pulse 2 to 3 more times. Squeeze a handful of dough in your palm. If it holds its shape, it is ready. If it crumbles and does not hold together, add more vinegar water, 1 tablespoon at a time, until the the crumbs come together when squeezed.

Next page

FRITO CRUMB CRUST

Continued

7 Butter 4 6-inch (15-cm) pie tins. Divide the crumbs evenly into the pie tins. Press the crumbs uniformly along the bottoms and sides of the tins. It is helpful to use another pie tin to press the crumbs down firmly, but a measuring cup will also work.

8 Preheat the oven to 375°F (190°C).

9 Bake the shells for 10 minutes. Prick each shell all over with a fork and bake 8 to 10 more minutes, until the shells are crisp, but not browned.

The unbaked shells can be stored in the freezer, tightly wrapped, for up to 2 weeks, or in the refrigerator for up to 3 days. The baked shells can be stored at room temperature for up to 2 days—do not refrigerate.

You can make corn chip crumbs without a food processor by placing the corn chips in a freezer bag and then crushing with a rolling pin. Stir the crumbs and other dry ingredients together, rub the butter into the dry ingredients, and then fold in the Cheddar cheese and 1 ounce (28g) of smashed corn chips. Add the vinegar water until the dough holds together.

CREAM CHEESE DOUGH

We use this melt-in-your-mouth dough for both our sweet turnovers and our savory hand pies. It is far too delicate to hold its shape in a pie shell, but it is perfect for snack-sized pastries. Large amounts of butter and cream cheese make it wonderfully tender and a little fussy to work with. Once again, the key to success is keeping the dough at just the right temperature. If it is too cold, the dough will crack and break when you try to bend and work it. Too warm and it becomes a melty mess incapable of holding its shape and unable to contain the weight of the filling. If you work quickly and methodically, you will find the ideal dough temperature and master this process.

At the shop, we store precut circles of dough in the freezer and take out a half dozen or so at a time. If the rounds are too cold to work with, we warm them between our hands for a few seconds.

Ingredients

Makes enough dough for 24
hand pies or turnovers

2 cups	**all-purpose flour**	296g
1 (8-ounce) package	**cream cheese, cut into 1-inch (2.5-cm) cubes**	226g
2 sticks	**unsalted butter, cut into ½-inch (13-mm) cubes**	224g
½ teaspoon	**granulated sugar**	2g
1 teaspoon	**kosher salt**	3g

1 Combine all the ingredients in the bowl of a stand mixer fitted with the paddle attachment. Using your hands, coat the butter and cream cheese cubes in flour. Pulse the mixer on and off until most of the butter and cream cheese is reduced to the size of peas. Place a dishtowel or a piece of plastic wrap around the mixer so the dough cannot escape. Turn the mixer to High and mix for 30 seconds, or until the dough comes together in 1 or 2 chunks.

2 Lightly dust a work surface with flour. Remove the dough from the mixer and knead into 2 smooth balls; flatten balls into discs and wrap in plastic wrap. Let the dough rest in the refrigerator overnight before rolling.

ROLLING CREAM CHEESE DOUGH

1 Take the dough out of the refrigerator and let stand at room temperature for 5 to 10 minutes. Dough should feel cool, but not cold.

2 Generously dust the work surface and rolling pin with flour. Roll the dough out so it is ⅛ inch (3mm) thick. Using a round pastry cutter or jar lid, punch out 4- to 5-inch (10–12.5-cm) diameter circles of dough.

3 Transfer the circles to a baking sheet lined with parchment paper, using additional parchment in between layers if you are stacking them. Let the dough rest in the refrigerator for at least 30 minutes before filling.

4 Gather up any leftover dough scraps and knead into a ball. Flatten the ball into a disc and let it rest in the refrigerator for 30 minutes.

5 Reroll the scrap dough and punch out more circles. Dough may be rerolled once.

The rested dough, filled or unfilled, can be stored in the refrigerator for up to 3 days. It can be stored in the freezer, tightly wrapped, for up to 2 weeks.

DOUGH CHEAT SHEET

IF THE RECIPE CALLS FOR ...

1 single-crust All-Butter Pie Dough shell

Roll out 1 ball of dough

Place one 14-inch (35-cm) dough round (16 inches [40cm] for lattice) into a pie tin that has been sprayed with cooking spray and dusted with flour

This is now your pie shell

Finish with a traditional crimp (p. 32)

Cream Cheese Dough circles

Follow the Cream Cheese Dough recipe and rolling instructions (p. 51)

Finish according to hand pie or turnover assembling and baking instructions, depending on which one you're making.

1 double-crust shell

(All-Butter Pie Dough, Thyme Dough, Peppery or Honey Cornmeal Dough)

Roll out 2 balls of dough

Place one 14" dough round into a pie tin that has been sprayed with cooking spray and dusted with flour

This is now your pie shell

When the filling is in the pie shell, center the second 14-inch pie dough round on top of it

Finish with a traditional or a fork crimp

Cut 4–6 vents to let steam escape

1 single-crust, blind-baked All-Butter Pie Dough shell

Follow instructions for single crust, then blind bake according to instructions on p. 34

Lattice strips

Roll out 1 ball of dough

Cut strips ½- to ¾-inch (13–19mm) wide by about 1 foot (30cm) long. Roll scrap dough if you need more lattice strips

After the filling is in the pie shell, affix the lattice strips on top per the lattice-top instructions on p. 42 finish with a traditional or fork crimp (p. 41)

1 single-crust, napkin-fold All-Butter Pie Dough shell

Follow instructions for single crust, but finish with a napkin fold (p. 36) instead of a traditional crimp

Shingles

Roll out 1 ball of dough

Punch out approximately 30 2-inch-diameter (5-cm) circles

After the filling is in the pie shell, affix shingles on top per the shingle-top instructions (p. 37)

1 Crumb Crust shell

Press crumb mixture into pie tin

Bake according to instructions on p. 44

PIE DOUGH TROUBLESHOOTING GUIDE

PROBLEM	CAUSE	SOLUTION
Dough cracks or falls apart when rolled.	*Dough is too cold.*	Let it warm up for 10 minutes and try again.
	Dough is too dry.	Do your best with it and add more water next time.
Dough springs back when rolled.	*Dough is not properly rested.*	Let it rest for 20 minutes and try again. *If resting does not solve the problem, then …*
	Dough is overworked.	Start over. Make sure the dough doesn't come together in the food processor and/or knead it less.
Dough sticks to the table or rolling pin.	*Not enough flour on the table or rolling pin.*	Add flour to both.
	Dough is too wet.	Do your best by adding flour to the table and rolling pin. Add less water next time.
Dough feels oily.	*Butter in the dough is melting because it is too warm.*	Throw it out and start over. Avoid leaving dough out too long or near a heat source.
Pie shrinks into pan when baked.	*Dough is overworked.*	Next time: Make sure the dough doesn't come together in the food processor and/or knead it less.
	Dough is not rested enough.	Next time: Make sure it rests after each time it is worked, both after kneading together and after rolling and crimpling.
	Dough was lifted off of bottom of the tin when crimped.	Make sure it is pressed into the corners of the pie tin when crimping.
	The dough or shell was not frozen enough.	Freeze it longer. Make sure the crust feels firm.
	Improper blind baking.	Add more beans or other pie weights. Make sure beans or other pie weights are pressed to the edges of the pie.

Sweet Pies

Farmers' Market Pies

These are the pies we sell at Chicago's Green City Market every Wednesday and Saturday in the spring, summer, and fall, and every Saturday in the winter. We make them with local ingredients, most of which we buy from other market vendors. They are grouped here by season because that is how we bake them.

Strawberry–Rhubarb Pie

SPRING

At Hoosier Mama, the new year doesn't start on January 1st. It starts when the first rhubarb shows up from our farmers. In late March, we start watching the weather, hoping for early spring days that are warm but not too warm, and rainy but not too rainy. By early April, I'm calling and emailing farmer René: "How is the rhubarb? Is anything up yet?" She takes it in stride.

By mid-April, our customers are calling the shop to ask if we'll have rhubarb for the first farmers' market in May. In good years, René arrives at our back door with the first scant bundles a few days before the first market Saturday. Other years, we tap our feet for a week or two, waiting for a new pie year to begin.

Rhubarb Pie

I love the sweet, tart flavor and the unlikely silky texture

of the rhubarb once it is baked. Rhubarb isn't nicknamed "pie plant" for nothing! Piewise, rhubarb is the first harbinger of spring, and the first lug of rhubarb from our farmers is usually greeted with cheers in the kitchen.

Ingredients

Makes one 9-inch (22.5-cm) pie

1	**double-crust All-Butter Pie Dough shell (recipe p. 24)**	
5 cups	**rhubarb, peeled and cut into 1-inch (2.5-cm) pieces**	568g
1 cup	**granulated sugar**	200g
¼ cup	**cornstarch**	35g
Pinch	**kosher salt**	
	Crust Dust (p. 21), for sprinkling	
	Pie Wash (p. 21), for brushing the top of the pie	
	Coarse-grained sugar, for sprinkling	

The unbaked pie can be stored in the freezer for up to 1 week. The baked pie can be stored at room temperature for up to 2 days and in the refrigerator for up to 3 days.

1 Place the rhubarb in a large bowl.

2 Combine the sugar, cornstarch, and salt in a small bowl. Pour over the rhubarb and toss until evenly coated. The rhubarb will not absorb all the dry ingredients.

3 Sprinkle Crust Dust into the empty pie shell. Pour in the rhubarb mixture, making sure to scrape out any dry ingredients that stick to the side of the bowl. Gently smooth the pie filling with a spatula. Finish the pie according to the double-crust instructions (p. 39), then freeze for at least 20 minutes.

4 Preheat the oven to 400°F (200°C).

5 Brush the top of pie with Pie Wash and sprinkle liberally with coarse-grained sugar.

6 Bake for 45 minutes to 1 hour, rotating 180 degrees every 20 minutes, until the crust is dark golden brown and the juices are bubbling thickly through the vents. Cool for at least 2 hours before slicing.

ELLIS FAMILY FARMS

It was while spraying for ants around the base of her house that René Gelder began her journey toward low-chemical farming. She was pregnant at the time, and the pet-safety warning label on the household pesticide raised a lot of other questions. Her research quickly expanded from household to orchard. After months of research, she approached her father, Jerry Ellis, about changing the farm's pest management plan. At the time, they were following a conventional pesticide-spraying plan, which involved regular preventative sprayings. It was a monumental decision to change, but after much discussion, her father agreed to give it a go.

A few months later, during a weekly orchard inspection, René and her father discovered a huge cluster of eggs on the bottom of an apple-tree leaf. Things looked bad; René's father was very

René Gelder

alarmed. They bagged the leaf and took it to the local cooperative extension office. The extension office was delighted—they were lady bug eggs. Lady bugs are a very beneficial aphid-eating insect, usually wiped out by spraying. These ladybugs were the beginning of a natural pest management system.

In addition to being great stewards of their land, Ellis Family Farms, located in Benton Harbor, MI, is

a perfect match for our pie company. They bring us their first rhubarb in the spring and their last Granny Smith apples in the winter, and in between they supply us with eggs, asparagus, honey, all kinds of berries, peaches, and pears. We maintain a continual year-round conversation about crops, weather, pie sales, and families—sometimes face to face, sometimes by phone, sometimes by text message in the middle of the night.

In 2011, we wanted to check out an elaborate apple-peeling machine at a farm and orchard trade show in Grand Rapids, MI. Unfortunately, we just could not get out of Chicago that week. We called René and asked her to check out the machine while she was at the show, take some pictures, and give us her opinion on it. In the end, she liked the machine and we trusted her judgment, so she and her husband Bruce negotiated a great deal on the demonstrator machine, made the purchase for us, and delivered the machine to us with our next order of apples. We love that apple-peeling machine and it has become an integral part of our operation.

The slogan of Chicago's Green City Market is "Know Your Farmer." We have found this to be excellent advice.

Strawberry–Rhubarb Pie

In springtime, Strawberry–Rhubarb rivals apple for most popular pie. Of course, once the rhubarb is up, it is hard to wait the extra few weeks for the local strawberries to pair it with. Don't be tempted to cheat with off-season berries from Mexico or South America. It takes a flavorful, field-ripened berry to stand up to rhubarb.

Ingredients

Makes one 9-inch (22.5-cm) pie

1	double-crust All-Butter Pie Dough shell (recipe p. 24)		¼ cup	cornstarch	35g
4 cups	rhubarb, peeled and cut into 1-inch (2.5-cm) pieces	454g	Pinch	kosher salt	
1 cup	Japanese-cut strawberries (sidebar p. 63)	113g		Crust Dust (p. 21), for sprinkling	
1 cup	granulated sugar	200g		Pie Wash (p. 21), for brushing the top of the pie	
				Coarse-grained sugar, for sprinkling	

The unbaked pie can be stored in the freezer for up to 1 week. The baked pie can be stored at room temperature for up to 2 days and in the refrigerator for up to 3 days.

1   Combine the rhubarb and strawberries in a large bowl.

2   Combine the sugar, cornstarch, and salt in a small bowl. Pour over the fruit and toss until evenly coated.

3   Sprinkle Crust Dust into the empty pie shell.

4   Pour the rhubarb and strawberries into the crust, making sure to scrape out any dry ingredients that stick to the side of the bowl. Gently smooth the pie filling with a spatula.

5   Finish the pie according to the double-crust instructions (p. 39), then freeze for at least 20 minutes.

6   Preheat the oven to 400°F (200°C).

7   Brush the top of pie with Pie Wash and sprinkle liberally with coarse-grained sugar.

8   Bake for 45 minutes to 1 hour, rotating 180 degrees every 20 minutes, until the crust is dark golden brown and the juices are bubbling thickly through the vents.

9   Cool for at least 3 hours before slicing.

JAPANESE-CUT STRAWBERRIES

Pastry chef Gale Gand taught this method to my former boss, Della Gossett, who taught it to me. I've never seen anyone else use it. With a little practice, it is a very fast way of slicing strawberries, and it ensures that each slice has a little bit of each part of the berry.

Rinse the berries under cold running water, then pat dry with paper towels or air dry. Cut straight across the top of the fruit, removing the stem and any "white shoulders" from the top of the berry. Next, place the berry cut-side down on a cutting board. Holding a paring knife at a 45-degree angle, slice diagonally through the strawberry. Rotate the berry a quarter turn counter-clockwise and make another cut. Repeat until the berry is sliced into bite-sized pieces.

Apple-Rhubarb with Oat Crumble Pie

This pie was born out of necessity one year, when we had

a few local apples and just a little rhubarb to work with for the first farmers' market of the season. We decided to stretch what little we had by combining the two. Taking inspiration from traditional English rhubarb crisps, we topped the pie with our Brown Sugar and Oat Crumble. The result was far better than anything we imagined, and the pie is a top seller every spring.

Ingredients

Makes one 9-inch (22.5-cm) pie

1	single-crust, blind-baked All-Butter Pie Dough shell (recipe p. 24, blind baking p. 34)	
4 cups	apples, peeled, cored, and chopped into bite-sized pieces (roughly 1 inch long by ¾ inch thick [2.5cm by 19mm])	480g
4 cups	rhubarb, peeled and cut into 1-inch (2.5-cm) pieces	454g

1¼ cups	granulated sugar	250g
¼ cup	cornstarch	35g
Pinch	kosher salt	
1 recipe	Brown Sugar and Oat Crumble (recipe follows)	

The unbaked pie can be stored in the freezer for up to 1 week. The baked pie can be stored at room temperature for up to 2 days and in the refrigerator for up to 3 days.

The crumble can be stored in the refrigerator for up to 1 week.

1   Preheat the oven to 400°F (200°C).

2   Combine the apples and rhubarb in a medium bowl.

3   Mix the sugar, cornstarch and salt in a small bowl until well combined. Pour over the fruit and toss until evenly coated.

4   Transfer the mixture to a 9x13-inch (22.5x32.5-cm) baking pan and bake for 20 minutes. Remove the pan from the oven and stir the ingredients gently, making sure to scrape down the sides of the baking dish. Do not break up the rhubarb.

5   Bake for another 20 to 30 minutes, until the fruit juices are thick and translucent and the apples are fork tender but still hold their shape. Cool to room temperature.

6   Spoon the cooled fruit into the pie shell and top with the Brown Sugar and Oat Crumble.

7   Bake for 25 to 30 minutes, until the crumble is dark golden brown and crispy on top.

8   Cool for at least 1 hour before slicing.

BROWN SUGAR AND OAT CRUMBLE

Makes enough to top one 9-inch (22.5-cm) pie

1 cup	**old-fashioned oats**	90g
½ cup	**dark brown sugar**	120g
Pinch	**kosher salt**	
4 Tablespoons	**unsalted butter, cut into 1-inch (2.5-cm) cubes**	56g

1   Combine all of the ingredients in the bowl of a stand mixer fitted with the paddle attachment.

2   Mix on Low until the mixture resembles fine crumbs. Increase the speed to Medium and mix until gravel-sized pieces form. Chill in the refrigerator for at least 30 minutes before using to top a pie.

PREP NOTE   *Make sure the fruit is cool when you add the crumble, otherwise the heat will melt the crumble before it can crisp in the oven, leaving a soggy layer.*

Strawberry Pie

Strawberry is the first berry of the year, and our first

strawberry pies at the farmers' market are greeted like old friends. The crop starts out with a trickle in late May and turns into a flood by July, when the farmers have more strawberries than we can keep up with. If you don't have a good source for freshly ground mace, buy mace blades (whole, unground mace) to grate yourself.

VANILLA PASTE

Vanilla has long been unfairly labeled as synonymous with "boring." At Hoosier Mama, we couldn't disagree more—we love the earthy, floral spice in everything, from strawberry and raspberry fruit pies to pumpkin pie and chocolate cream.

We are not alone. Vanilla is the most popular flavor in the world—and second only to saffron in its high price. But that is no excuse not to get the good stuff; artificial vanilla is made from wood pulp and paper processing byproducts, while real vanilla beans are the fruit of the climbing vanilla orchid. They spend four to six months ripening on the vine, then another six months curing before they are ready to use.

You may buy vanilla as a whole bean, an extract, a paste, or a powder. We prefer the paste, which is a mixture of vanilla bean seeds; vanilla extract; and a natural gum that's used as a thickener, which helps the vanilla stay suspended in the pie filling, so there's vanilla flavor in each bite. You can use whichever version you prefer, however.

If you opt for something other than vanilla paste, Nielsen-Massey (purveyor of fine vanilla products) recommends a 1:1 ratio for all vanilla products:

---

1 vanilla bean = 1 tablespoon vanilla extract, powder, or paste.

Ingredients

Makes one 9-inch (22.5-cm) pie

1	**double-crust All-Butter Pie Dough shell (recipe p. 24)**	
5 cups	**Japanese-cut strawberries (sidebar p. 63)**	567g
½ teaspoon	**vanilla paste**	3g
¾ cup	**granulated sugar, plus more for sprinkling**	150g
3 Tablespoons plus 1 teaspoon	**cornstarch**	30g

¼ teaspoon	**ground mace**	.4g
Pinch	**kosher salt**	
Pinch	**freshly ground black pepper**	
	Crust Dust, for sprinkling (p. 21)	
1 Tablespoon	**unsalted butter, cut into small pieces**	14g
	Pie Wash (p. 21), for brushing the top of the pie	

1   Place the strawberries in a medium bowl. Add the vanilla paste and mix gently to coat the berries.

2   Place the sugar, cornstarch, mace, salt, and black pepper in a small bowl and whisk to combine. Pour the dry ingredients over the berries and mix very gently to combine. The strawberries will not absorb all the dry ingredients.

3   Sprinkle Crust Dust into the empty pie shell. Pour in the strawberries, making sure to scrape out any dry ingredients that stick to the side of the bowl. Smooth the pie filling with a spatula and dot with the butter.

4   Finish the pie according to the double-crust instructions (p. 39), then freeze for at least 20 minutes.

5   Preheat the oven to 400°F (200°C).

6   Brush top of pie with Pie Wash and sprinkle liberally with granulated sugar.

7   Bake for 45 minutes to 1 hour, rotating 180 degrees every 20 minutes, until the crust is dark golden brown and the juices are bubbling thickly through the vents.

8   Cool for at least 2 hours before slicing.

The unbaked pie can be stored in the freezer for up to 1 week. The baked pie can be stored at room temperature for up to 2 days and in the refrigerator for up to 3 days.

Triple-Berry Pie

SUMMER

Summer arrives overnight. Suddenly, we are overwhelmed with cherries, peaches, nectarines, apricots, and at least five kinds of berries. The farmers look harried and we struggle to keep up as fruit goes in and out of season and back again.

Blueberry Pie

From the first crop of Dukes in the spring to the last

picking of Elliotts in the fall, we go through eight different varieties of blueberries in just one blueberry pie season—so the pie you buy in June may taste a little different from the pie you bring home in August. At first, I was afraid this would put off our customers, but instead they have embraced it. Last summer I overheard two customers in the shop debating when the "best" blueberry pies were available.

Ingredients

Makes one 9-inch (22.5-cm) pie

1	single-crust All-Butter Pie Dough shell (recipe p. 24)	
10	All-Butter Pie Dough lattice strips (p. 42)	
5 cups	blueberries	750g
1	lemon, for zesting	
2 teaspoons	fresh lemon juice	11g
1 cup plus 3 Tablespoons	granulated sugar	239g
6 Tablespoons	tapioca starch	42g
Pinch	kosher salt	
	Crust Dust (p. 21), for sprinkling	
	Pie Wash (p. 21), for brushing the top of the pie	
	Coarse-grained sugar, for sprinkling	

The unbaked pie can be stored in the freezer for up to 1 week. The baked pie can be stored at room temperature for up to 2 days and in the refrigerator for up to 3 days.

1   Sort through the blueberries, picking out stems and leaves. Place in a medium bowl. Zest the lemon over the bowl, add the lemon juice, and toss to combine.

2   Place the sugar, tapioca starch, and salt in a separate bowl and whisk to combine. Pour the dry ingredients over the blueberries and mix gently. The berries will not absorb all the dry ingredients.

3   Sprinkle Crust Dust into the empty pie shell. Pour in the blueberries, making sure to scrape out any dry ingredients that stick to the side of the bowl. Gently smooth the pie filling with a spatula. Finish the pie according to the lattice-top instructions (p. 42), then freeze for at least 20 minutes.

4   Preheat the oven to 400°F (200°C).

5   Brush top of the pie with Pie Wash and sprinkle liberally with coarse-grained sugar.

6   Bake for 45 minutes to 1 hour, rotating 180 degrees every 20 minutes, until the crust is dark golden brown and the juices are bubbling thickly.

7   Cool for at least 2 hours before slicing.

END-OF-THE-DAY VARIATIONS

Back when Hoosier Mama rented kitchen time by the hour, fruit that didn't make it into pies during the baking shift often went to waste. This was especially true during the summer months, when we would end the day with odd amounts of three or four kinds of farmers' market berries and cherries left over. One night, we took inspiration from Venetian glass blowers, who would gather up all the different colored glass scraps at the end of the day and fire them together into beautiful "end-of-the-day glass." We decided to gather all the leftovers and throw them into one pie.

Initially, I thought I might sell these one-off pies to our café and coffeehouse customers at a discount. Instead, we offered them to our farmers' market customers, who enthusiastically bought the "odd" pies first.

These are three of our best, and best-selling, inventions, which you can use instead of the 5 cups blueberries. The fruit amounts are just suggestions. If, like us, you find yourself with odd amounts, feel free to improvise. Just make sure your mix adds up to 5 cups (between 650 and 750 grams, depending on the ingredients) so the ratio of fruit to sugar and thickener is correct.

CHERRY-BERRY VARIATION

2 cups (276g) sweet cherries, 1½ cups (185g) raspberries or blackberries, and 1½ cups (218g) blueberries. Omit the lemon juice.

TRIPLE-BERRY VARIATION

2 cups (290g) blueberries, 1½ cups (185g) raspberries, and 1½ cups (216g) blackberries. Omit the lemon zest and the lemon juice.

BLACK-AND-BLUE VARIATION

2½ cups (363g) blueberries and 2½ cups (360g) blackberries. Omit the lemon zest and the lemon juice.

CHICAGO'S GREEN CITY MARKET

In Chicago, we are lucky to have nearly 50 farmers' markets spread across the city. In the summer, you can find a market any day of the week. They range from small neighborhood affairs with four or five vendors to the Green City Market, which boasts some 58 vendors and runs year-round—Wednesdays and Saturdays in the summer, and Saturdays-only in the winter.

Green City was the brainchild of the late cookbook author and Chicago Tribune food columnist Abby Mandel, who modeled it after the sustainable markets she saw in Europe. Sustainable agriculture promotes farming methods that provide healthy food for the consumer, protect the environment, respect workers, use resources more efficiently, maintain the land, and treat animals humanely. No chemical pesticides, synthetic fertilizers, or genetically modified crops are used.

Green City is the only market in the country that requires its farmers to be certified sustainable. The rules for prepared-food vendors like us are strict as well. All of the pies we sell at the market are made with local ingredients, from the flour in the crust to the fruit in the filling. (A few exceptions are made for necessary ingredients like sugar, which cannot be grown locally.) Each year at application time, we submit the recipes and ingredients sources for every item we sell. Last year our application ran close to forty pages.

While we are certainly proud to be a part of the market's fine mission, we also think it's just a lot of fun! There are farmers selling everything from Asian greens to free-range chickens and from pawpaws to foraged puffball mushrooms. There are cheesemakers, beekeepers, an ice cream vendor, a tamale stand, fresh cider, handmade soda, flowers, chef demos, and, of course, bakeries.

Now in its 14th season, the market has a permanent summer home in Chicago's Lincoln Park, which is landscaped specifically to accommodate vendors and 8,000 visitors a week. Before that, the market moved up and down the park each year and the ever-growing market left trampled grass in its wake. In the winter, two thousand people a week visit the market in its indoor home at the nearby Peggy Notebaert Nature Museum.

Hopefully you can find a market in your area; we have provided links to lists of farmers' markets in the US in the Resources section of this book (p. 336). If there is no market nearby, why not start one yourself?

ENJOYING THE GREEN CITY MARKET

Top left: Tim Burton of Burton's Maplewood Farms, where we get our maple syrup.

Top right: Pie slinger Courtney Behrens at our Green City Market stand.

Bottom left: Hadley (left) and Colleen enjoy a treat.

Bottom right: Joel Masters sells vegetables from Green Acres Farm.

Cherry Pie

At the pie shop, we are often bewildered by the cherry-pie lovers who will leave the shop empty-handed if we don't have their favorite pie—even when there are other kinds of pie on hand.

As we write this book, we are coming off the worst cherry season in years. Seventy-five percent of all the pie cherries in the US are grown along the eastern shore of Lake Michigan, between the Michigan towns of Benton Harbor and Traverse City. Normally, we have six weeks of tart, juicy, flavorful cherries straight from the orchard, but in 2012 freakish weather—80-degree March days followed by an April freeze—killed 95 percent of Michigan's cherry crop. Our farmers were lucky to have a few cherries to bring to market, but when they were gone, we pondered our options. How do you bake local when there is no local produce? Should we bring in cherries from across the country? Buy frozen commercial cherries?

In the end, we took a cue from those single-minded cherry pie lovers. We would walk away empty-handed and keep our fingers crossed for next year.

IT'S THE PITS!

I hate pitting cherries. It is time-consuming and messy, and missing even one pit can mean an angry phone call from a customer with a dental bill to settle. We buy cherries already pitted from our farmers whenever possible, but we have found a few tools to make the job easier when we have to do it ourselves.

For one or two pies, I prefer a simple hand pitter. OXO makes a nice one with a little plastic shield that keeps cherry juice from splattering everywhere. For bigger jobs, we love the cherry stoner by the German brand Leifheit. Just fill the hopper with cherries, hit the plunger, and the pits fall into an attached bin. The cherries themselves come out whole and full of juice. Leifheit claims the stoner can pit 25 pounds of cherries per hour. I don't know if that's true, since I usually give out long before then.

Ingredients

Makes one 9-inch (22.5-cm) pie

1	**single-crust All-Butter Pie Dough shell (recipe p. 24)**			1½ Tablespoons	**cornstarch**	13.5g
10	**All-Butter Pie Dough lattice strips (p. 42)**			Pinch	**kosher salt**	
4 cups	**pitted sour cherries**	650g			**Crust Dust (p. 21), for sprinkling**	
¼ cup (59mL)	**cherry juice**	55g			**Pie Wash (p. 21), for brushing the top of the pie**	
¼ teaspoon	**almond extract**	.5g			**Coarse-grained sugar, for sprinkling**	
½ cup	**granulated sugar**	100g				

1   Sort through the pitted cherries, removing any rogue pits or stems. Combine with the cherry juice and almond extract in a medium bowl and toss until the cherries are well coated.

2   Place the sugar, cornstarch, and salt in a small bowl and whisk to combine. Pour the dry ingredients over the cherries and mix gently. The cherries may not absorb all the dry ingredients.

3   Sprinkle Crust Dust into the empty pie shell. Pour in the cherries, making sure to scrape out any dry ingredients that stick to the side of the bowl. Gently smooth the pie filling with a spatula. Finish the pie according to the lattice-top instructions (p. 42), then freeze for at least 20 minutes.

4   Preheat the oven to 400°F (200°C).

5   Brush top of the pie with Pie Wash and sprinkle liberally with coarse-grained sugar.

6   Bake for 45 minutes to 1 hour, rotating 180 degrees every 20 minutes, until the crust is dark golden brown and the juices are bubbling thickly.

7   Cool for at least 2 hours before slicing.

The unbaked pie can be stored in the freezer for up to 1 week. The baked pie can be stored at room temperature for up to 2 days and in the refrigerator for up to 3 days.

Blackberry Pie

Be sure to taste your blackberries! The sweetness of blackberries can vary throughout a season and also from year to year. This recipe works great for berries that have just a touch of acidity. If your berries are on the sweet side, add the zest of half a lemon. If they are very sweet, add the zest plus one teaspoon of fresh lemon juice.

Ingredients

Makes one 9-inch (22.5-cm) pie

1	double-crust All-Butter Pie Dough shell (recipe p. 24)		1 teaspoon	tapioca starch	2.5g
4 cups	blackberries	454g	Pinch	kosher salt	
	Zest of ½ lemon (optional)			Crust Dust (p. 21), for sprinkling	
1 teaspoon	fresh lemon juice (optional)	10g	1 Tablespoon	unsalted butter, cut into small pieces	14g
¼ teaspoon	vanilla paste	1g		Pie Wash (p. 21), for brushing the top of the pie	
¾ cup	granulated sugar	150g		Coarse-grained sugar, for sprinkling	
2 Tablespoons plus 2 teaspoons	cornstarch	23g			

1   Pick through the blackberries, discarding any stems, leaves, or shriveled berries.

2   Place the blackberries in a medium bowl and add the optional lemon juice and/or lemon zest, if the berries are on the sweet side, and the vanilla paste. Gently mix with a spatula to coat berries.

3   Place the sugar, cornstarch, tapioca starch, and salt in a small bowl and whisk to combine.

4   Pour the dry ingredients over the berries and mix very gently. The berries will not absorb all of the dry ingredients.

5   Sprinkle Crust Dust into the empty pie shell.

6   Pour in the blackberries, making sure to scrape out any dry ingredients that stick to the side of the bowl. Gently smooth the pie filling with a spatula and dot with the butter.

7   Finish according to the double-crust instructions (p. 39), then freeze for at least 20 minutes.

8   Preheat the oven to 400°F (200°C).

9   Brush the top of pie with Pie Wash and sprinkle liberally with coarse-grained sugar.

10 Bake 45 minutes to 1 hour, rotating 180 degrees every 20 minutes, until the crust is dark golden brown and the juices are bubbling thickly through the vents.

11 Cool for at least 2 hours before slicing.

The unbaked pie can be stored in the freezer for up to 1 week. The baked pie can be stored at room temperature for up to 2 days and in the refrigerator for up to 3 days.

Peach Pie

Ingredients

Makes one 9-inch (22.5-cm) pie

1	**double-crust All-Butter Pie Dough shell (recipe p. 24)**	
5½ cups	**peeled peach slices (sidebar p. 78)**	845g
1 Tablespoon	**fresh lemon juice**	12g
¼ teaspoon	**almond extract**	.5g
1 cup	**granulated sugar**	200g
3½ Tablespoons	**potato starch**	37g
Pinch	**kosher salt**	
	Crust Dust (p. 21), for sprinkling	
	Pie Wash (p. 21), for brushing the top of the pie	
	Granulated sugar or coarse-grained sugar, for sprinkling	

·········· **HOW TO PEEL A PEACH** ··········

The easiest way to peel a peach is to blanch it in boiling water until the skin easily rubs off. While this method is blithely promoted in food magazines and newspaper articles each peach season, the truth is it only works about half the time. I'm including it here because it is fast and fun when it does work. Otherwise, we use a vegetable peeler or paring knife—and a willing kitchen intern or two. For best results, use ripe freestone peaches.

1. *Bring a large, shallow pot of water to a boil. Position a bowl of ice water nearby.*
2. *Cut an x on the bottom of the peaches (opposite the stem end) and place them in the boiling water for 45 seconds.*
3. *Using a slotted spoon, transfer the peaches to the bowl of ice water. The skin should start to separate from the peach at the X. Peel or rub the skin off in strips. The skin should come off easily; if it does not, place it in the boiling water for 30 more seconds and repeat the process.*

The unbaked pie can be stored in the freezer for up to 1 week. The baked pie can be stored at room temperature for up to 2 days and in the refrigerator for up to 3 days.

1   Place the peach slices in a medium bowl. Add the lemon juice and almond extract; toss until the peaches are well coated.

2   Place the sugar, potato starch, and salt in a small bowl and whisk until thoroughly combined. Pour the dry ingredients over the peaches. Gently toss with a spatula or wooden spoon until most of the dry ingredients cling to the peaches.

3   Sprinkle Crust Dust into the empty pie shell. Pile the peaches into the pie shell and smooth the top with a spatula. Finish the pie according to the double-crust instructions (p. 39), then freeze for at least 20 minutes.

4   Preheat the oven to 400°F (200°C).

5   Brush top of pie with Pie Wash and sprinkle liberally with granulated sugar or coarse-grained sugar.

6   Bake for 1 hour to 1 hour and 20 minutes, rotating 180 degrees every 20 minutes, until the crust is dark golden brown and the juices are bubbling thickly through the vents.

7   Cool for at least 2 hours before slicing.

WHAT'S YOUR FAVORITE PEACH?

Some 300 varieties of peaches are grown in North America, and as far as I can tell, they are all yummy! Peaches are divided into two main categories: freestone and clingstone. (There is a vague third variety called semi-freestone, but for all practical purposes, we can count that as clingstone as well.)

*A **clingstone peach**, as the name implies, has flesh that clings tenaciously to its pit or stone. They are the first peaches to ripen in the spring, and tend to be sweeter and juicier than their freestone cousins. Look for them at farm stands and farmers' markets. They are almost never sold commercially.*

***Freestone peaches** separate easily from the pit, making them a dream for pie makers to work with. They are usually bigger than clingstones with a firmer, less juicy texture. Either kind will make a fine pie as long as it is ripe.*

*While I normally champion old-fashioned and heirloom-fruit varieties, I have to admit my favorite peach is a commercial darling. The **Baby Gold** peach (a clingstone) was developed in the 1950s specifically for the peach canning industry, and most end up as—you guessed it—peach baby food.*

Farmers in southwest Michigan planted acres and acres of Baby Gold peaches at the request of the Gerber Product Company, who for several years had a large cannery in Fremont, Michigan. Today, the area is still known as the "Baby Food Capital of the World." These days there is a good supply of Baby Gold peaches at farmers' markets in Illinois, Michigan, and Wisconsin.

Baby Gold peaches are difficult to peel (see page 78), but they make the tastiest pies of the season. The raw flesh, which is almost rubbery, bakes up soft but still holds it shape. The flavor is intensely peachy with an almost floral aroma. Perhaps it is just some long-forgotten childhood food memory, but to me it just tastes more like a peach than the other varieties.

Raspberry Pie

One summer day, I happened to lament that I had never had a good raspberry pie. A few days later, my assistant, Anne, came in with her grandmother's recipe. I could tell it was going to be good because it was simply a list of ingredients with very few measurements. Like so many great pie makers before her, Grandma Esther made pie by feel, adjusting her recipe for each batch of fruit.

Esther grew up in Fremont, Ohio, and learned pie making by watching her mom bake several a week to feed the workmen who came to help out on their farm. Soon she was helping, making the pies from fruit they grew themselves: apples, grapes, apricots, rhubarb, elderberries, and even watermelon!

When her mother died many, many years later, she took over the role of family pie maker. Pies were her go-to dish. She baked pies for everything, from dinner parties to funeral luncheons. Until the age of 89, she offered one pie a month to the highest bidder at the local high school's benefit auction. She was so embarrassed by the high price paid for her pies the first year that she made extra dishes to go with them—a ham loaf one month, crackers and cheese spread the next.

Anne's mother Margaret says her mom had very practical advice for aspiring pie makers. When Margaret complained that she couldn't make a good pie crust, Esther told her again and again, "Roll it out and don't fuss with it!"

The unbaked pie can be stored in the freezer for up to 1 week. The baked pie can be stored at room temperature for up to 2 days and in the refrigerator for up to 3 days.

Ingredients

Makes one 9-inch (22.5-cm) pie

1	**double-crust All-Butter Pie Dough shell (recipe p. 24)**	
4 cups	**raspberries**	500g
2 teaspoons	**fresh lemon juice**	11g
¼ teaspoon	**vanilla paste**	1g
1 cup	**granulated sugar, plus more for sprinkling**	200g
2 Tablespoons	**cornstarch**	18g
1 teaspoon	**ground cinnamon**	2g
1 teaspoon	**tapioca starch**	3g
Pinch	**kosher salt**	
	Crust Dust (p. 21), for sprinkling	
1 Tablespoon	**unsalted butter, cut into small pieces**	14g
	Pie Wash (p. 21), for brushing the top of the pie	

Grandma Esther

1 Pick through the raspberries, discarding any stems, leaves, or shriveled berries. Place berries in a medium bowl. Add the lemon juice and vanilla paste and gently mix with a spatula to coat the berries.

2 Place the sugar, cornstarch, cinnamon, tapioca starch, and salt in a small bowl and whisk to combine.

3 Pour the dry ingredients over the berries and mix very gently, until the berries absorb roughly 2/3 of the dry ingredients. Do not overmix or the pie filling will be soupy.

4 Sprinkle Crust Dust into the empty pie shell. Pour in the raspberries, making sure to scrape out any dry ingredients that stick to the side of the bowl. Gently smooth the pie filling with a spatula and dot with the butter. Finish the pie according to the double-crust instructions (p. 39), then freeze for at least 20 minutes.

5 Preheat the oven to 400°F (200°C).

6 Brush the top of pie with Pie Wash and sprinkle liberally with granulated sugar. Bake for 45 minutes to 1 hour, rotating 180 degrees every 20 minutes, until the crust is dark golden brown and the juices are bubbling thickly through the vents. Cool for at least 2 hours before slicing.

Sweet Corn Custard with Tomato Jam

Ingredients

Makes one 9-inch (22.5-cm) pie

1	single-crust, blind-baked All-Butter Pie Dough shell (recipe p. 24, blind baking p. 34)	
1½ cups	fresh sweet corn kernels, divided	240g
1⅓ cups (316mL)	heavy cream, divided	309g
⅓ cup (79mL)	whole milk	80g
½ cup plus 2 teaspoons	granulated sugar	109g

1 teaspoon	vanilla paste	5g
Pinch	kosher salt	
Pinch	freshly ground black pepper	
Pinch	ground nutmeg	
4	large egg yolks	60g
2	large egg whites	40g
1 recipe	Tomato Jam (recipe follows)	

1   Preheat the oven to 325°F (165°C).

2   Place ¾ cup (120g) of the corn kernels, ⅓ cup (79mL) of the heavy cream, the milk, and the sugar in the bowl of a food processor. Pulse 2 to 3 times until the corn is finely chopped.

3   Transfer the mixture to a medium bowl. Stir in the remaining 1 cup (237mL) of the heavy cream, the vanilla paste, the salt, the black pepper, and the nutmeg. Add the egg yolks one at a time. Stir in the remaining ¾ cup (120g) of the corn kernels.

4   Whip the egg whites into soft peaks and fold into the corn mixture in 2 additions.

5   Pour the filling into the pie shell and bake immediately for 50 to 55 minutes, until the edges of the pie are slightly puffed and the custard moves in 1 piece when the pie is gently shaken.

6   Cool to room temperature, then chill in the refrigerator overnight before slicing.

7   Serve with Tomato Jam (recipe follows).

TOMATO JAM

½ cup plus 2 Tablespoons	**granulated sugar**	126g			Juice of 1 orange	
4 pinches	**cayenne pepper**				Juice of 1 lemon	
4 pinches	**freshly ground black pepper**			20	**cherry tomatoes, halved**	280g
2 pinches	**kosher salt**					

1 Preheat the oven to 275°F (140°C).

2 Combine the sugar, spices, salt, orange juice, and lemon juice in a medium saucepan. Take care to remove any stray citrus seeds.

3 Cook over medium-high heat, stirring often, until the mixture comes to a boil.

4 Turn the heat down to low and simmer for 1 to 2 minutes, until the mixture has thickened slightly. Remove from the heat.

5 Gently toss the tomato halves into the hot mixture. Pour everything onto a parchment paper-lined baking sheet.

6 Bake for 25 to 30 minutes. Cool to room temperature. Serve with the Sweet Corn Custard.

The baked pie can be stored in the refrigerator for up to 3 days.

The Tomato Jam can be stored in the refrigerator, in an airtight container, for up to 1 week.

Peach–Raspberry Pie with Pecan Crumble

This is our most-requested summertime pie. It's on the menu nearly every day once ripe peaches show up at the farmers' market. It's equally popular at backyard barbecues and summer weddings.

Ingredients

Makes one 9-inch (22.5-cm) pie

1	single-crust, blind-baked All-Butter Pie Dough shell (recipe p. 24, blind baking p. 34)	
1 cup	raspberries	125g
8 cups	peeled peach slices (sidebar p. 78)	1230g
1 Tablespoon	fresh lemon juice	15g
¼ teaspoon	almond extract	.5g
1 cup	granulated sugar	200g
3 Tablespoons	potato starch	31g
Pinch	kosher salt	
1 recipe	Pecan Crumble (recipe p. 306)	

The baked pie can be stored at room temperature for up to 2 days and in the refrigerator for up to 3 days. This pie should not be stored unbaked, as the crumble gets gummy.

1   Preheat the oven to 400°F (200°C).

2   Pick through the raspberries, discarding any stems, leaves, or shriveled berries. Set aside.

3   Place the peach slices in a large bowl. Add the lemon juice and almond extract and toss until the peaches are well coated.

4   Place the sugar, potato starch, and salt in a small bowl and whisk until thoroughly combined. Pour the dry ingredients over the peaches and gently toss until most of the dry ingredients cling to the peaches.

5   Spray a 9x13-inch (22.5x32.5-cm) baking pan with cooking spray. Transfer the peaches to the baking pan and bake for 20 minutes.

6   Remove the pan from the oven and stir the peaches, making sure to scrape out any ingredients that stick to the sides of the baking dish.

7   Return the pan to the oven and bake for 20 more minutes. Repeat this step until the peach juices are thickened and translucent. The peach slices should be tender but still hold their shape.

8   Stir the raspberries directly into the hot peaches and cool to room temperature.

9   Once cooled, spoon the fruit into the pie shell and top with ½ of the Pecan Crumble.

10 Bake for 25 to 30 minutes, until the crumble is lightly toasted.

11 Top the pie with remaining crumble and bake 20 to 25 minutes more, until the top is crispy.

12 Cool for at least 1 hour before slicing.

BLUEBERRY VARIATION

Replace the raspberries with 1 cup (145g) of blueberries. After stirring the blueberries into the hot peaches, return the fruit to the oven for 5 to 10 more minutes, until the blueberries are just starting to burst.

FALL

Fall is my favorite season at the market. The city is still dark as we unpack our pies, and the farmers set up their booths by lantern light. The market seems, if anything, even more abundant than in summer. Perhaps it's all the varieties of apples with which to make pie, or the scent of warm cider in the air.

THE HOOSIER MAMA APPLE PIE METHOD

Top, left to right: Toss the apples; pour the juice into a saucepan.
Middle, left to right: Bring the juices to a boil; juice will thicken into a goo.
Bottom, left to right: Sprinkle the pie shell with Crust Dust; add the apples.

Top, left to right: Pour in the apple goo; dot with the butter.

Middle, left to right: Roll the dough under; shape the edge.

Bottom, left to right: Crimp the edge; brush with Pie Wash.

Classic Apple Pie

I knew I couldn't open a pie shop without a great apple pie.

So once the pie dough recipe was finished, I started peeling apples. Apple pie poses some special challenges and honestly, if all our recipes had taken as many trials as the pie dough and apple pie did, I would have abandoned the whole idea! In a great apple pie, the juice from the apples combines with the sugar, spices, and thickener to create a dense sauce as it bakes, while the dough remains firm and flaky. The apple pieces themselves should be tender but hold their shape, giving way only as you bite into them.

There are, of course, lots of ways to make an apple pie. The method we finally settled on may seem overly complex, but each of the steps is crucial for a perfectly baked pie: macerating the apples with the sugar, starches, and spices brings out the juices; cooking the apple juices on the stove ahead of time activates the starches and ensures a thick sauce every time; and briefly freezing the pie before baking gives the dough time to cook before the fruit juices thaw and soak into the crust. Freezing also helps the pie hold its shape, because the surface of the dough, which is closest to the heat, cooks before the interior of the dough can thaw and become misshapen. The baked exterior and perfectly crimped edges you've labored over then hold their form as the interior thaws and cooks.

This is the method we use to make several thousand apple pies each year. If we believed we could simplify it and get the same results, we definitely would!

Next page

CLASSIC APPLE PIE

Continued

Makes one 9-inch (22.5-cm) pie

1	double-crust All-Butter Pie Dough shell (recipe p. 24)		1 Tablespoon	cornstarch	9g
8 cups	apples, peeled and chopped into bite-sized pieces (roughly 1 inch long by ¾ inch thick [2.5cm by 19mm])	960g	1 teaspoon	Chinese five-spice powder	2g
			½ teaspoon	kosher salt	1.5g
1 Tablespoon	lemon juice	16g		Crust Dust (p. 21), for sprinkling	
¾ cup	granulated sugar	150g	1 Tablespoon	unsalted butter, cut into small pieces	14g
3 Tablespoons	dark brown sugar	45g		Pie Wash (p. 21), for brushing the top of the pie	
1 Tablespoon plus 1 teaspoon	tapioca starch	10g			

The unbaked pie can be stored in the freezer for up to 1 week. The baked pie can be stored at room temperature for up to 2 days and in the refrigerator for up to 3 days.

APPLES

For apple pie, I like Granny Smith apples. They are tart enough to stand up to a good amount of sugar and spice, and firm enough to hold their shape when baked in a pie. They also store well, ensuring a long supply of local apples from our farmers.

In the early fall, before the Grannies are ripe, we use a mix of heirloom varieties. Empire, Cortland, black twig, mutsu, Northern Spy, and Cox's orange pippen all make delicious pie. If you are lucky enough to have an orchard or farmers' market nearby, you can create your own apple pie mix. But don't just go for the beauty queens of the apple stand. Modern apple varieties were bred to be perfectly round, resist bugs and disease, and withstand long trips cross-country (or even continents) without bruising. These advances usually came at the expense of flavor. The best-tasting heirloom apples are often pretty ugly!

That farmers' market rock star, honeycrisp, must also be avoided. It may taste great raw, but it is too sweet and too soft to make an interesting pie.

1   Place the apples in a medium bowl. Add the lemon juice and toss with a spatula until the apples are well coated.

2   Place the granulated sugar, brown sugar, tapioca starch, cornstarch, Chinese five-spice powder, and salt in a small bowl and whisk to combine. Pour the dry ingredients into the bowl of apples and mix until the apples are again well coated. Set aside to macerate for at least 25 minutes.

3   Place a colander over a medium bowl and transfer the macerated apples to the colander, making sure to scrape down the side of the bowl to get all the juices, sugars, and starches. Let the apples drain for 25 minutes.

4   Pour the drained juice into a small saucepan, scraping down the side and bottom of the bowl to get every drop. Bring the apple juice to a boil over medium-high heat, stirring constantly. Reduce heat and continue to boil the apple juice gently until it thickens, about 2 minutes. Remove from the heat and set aside to cool. Once it is room temperature, chill the saucepan in the refrigerator for about 20 minutes.

5   Sprinkle Crust Dust into the empty pie shell. Pour in the apples, making sure to scrape out any dry ingredients or juices that stick to the side of the bowl. Make a well in the middle of the apples and pour in the thickened apple juice. Gently smooth the pie filling with a spatula and dot with the butter. Finish the pie according to the double-crust instructions (p. 39), then freeze for at least 20 minutes.

6   Preheat the oven to 400°F (200°C).

7   Brush the top of pie with Pie Wash and bake for 45 minutes to 1 hour, rotating 180 degrees every 20 minutes, until the crust is dark golden brown and the juices are bubbling thickly through the vents. Cool for at least 2 hours before slicing.

APPLE–QUINCE PIE VARIATION

Woody and astringent, raw quince is nearly inedible, but cook it and something magical happens. The flesh becomes silky and tender, and the flavor is a cross between apples, pineapples, and pears, with a good deal of honey thrown in. The aroma is testament to the fact it is related to the rose.

We like to make this apple pie variation in late fall and early winter, when a few local quinces appear at the farmers' market. Replace 3 cups (360g) of the chopped apples with the same quantity of chopped quince, bring the Chinese five-spice powder down from 1 teaspoon (2g) to ½ teaspoon (1g) , and use only 1 teaspoon (2g) of tapioca starch. Follow the rest of the recipe as directed.

Apple, Honey, and Currant Pie

I like to use buckwheat honey for this recipe because it is the only honey I have found whose flavor does not fade as it bakes. It has a strong, malty, almost molasses-like flavor that pairs well with the currants, but unfortunately smells quite pungent as it cooks (Allison compares it to wet dog)! The finished pie tastes and smells great though!

Ingredients

Makes one 9-inch (22.5-cm) pie

1	double-crust All-Butter Pie Dough shell (recipe p. 24)	
7 cups	apples, peeled and chopped into bite-sized pieces (roughly 1 inch long by ¾ inch thick [2.5cm by 19mm])	840g
½ cup	dried currants	80g
1 Tablespoon plus ½ teaspoon	fresh lemon juice	17.5g
½	lemon, for zesting	
2½ Tablespoons	all-purpose flour	23g
2 Tablespoons	granulated sugar	26g
½ teaspoon	ground cinnamon	1g
⅓ cup (79mL)	buckwheat honey	160g
	Crust Dust (p. 21), for sprinkling	
1 Tablespoon	unsalted butter, cut into small pieces	14g
	Pie Wash (p. 21), for brushing the top of the pie	
	Granulated sugar, for sprinkling	

1 Combine the apples, currants, and lemon juice in a medium bowl. Zest the lemon over the apples and currants. Set aside.

2 Place the flour, sugar, and cinnamon in a small bowl and whisk to combine.

3 Pour the dry ingredients over the apples and currants and mix until well coated.

4 Stir in the honey.

5 Sprinkle Crust Dust into the empty pie shell.

6 Pour in the apples and currants, making sure to scrape out any dry ingredients that stick to the side of the bowl. Gently smooth the pie filling with a spatula and dot with the butter.

7 Finish the pie according to the double-crust instructions (p. 39), then freeze for at least 20 minutes.

8 Preheat the oven to 400°F (200°C).

9 Brush top of pie with Pie Wash and sprinkle liberally with granulated sugar.

10 Bake for 45 minutes to 1 hour, rotating 180 degrees every 20 minutes, until the crust is dark golden brown and the juices are bubbling thickly through the vents.

11 Cool for at least 2 hours before slicing.

The unbaked pie can be stored in the freezer for up to 1 week. The baked pie can be stored at room temperature for up to 2 days and in the refrigerator for up to 3 days.

 PREP NOTE *Cold honey can be awkward to work with. Heat it for a few seconds in a microwave or on the stovetop before stirring into the apples.*

Apple Pie with Raspberries and Rosewater

I developed this recipe for an edible-flower-themed demo

at the Macy's Flower Show. The addition of rosewater makes the apples taste wonderfully exotic.

This pie smells amazing as it bakes!

Ingredients

Makes one 9-inch (22.5-cm) pie

1	double-crust All-Butter Pie Dough shell (recipe p. 24)	
7 cups	apples, peeled and chopped into bite-sized pieces (roughly 1 inch long by ¾ inch thick [2.5cm by 19mm])	840g
1 Tablespoon	fresh lemon juice	16g
1 Tablespoon	rosewater	12g
½	lemon, for zesting	
¾ cup	granulated sugar	150g
¼ cup	all-purpose flour	37g
¼ teaspoon	ground cardamom	.5g

Pinch	kosher salt	
Pinch	freshly ground black pepper	
2 cups	raspberries	250g
	Crust Dust (p. 21), for sprinkling	
1 Tablespoon	unsalted butter, cut into small pieces	14g
	Pie Wash (p. 21), for brushing the top of the pie	
	Coarse-grained sugar, for sprinkling	

1 Place the apples in a large bowl. Add the rosewater and lemon juice and toss until the apples are well coated.

2 Zest the lemon over the apples. Set aside.

3 Place the sugar, flour, cardamom, salt, and black pepper in a small bowl and whisk to combine.

4 Pour the dry ingredients over the apples and mix well, then gently fold in the raspberries.

5 Sprinkle Crust Dust into the empty pie shell.

6 Gently pour in the pie filling, making sure to scrape in any dry ingredients that stick to the side of the bowl. Smooth with a spatula and dot with the butter.

7 Finish the pie according to the double-crust instructions (p. 39), then freeze for at least 20 minutes.

8 Preheat the oven to 400°F (200°C).

9 Brush the top of pie with Pie Wash and sprinkle liberally with coarse-grained sugar.

10 Bake for 1 hour to 1 hour and 20 minutes, rotating 180 degrees every 20 minutes, until the crust is dark golden brown and the juices are bubbling thickly through the vents.

11 Cool for at least 2 hours before slicing.

The unbaked pie can be stored in the freezer for up to 1 week. The baked pie can be stored at room temperature for up to 2 days and in the refrigerator for up to 3 days.

 **PREP NOTE**

Rosewater can be a bit pricey, but it is much less expensive in Middle Eastern groceries. The intensity of flavor varies across brands, so you may have to adjust the amount to suit your taste.

Pear Pie

The key to this pie is using perfectly ripe pears. Choose a Bartlett, Anjou, or other soft, juicy variety. This is not the place for a Bosc or a moonglow, both of which stay firm as they bake. Many of our customers tell us that they thought pears were bland and boring. If you fall into that camp, this pie will amaze you!

Ingredients

Makes one 9-inch (22.5-cm) pie

1	**single-crust, blind-baked All-Butter Pie Dough shell (recipe p. 24, blind baking p. 34)**	
30	**All-Butter Pie Dough shingles (p. 37)**	
8 cups	**pears, peeled, cored, and chopped into bite-sized pieces (roughly 1 inch long by ¾ inch thick [2.5cm by 19mm])**	1200g
1 Tablespoon	**fresh lemon juice**	16g
¾ cup	**granulated sugar**	150g
3 Tablespoons	**dark brown sugar**	45g
1 Tablespoon plus 1 teaspoon	**tapioca starch**	9g

1 Tablespoon	**cornstarch**	9g
½ teaspoon	**kosher salt**	1.5g
½ Tablespoon	**bourbon**	4g
¼ teaspoon	**vanilla paste**	1g
	Crust Dust (p. 21), for sprinkling	
1 Tablespoon	**unsalted butter, cut into small pieces**	14g
	Pie Wash (p. 21), for brushing the top of the pie	
	Coarse-grained sugar, for sprinkling	

1   Place the pears in a medium bowl. Add the lemon juice and toss until the pears are well coated.

2   Place the granulated sugar, brown sugar, tapioca starch, cornstarch, and salt in a small bowl and whisk to combine. Pour the dry ingredients into the bowl of pears and mix until the pears are again well coated. Set aside to macerate for 25 minutes.

3   Transfer the macerated pears to a colander set over a medium bowl, making sure to scrape down the side of the bowl to get all the pear juice, sugar, and starches. Set the pears aside to drain for another 25 minutes.

4   Transfer the drained pear juice to a small saucepan, making sure to scrape down the side and bottom of the bowl to get every drop. Cook over medium-high heat, stirring constantly, until it comes to a boil. Reduce heat and boil gently until the juice thickens, about 2 minutes.

5   Remove from the heat stir in the bourbon and vanilla paste. Set aside to cool. Once the pan has cooled to room temperature, chill it in the refrigerator for about 20 minutes.

6   Sprinkle Crust Dust into the empty pie shell. Pour the pears into the pie shell, making sure to scrape out any dry ingredients or juices that stick to the side of the bowl. Make a well in the middle of the pears and pour the thickened pear juice into the well. Gently smooth the pie filling with a spatula and dot with the butter.

7   Finish the pie according to the shingle-top instructions (p. 37), then freeze for at least 20 minutes.

8   Preheat the oven to 400°F (200°C).

9   Brush top of pie with Pie Wash and sprinkle generously with coarse-grained sugar.

10 Bake for 1 hour to 1 hour and 20 minutes, rotating 180 degrees every 20 minutes, until the crust is dark golden brown and the juices are bubbling thickly. After 45 minutes, you may need to cover the top crust to prevent overbrowning. Cut a hole, no bigger than a quarter, in the center of a disposable aluminum pie tin and invert it on top of the pie; the hole allows steam to escape.

11 Cool for at least 2 hours before slicing.

The unbaked pie can be stored in the freezer for up to 1 week. The baked pie can be stored at room temperature for up to 2 days and in the refrigerator for up to 3 days.

Pear-Raspberry Pie

This is a wonderful pie, made even more special by its

short season. Each year, I look forward to the few weeks in early fall when the first pears and the last raspberries share table space at the farmers' market. If you are patient enough to wait for perfectly ripe pears, the results are spectacular.

Ingredients

Makes one 9-inch (22.5-cm) pie

1	single-crust All-Butter Pie Dough shell (recipe p. 24)		2½ Tablespoons	cornstarch	22.5g
10	All-Butter Pie Dough lattice strips (p. 42)		¼ teaspoon	ground ginger	.5g
5 cups	pears, peeled, cored, and chopped into bite-sized pieces (roughly 1 inch long by ¾ inch thick [2.5cm by 19mm])	750g	Pinch	kosher salt	
				Crust Dust (p. 21), for sprinkling	
2 cups	raspberries	250g		Pie Wash (p. 21), for brushing the top of the pie	
1 Tablespoon	fresh lemon juice	16g		Coarse-grained sugar, for sprinkling	
¾ cup	granulated sugar	150g			

1   Place the pears, raspberries, and lemon juice in a medium bowl. Do not mix.

2   Place the sugar, cornstarch, ginger, and salt in a small bowl and whisk until thoroughly combined.

3   Gently fold the dry ingredients into the fruit, until most of the mixture is absorbed. Take care not to break up the raspberries.

4   Sprinkle Crust Dust into the empty pie shell.

5   Pile the pears and raspberries into the pie shell and smooth the top with a spatula.

6   Finish the pie according to the lattice-top instructions (p. 42), then freeze for at least 20 minutes.

7   Preheat the oven to 400°F (200°C).

8   Brush the lattice with Pie Wash and sprinkle liberally with coarse-grained sugar.

9   Bake for 1 hour to 1 hour and 20 minutes, rotating 180 degrees every 20 minutes, until the crust is dark golden brown and the juices are bubbling thickly.

10 Cool for at least 2 hours before slicing.

The unbaked pie can be stored in the freezer for up to 1 week. The baked pie can be stored at room temperature for up to 2 days and in the refrigerator for up to 3 days.

American Persimmon Pie

The American persimmon, *Diospyros virginiana*, tastes
amazing—like a cross between pumpkins and apricots, with some orange zest and allspice thrown
in. But what's really amazing is that we know what persimmons taste like at all. The fruit itself is
quite striking; it looks like a deep-orange tomato with pretty green scalloped leaves. You want to
pick it off the tree and eat it, but don't. It is underripe and almost unbearably tannic—so astringent
it will pucker your lips and dry out your mouth. It is only after the skin shrivels and the fruit falls off
the tree that the flesh turns sweet and pudding-like. For this reason, native persimmons have never
been cultivated commercially. The persimmons you find in the grocery store are an Asian variety
that was transplanted to California.

American persimmons are abundant and beloved in southern Indiana. The tiny town of Mitchell
(pop 4,357) hosts a persimmon fest each year that runs for ten days, complete with a parade, carni-
val, persimmon queen, and persimmon pudding contest (after the judging, the winners' names are
posted in the window of the hardware store).

In many southern Indiana homes, including the one my husband grew up in, persimmon pudding—not pumpkin pie—is the holiday dessert de rigueur.

If you'd like to try persimmons for yourself, you'll need to buy the fruit directly from a small
farmer. American persimmon growers string nets under the trees to keep the fruit off the ground,
then scoop out the pulp and sell it frozen. It is a good idea to keep the pulp frozen until you plan
to use it. Thaw it in the refrigerator overnight or under cool running water. Thaw only what you
plan to use and refreeze any unused portions. Several sources for frozen persimmon pulp are
listed in the Resources section of this book (p. 336).

Ingredients

Makes one 9-inch (22.5-cm) pie

1	**single-crust, blind-baked All-Butter Pie Dough shell (recipe p. 24, blind baking p. 34)**	
1 cup	**strained American persimmon pulp**	240g
	Zest of ½ orange	
3	**large eggs**	150g
1 cup (237mL)	**heavy cream**	232g
1 Tablespoon	**unsalted butter, melted**	14g

1 teaspoon	**vanilla paste**	5g
⅔ cup	**granulated sugar**	133g
2 Tablespoons	**dark brown sugar**	30g
1 teaspoon	**ground cinnamon**	2g
¼ teaspoon	**ground mace**	.5g
¼ teaspoon	**kosher salt**	1g

1 Preheat the oven to 350°F (180°C).

2 Using a spatula or the back of a serving spoon, press the pulp through a tami or fine-mesh strainer.

3 Place the persimmon pulp in a medium bowl and sprinkle the orange zest over it.

4 Whisk in the eggs, cream, butter, and vanilla paste, stirring well after each addition.

5 In a separate bowl, combine the granulated sugar, brown sugar, cinnamon, mace and salt. Whisk or mix with your hands to break up the brown sugar until thoroughly combined.

6 Add the dry ingredients to the persimmon mixture and whisk until just combined.

7 Pour the filling into the pie shell and bake for 45 minutes to 1 hour, or until the edge of the pie is slightly puffed and the center of the pie is dry to the touch. The top of the pie will color slightly.

8 Cool to room temperature and then chill in the refrigerator for at least 2 hours, up to overnight, before slicing.

The baked pie can be stored in the refrigerator for up to 3 days. Do not store the pie at room temperature.

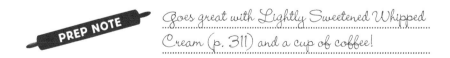

PREP NOTE *Goes great with Lightly Sweetened Whipped Cream (p. 311) and a cup of coffee!*

Maple-Pecan Pie

When I asked why her pecan pie was so much better than everyone else's, JoAnn Clevenger, owner of the wonderful New Orleans restaurant Upperline, advised me to lightly toast the pecans. So I always do. I also replace the cloyingly sweet corn syrup you find in most pecan pies with grade B maple syrup. The result is a rich, not-too-sweet pie that tastes of toasted pecans and just a hint of maple. I like to roughly chop the pecans so they end up mixed throughout the pie, rather than in just a single layer on top. Leave them whole if you prefer. If you don't want to use maple syrup, another good option is that southern staple, Steen's cane syrup. Again, it is not as cloying as corn syrup, and I suspect it is the second secret to JoAnn's delicious pie.

You will need a thermometer to make sure the maple syrup and eggs are heated to the proper temperature in step 11.

Ingredients

Makes one 9-inch (22.5-cm) pie

1	single-crust, blind-baked All-Butter Pie Dough shell (recipe p. 24, blind baking p. 34)		2 Tablespoons	dark brown sugar	30g
1½ cups	toasted pecan halves (sidebar p. 105)	150g	½ teaspoon	kosher salt	1.5g
4 Tablespoons	unsalted butter	56g	3	large eggs	150g
½ cup	granulated sugar	100g	1 cup (237mL)	grade B maple syrup	311g

1 Preheat the oven to 350°F (180°C).

2 Roughly chop the pecans in a food processor, or by hand.

3 Place the pie shell on a baking sheet lined with parchment paper.

4 Spread the pecans over the bottom of the pie shell and set aside.

5 Fill a medium saucepan halfway with water and bring to a simmer over medium-high heat.

6 Place the butter in a medium, heatproof bowl and rest it on top of the saucepan of simmering water. Stir the butter occasionally until it is melted.

7 Meanwhile, mix the granulated sugar, brown sugar, and salt in a small bowl until thoroughly combined.

8 Remove the butter from the heat and work the sugar mixture into the butter with a spatula until the butter is well absorbed.

9 Add the eggs one at a time, beating well after each addition.

10 Whisk in the maple syrup.

11 Place the bowl back on top of the saucepan of simmering water and heat, whisking constantly, until the maple syrup mixture reaches 140°F (60°C) on an instant-read thermometer.

12 Pour through a fine-mesh strainer into the prepared pie shell, over the pecans.

13 Bake for 50 to 60 minutes, until the pie is slightly puffed and the center is set.

14 Cool to room temperature before slicing.

> ⸻ TOASTING ⸻
> *To toast nuts of any kind, just spread the nuts on a baking sheet and bake at 300°F (150°C) for 10 minutes. To toast coconut flakes, bake them at 350°F (180°C) for 10 minutes.*

The baked pie can be stored at room temperature up to 2 days and in the refrigerator up to 3 or 4 days.

 **PREP NOTE** *It's important that the pie shell not have holes near the crimp. Patch any small holes with raw pie dough before filling the shell.*

JEFFERSONVILLE PIE VARIATION

We hear they make something kind of similar across the river in Louisville, but we don't really know anything about that. Add 2 tablespoons of bourbon to the maple syrup mixture, and replace the 1½ cups (150g) of pecans with 1 cup (100g) of pecans plus ¼ cup (45g) of semisweet chocolate chips. After the pie has cooled, stripe it with Chocolate Ganache (p. 310).

Jeffersonville Pie

BURTON'S MAPLEWOOD FARM

I was a bit dubious when I first heard about maple syrup from southern Indiana. We had already eschewed the iconic Vermont and Canadian maple syrups in favor of Midwestern syrup from Wisconsin and Michigan, but southern Indiana just seemed , well, too southern. Maple syrup is a northern thing, right? Well, usually, but the glaciers left a unique geography of high hills surrounding tiny Medora, Indiana. These hills, known locally as knobs, provide a surprising maple sugar microclimate. Late January brings the cold nights and warm days that are necessary to start the maple sap flowing—it's the earliest "sugar season" in the world.

Burton's Maplewood Farm sits among the trees atop one of these knobs. The farm's sugar shack is an oversized log cabin with a giant stone fireplace. It houses a big copper and stainless steel evaporator, which reduces 40 gallons of maple sap to make each gallon of maple syrup. There are few better places to spend a late-winter afternoon.

Proprietors Tim and Angie Burton sell their syrup at farmers' markets in the Indiana cities of Bloomington and Indianapolis, as well as in Chicago. They also sell it online (see Resources, p. 336). Here in Chicago their grade A maple syrup is served alongside pancakes at the Ritz-Carlton, and their oak-barrel-aged, bourbon-infused maple syrup appears on trendy cocktail bar menus. You can also find their Grade B syrup in our Maple–Pecan Pie.

KERN'S DERBY–PIE®

In 1950, George Kern and his parents, Walter and Leaudra Kern, created a chocolate walnut pie for their family restaurant in Prospect, Kentucky. After much debate, they called it Derby-Pie® for the famous horse race in nearby Louisville. The pie quickly became popular—so popular that in 1969, upon the advice of friends and colleagues, Walter and Leaudra sought state and federal trademark protection. No one knows what's in the Kern family's closely guarded recipe other than semisweet chocolate chips and English walnuts. The numerous knock-off recipes often include pecans, Kentucky bourbon, butterscotch, and flaked coconut, among other ingredients.

Alan Rupp, George's nephew and Walter and Leaudra's grandson, still makes the pies and tenaciously defends the trademark from a production facility in Louisville (the restaurant closed years ago). Employees at the company's plant all sign confidentiality agreements, and in 2004 Rupp told the Cincinnati Enquirer that besides himself, just his brother, ex-sister-in-law, and production manager know the true recipe.

Rupp's lawyers have won lawsuits against dozens of trademark infringers, including PBS and Rupp's own chocolate-chip supplier, Nestlé, when the company printed a "Tollhouse Derby Pie" recipe on hundreds of thousands of bags of chocolate morsels. In 1988, he won a lawsuit against Bon Appétit magazine when they published a cookbook that included a Derby–Pie® recipe.

You can pick up an authentic slice of Derby-Pie® at Churchill Downs on the first Saturday in May, or order a whole pie from the Kern's Kitchen website, derbypie.com. While you're there, be sure to check out the trademark FAQ page.

Pear, Apple, and Cranberry Pie with Walnut Crumble

Problems arise when one of your most popular pies also has the longest name. To save time in the shop, we've nicknamed it "PAC," to the confusion of customers and new pie slingers alike, since we invariably forget to use its proper name. Whatever you choose to call it, it's a very satisfying pie, especially on a blustery fall day. The apples and pears take on a honey-like flavor as they bake, and the cranberries add a hint of tartness and color. Long-term customers now know to ask for it by nickname as well. Feel free to substitute pecans for the walnuts in the crumble.

Ingredients

Makes one 9-inch (22.5-cm) pie

1	single-crust, blind-baked All-Butter Pie Dough shell (recipe p. 24, blind baking p. 34)		1 Tablespoon	fresh lemon juice	16g
¾ cup	fresh cranberries	74g	¾ cup	granulated sugar	150
4 cups	apples, peeled and chopped into bite-sized pieces (roughly 1 inch long by ¾ inch thick [2.5cm by 19mm])	480g	3 Tablespoons	dark brown sugar	45g
			2 Tablespoons	cornstarch	18g
			½ teaspoon	Chinese five-spice powder	1g
			½ teaspoon	kosher salt	1.5g
4 cups	pears, peeled and chopped into bite-sized pieces (roughly 1 inch long by ¾ inch thick [2.5cm by 19mm])	600g	1 recipe	Walnut Crumble (recipe p. 306)	

1 Preheat the oven to 400°F (200°C).

2 Sort through the cranberries, discarding any stems or leaves. Set aside.

3 Place the apples and pears in a large bowl and toss with the lemon juice.

4 Place the granulated sugar, brown sugar, cornstarch, Chinese five-spice powder, and salt in a small bowl and whisk to combine. Pour the dry ingredients into the bowl of apples and pears and mix until the fruit is well coated.

5 Lightly coat a 9x13-inch (22.5x32.5cm) baking pan with cooking spray.

6 Transfer the fruit to the baking pan, making sure to scrape out any dry ingredients that stick to the side of the bowl, and bake for 20 minutes.

7 Stir and return to the oven for 20 more minutes. Repeat this step until the fruit juices are thickened and translucent, and fruit pieces are tender but still hold their shape.

8 Stir in the cranberries and return to the oven. Bake 10 more minutes, or until the cranberries burst. Set aside to cool to room temperature.

9 Spoon the filling into the pie shell and top with ½ of the Walnut Crumble.

10 Bake for 25 to 30 minutes, until the crumble is lightly toasted.

11 Top with the remaining crumble and bake 20 more minutes, until the top is crispy.

12 Cool for at least 1 hour before slicing.

The baked fruit filling can be stored in the refrigerator overnight before building the pie. The baked pie can be stored at room temperature for up to 2 days and in the refrigerator for up to 3 days. It should not be stored unbaked, as the crumble gets gummy.

Sweet Potato Pie

WINTER

Winter at the farmers' market starts out festively, with customers lined up and waiting for Thanksgiving pies long before we arrive. At Christmastime, farmers roast chestnuts and sell wreaths and swags of evergreen. It ends quietly, as Chicagoans hibernate through the worst of winter and farmers run low on produce. A sunny Saturday morning, however, will still bring a crowd, and it's a nice reminder that spring is not as far away as it seems.

Sweet Potato Pie

There are hundreds of ways to make a sweet potato pie,

which is why it took us three years to settle on our own version. We knew we wanted the sweet potato flavor to come through first, so we settled on a lightly spiced filling with plenty of butter, salt, and pepper to bring out the roasted sweet potato flavor. Next, we finish it with a light Bourbon-Maple Glaze and a scattering of Candied Pecans. You might be tempted to skip the Candied Pecans, but don't!

Ingredients

Makes one 9-inch (22.5-cm) pie

1	single-crust, blind-baked All-Butter Pie Dough shell (recipe p. 24, blind baking p. 34)	
½ cup	granulated sugar	100g
½ cup	dark brown sugar	120g
¾ teaspoon	kosher salt	2.25g
¼ teaspoon	freshly ground black pepper	.5g
¼ teaspoon	ground cinnamon	.5g
¼ teaspoon	ground nutmeg	1g
⅛ teaspoon	ground cloves	.5g
½	orange, for zesting	
2½ cups	Sweet Potato Purée (recipe follows)	545g
2	large eggs	100g
1	large egg yolk	20g
1 cup (237mL)	heavy cream	232g
3 Tablespoons	unsalted butter, melted	42g
3 Tablespoons (45mL)	bourbon	27g
1 Tablespoon	vanilla paste	15g
	Bourbon–Maple Glaze, for brushing (recipe follows)	
2–3 Tablespoons	roughly chopped Candied Pecans (recipe p. 307)	

1   Preheat the oven to 350°F (180°C).

2   Combine the granulated sugar, brown sugar, salt, black pepper, cinnamon, nutmeg, and cloves in a small mixing bowl and mix with a whisk or your fingers until thoroughly combined. Set aside.

3   Zest the ½ orange over the Sweet Potato Purée. Stir in the dry ingredients.

4   Whisk in the eggs, egg yolk, and cream.

5   Mix 1 to 2 tablespoons of sweet potato batter into the melted butter to cool it slightly. Stir this mixture back into the sweet potato batter.

6   Whisk in the bourbon and vanilla paste.

7   Pour the batter into the pie shell. You may have extra batter.

8   Bake for 45 minutes to 1 hour, until the pie appears set and the center of the pie is dry to the touch. The edges of the pie will puff and crack slightly.

9   Cool to room temperature.

10 Brush the hot Bourbon–Maple Glaze generously over the top of the cooled pie. Don't pour the glaze on or allow it to pool.

11 Chill in the refrigerator overnight to allow the pie to set.

12 Scatter the Candied Pecans over the set pie.

The baked pie can be stored in the refrigerator for up to 3 days. It should be baked immediately and should not be stored at room temperature.

SWEET POTATO PURÉE
Makes about 2½ cups (545g)

3	**jumbo sweet potatoes**	

1 Preheat the oven to 350°F (180°C).

2 Pierce the skin of the sweet potatoes all over and roast on a baking sheet for 2 hours, or until they are soft.

3 Cut in half lengthwise and scoop out the flesh. Place the flesh in the bowl of a food processor and purée until smooth.

4 Press the purée through a fine-mesh strainer into a medium bowl, using a spatula or the back of a ladle.

The purée can be stored in the freezer for up to 2 weeks.

BOURBON–MAPLE GLAZE
Makes ¼ cup (60mL or 60g)

3 Tablespoons (45mL)	**maple syrup**	45g
1 Tablespoon	**bourbon**	9g

1 Combine the ingredients in a saucepan and bring to a boil over medium heat.

Funeral Pie

Funeral pies got their name from the Pennsylvania Amish

tradition of taking pies to wakes. Raisin pies were the popular choice since they traveled well, kept for days, and could be thrown together quickly with ingredients most people kept in the pantry year-round. Indiana Amish, on the other hand, consider this a wedding pie. Either way, it's scary good! Baker Juli developed this pie based on traditional Amish recipes then added some very non-Amish spiced rum!

Ingredients

Makes one 9-inch (22.5-cm) pie

1	double-crust All-Butter Pie Dough shell (recipe p. 24)	
1 cup	golden raisins	150g
1 cup	dark raisins	150g
2 cups (474mL)	apple cider	493g
¼ cup plus 2 Tablespoons	granulated sugar, plus more for sprinkling	76g

3 Tablespoons	all-purpose flour	27g
¼ teaspoon	kosher salt	1g
¼ cup (49mL)	spiced rum	59g
3 Tablespoons (45mL)	fresh lemon juice	47g
	Pie Wash (p. 21), for brushing the top of the pie	

Next page

FUNERAL PIE

Continued

1   Combine golden and dark raisins with the cider in a medium, heavy saucepan. Bring to a boil over medium heat, stirring occasionally. Remove from the heat.

2   Combine the sugar, flour, and salt in a small, heatproof bowl.

3   Whisk in a few ladles of the raisin liquid and mix to form a smooth, thin paste. Pour the paste into the saucepan full of raisin liquid and mix well.

4   Bring to a boil over medium heat, stirring often. Boil 2 to 3 minutes, until the mixture starts to thicken, then remove the pan from the heat and stir in the rum and lemon juice. Set the filling aside to cool completely.

5   Pour the cooled pie filling into the pie shell and finish according to the double-crust instructions (p. 39) with a fork crimp (p. 41), then freeze for at least 20 minutes.

6   Preheat the oven to 350°F (180°C).

7   Brush top of pie with Pie Wash and sprinkle liberally with granulated sugar.

8   Bake for 1 hour and 20 minutes, until the crust is dark golden brown and the juices are bubbling thickly through the vents. Cover the edge of the pie with strips of foil or a crust guard if it starts to overbrown before the pie is done.

9   Cool for at least 2 hours before slicing.

The pie filling can be stored in the refrigerator overnight before using. The unbaked pie can be stored in the freezer for up to 1 week. The baked pie can be stored at room temperature for up to 2 days and in the refrigerator for up to 3 days.

Mincemeat Pie

Believe it or not, we have the crusades to thank for

mincemeat pie. In the 13th century, soldiers returning from the Middle East brought back recipes for exotic dishes made with meat, fruit, and spices. Industrious English cooks, seeing a way of preserving meat without salting or smoking it, added alcohol and baked the ingredients into pies. The first pies contained more minced meat than fruit (thus the name); it wasn't until the Victorian age that the pie became more of a dessert.

Mince pies are a Christmas tradition in England. According to folklore, early mincemeat recipes called for 13 ingredients, to represent Christ and the 12 apostles. Our recipe doubles the number of ingredients and substitutes butter for the traditional suet. It's worth it to take the time to candy the orange peel yourself.

Next page

MINCEMEAT PIE

Continued

Makes one 9-inch (22.5-cm) pie

1	**double-crust All-Butter Pie Dough shell (recipe p. 24)**	
3	**Granny Smith apples, peeled and diced**	317g
3	**Braeburn or McIntosh apples, peeled and diced**	317g
¾ cup	**dark brown sugar**	180g
1 stick	**unsalted butter**	112g
¼ cup	**golden raisins**	32g
¼ cup	**dried currants or raisins**	32g
¼ cup	**diced dried apricots**	35g
¼ cup	**diced dried apples**	64g
¼ cup	**dried figs**	42g
¼ cup	**dried cherries**	26g
¼ cup	**diced dried pears**	32g
¼ cup	**finely chopped Candied Orange Peel (recipe follows)**	51g

1 teaspoon	**ground cinnamon**	2g
½ teaspoon	**ground mace**	1g
½ teaspoon	**ground ginger**	1g
½ teaspoon	**ground cloves**	1g
½ teaspoon	**kosher salt**	1.5g
1	**lemon, for zesting and juicing**	
1	**orange, for zesting and juicing**	
1½ cups (356mL)	**apple cider, divided**	369g
¼ cup (59mL)	**rum**	55g
¼ cup (59mL)	**brandy**	55g
	Pie Wash (p. 21), for brushing the top of the pie	
	Granulated sugar, for sprinkling	

1 Place all ingredients beginning with the apples and ending with the salt and ½ cup (119mL or 55g) of the apple cider in a medium, heavy saucepan.

2 Zest the orange and lemon over the saucepan, then add the juice from each fruit.

3 Bring to a boil over medium heat, stirring occasionally until the sugar and spices dissolve.

4 Reduce the heat and simmer, covered, for 3 to 4 hours, until the mixture has a jamlike consistency and has darkened in color. As it is simmering, check the mixture periodically. If the fruit begins to scorch, add 2 to 3 more tablespoons (30–45mL) of cider and further reduce the heat.

5 Stir in the remaining apple cider, the rum, and the brandy and cook until syrupy, about 10 minutes. Cool to room temperature.

6 Transfer the filling to the pie shell and finish the pie according to the double-crust instructions (p. 39), then freeze for at least 20 minutes.

7 Preheat the oven to 400°F (200°C).

8 Brush top of pie with Pie Wash and sprinkle liberally with granulated sugar.

9 Bake for 30 to 40 minutes, rotating 180 degrees every 20 minutes, until the crust is dark golden brown and the juices are bubbling thickly through the vents.

10 Cool for at least 2 hours before slicing.

The unbaked pie can be stored in the freezer for up to 1 week. The baked pie can be stored at room temperature for up to 2 days and in the refrigerator for up to 3 days.

PREP NOTE

I like this pie best when the top crust is a little darker than usual. The granulated sugar on top caramelizes, providing a slightly bitter crunch.

CANDIED ORANGE PEEL
Makes about 1½ cups (114g)

Candying orange peels is time-consuming, but quite simple—and the result is worlds away from the gummy, bitter candied citron you buy at the grocery store. This recipe makes more than you will need for one pie, but smaller batches are harder to control and tend to over-caramelize quickly. You can use the extra in cookies, muffins and quick breads. Slice thin strips to garnish cocktails or dip it in sugar or melted chocolate to make your own candy.

3	**large oranges, rinsed and quartered**	447g
4 cups	**granulated sugar**	800g

1 Remove the orange peels by running your thumb between the white pith and orange pulp. Set the pulp aside for another use, or discard.

2 Place the orange peels in a 4-quart (3.8-L) saucepan. Cover with 8 cups (1.9L) of cold water and add a few ice cubes. Bring to a boil over medium heat.

3 Remove the pot from the stove and carefully drain the boiling water. Re-cover with 8 cups (1.9L) of cold water and ice cubes, bring to a boil, and drain. Repeat 3 more times, so that the peel has been boiled 5 times.

4 After the 5th boil, drain the hot water and add the granulated sugar and 4 cups (948mL) of cold water. Stir just until the sugar is suspended in the water.

5 Return the pan to the stove and bring to a boil over high heat. Reduce the heat and simmer until the sugar syrup thickens and reduces by roughly half, about 35 minutes. The syrup will be golden brown and smell like caramel and the orange pith will be translucent. Cool to room temperature.

6 Remove the orange peels from the syrup and chop for immediate use. If you are not using right away, store the peels along with syrup in an airtight container.

The candied orange peel can be stored in the refrigerator in an airtight container with the syrup for up to 3 weeks.

ORANGE PEEL CANDY VARIATION

Remove 2 to 3 orange peel quarters from the syrup and gently pull the peel through your thumb and forefinger to remove any excess syrup. Slice the peel into ¼- to ½-inch (6–13-mm) strips. Place a baking or cooling rack over a baking sheet lined with parchment or wax paper and arrange the strips on the rack, ½ inch (13mm) apart. Let the peel dry at room temperature at least 6 hours or up to overnight. When the peels feel tacky to the touch, toss them in a bowl of granulated sugar until well coated, then arrange them on a clean baking rack, or a baking pan lined with parchment or wax paper, and dry for 1 to 2 more hours. Store at room temperature in an airtight container for up to 1 week.

SPICES

The entire time I was growing up, we owned the same metal tin of McCormick-brand ground cloves. My mom got it down from the spice shelf every Christmas, Thanksgiving, and any time we made gingersnap cookies. I don't know how old that tin was, but the packaging looked old fashioned to me even then, and the price stamped on the bottom was just 53 cents.

Patty Erd, a second-generation spice merchant, runs the Spice House with her husband, Tom. They recommend replacing ground spices once a year and whole spices every two years. While old spices won't hurt you, she says, they definitely lose their flavor.

The Spice House has locations throughout Chicagoland as well as in Milwaukee, and each store grinds its own spices in small batches to make sure customers get them as fresh as possible. The Erds have even overnighted freshly ground spices to Pastry Team USA when they were competing in France.

Patty recommends storing spices in airtight glass jars, away from direct light and heat. Red spices, like cayenne pepper or chili powder, are high in volatile oils and should go in the refrigerator. So should seeds, like poppy or sesame, which can turn rancid if left at room temperature too long. Patty says the worst place to store spices is above the stove, because the heat destroys the essential oils that give spices their flavor.

At the pie shop, we buy our spices once or twice a month to make sure they are as flavorful as possible, and we wrote all of the recipes in this book using those spices. If you are using grocery store spices you may have to increase the amount the recipes call for to get the same amount of flavor. If there is a spice store in your town, we urge you to visit. It will be the best-smelling store you have ever been to. If not, you can find information about ordering from the Spice House in the Resources section of this book (p. 336).

Creams, Custards, and Curds

These are the staples of the pie shop. While they require a bit more technique than other pies, once mastered they offer endless variations. They're based on classic pastry building blocks like curds and pastry creams, so you could use your newfound skills to make non-pie desserts too—though I don't know why you'd want to!

GELATIN

Gelatin comes in two forms, and most of our cream pie recipes call for both of them. Powdered gelatin is the form most home cooks are familiar with. It's easy to find; you can buy it at most grocery stores and typically it comes in boxes of individual packets. In fact, many home recipes measure gelatin by the packet. Just make sure you buy the unflavored kind, and not Jell-O®, which has sugar, flavorings, and colorings added.

Professional cooks prefer leaf gelatin, because it's easier to use and more accurate to measure. It comes in clear sheets that look and feel like thin, brittle plastic. Our recipes call for the standard 2.5-gram sheets, also known as silver strength, which you can find online or at specialty cooking stores.

Both forms must be bloomed, or softened, in liquid before use. To bloom powdered gelatin, sprinkle it over a cool liquid (your recipe will specify the amount) and let stand for 5 to 10 minutes. Do not stir, or clumps may form that will be hard to dissolve later. The powder will absorb some of the liquid and form a lumpy, wrinkly skin on top. Once this happens, give it a good stir before adding it to your preparation.

To bloom leaf gelatin, simply soak the sheets in a bowl of cold water for 10 minutes. The amount of water is not important, as long as the sheets are submerged. The sheets will soften and become pliable as they absorb the water. Gently squeeze the excess water out of the sheets before adding them to your preparation.

In theory, the two forms can be used interchangeably, but there are slight differences in the textures they produce. Powdered gelatin sets more firmly, but can turn rubbery and mask flavor if you use too much. Leaf gelatin produces a silkier texture and has less effect on flavor. We use both in our cream pies to make sure they have a creamy, luxurious texture but are firm enough to hold up when sliced. To substitute powdered gelatin for leaf gelatin, or vice versa, use the following conversions:

1 envelope powdered gelatin = ¼ oz (7g) = 2¾ teaspoons =3½ sheets leaf gelatin.

All gelatin is derived from animal collagen. The closest vegetarian option is agar agar, which comes from seaweed. The powdered form is the easiest to work with; the ratio for substituting for powdered gelatin is simply 1:1, but it will produce a denser texture than the gelatin. Agar agar doesn't need to bloom; simply dissolve it in hot liquid.

CREAM PIES

Cream pies are the stars of the pie case. Piled high with fluffy pastry cream, they manage to be luxurious and comforting at the same time. We make at least two kinds of cream pie every day at the shop, and more on weekends and holidays, when customers special order them for parties and family gatherings. Making pastry cream may seem a bit tricky at first, but once you master the technique, the flavor options are limitless. Want orange pastry cream? Infuse orange zest into the hot milk and the cream. For a white- or milk-chocolate flavor, simply melt the chocolate into the finished pastry cream. In the summer, layer pastry cream over ripe berries.

Basic Pastry Cream

Make sure you read the individual pie recipes carefully,

because while this is the basic pastry cream you will be making, there are some variations in the steps depending on the pie.

Ingredients

Makes enough to fill one 9-inch (22.5-cm) pie

½ sheet	**leaf gelatin (silver strength)**	1.25g		3	**large egg yolks**	60g
3 cups (711mL)	**whole milk, divided**	726g		1	**large egg**	50g
1 Tablespoon	**unflavored powdered gelatin**	7g		2 Tablespoons	**unsalted butter**	28g
1 cup	**granulated sugar**	200g		1 Tablespoon	**vanilla paste**	15g
¼ cup	**cornstarch**	35g		1 cup (237mL)	**heavy cream**	232g

Pastry cream can be made 1 day ahead and stored in the refrigerator. Do not store at room temperature.

 **PREP NOTE** See the gelatin sidebar (p. 124) for more information on the different types of gelatin.

1   Place the leaf gelatin in a small bowl of ice water. Set aside to bloom for 10 minutes.

2   Pour ½ cup (119mL or 121g) of the milk into a small bowl. Sprinkle the powdered gelatin over the milk and let stand for 10 minutes.

3   Combine the milk–gelatin mixture with the remaining 2½ cups (592mL or 605g) of the milk in a medium, heavy saucepan.

4   Whisk over medium-high heat until the powdered gelatin dissolves, about 1 minute.

5   Continue to heat, whisking occasionally, until the mixture is just below a boil and small bubbles are forming along the side of the saucepan, about 4 minutes.

6   Meanwhile, place the sugar and cornstarch in a bowl and whisk to combine.

7   In a separate heatproof bowl, combine the egg yolks and egg.

8   Whisk in the sugar and cornstarch.

9   Gradually, in several additions, whisk in the hot milk mixture.

10   Pour everything back into the saucepan and whisk constantly over medium heat until the mixture starts to thicken and boil, about 1½ to 2 minutes. Whisk at a boil for 2 more minutes. Remove from the heat.

11   Remove the leaf gelatin from the water. Wring out the excess water, then whisk the gelatin into the pastry cream until it dissolves.

12   Whisk in the butter and vanilla paste.

13   Pour the pastry cream through a fine-mesh strainer into a heatproof bowl. Place a piece of plastic wrap directly onto the surface of the pastry cream and gently smooth with your fingers. This will prevent a skin from forming on top of the pastry cream.

14   Chill in the refrigerator until the pastry cream is firm, about 2 hours. You can speed up this process by placing the pastry cream over an ice-water bath.

15   Pour the heavy cream into the bowl of a stand mixer fitted with the whisk attachment. Whip on Medium for 30 seconds. Mix on High until soft peaks form, about 1½ to 2 minutes.

16   Remove the firm pastry cream from the refrigerator. Remove the plastic wrap and set it aside. Whisk the pastry cream until smooth, then gradually fold in the whipped cream until no streaks remain. Smooth the top of the pastry cream and re-cover with the plastic wrap.

17   Chill in the refrigerator until the pastry cream is set, about 1 hour.

Banana Cream Pie

When we decided to start a pie company, Craig and I sat down and made a list of six iconic pies we knew we had to master in order to call ourselves pie makers. Banana cream was second only to apple on that list, and now it is usually second only to apple in terms of popularity at the pie shop.

All the banana flavor in the recipe comes from the fresh bananas that are layered in the bottom of the pie shell, so be sure to use bananas that are ripe but not bruised. Nutmeg does an amazing job of bringing out the banana flavor. It is worth the extra time to buy whole nutmeg and grate it yourself.

Ingredients

Makes one 9-inch (22.5-cm) pie

1	single-crust, blind-baked All-Butter Pie Dough shell (recipe p. 24, blind baking p. 34)		2 Tablespoons	fresh orange juice	30g
1 recipe	Pastry Cream (recipe p. 126)		1 Tablespoon	fresh lemon juice	15g
¼ teaspoon	ground nutmeg	1g		Melted white chocolate, for coating the pie shell	
3	medium, ripe bananas	360g		White chocolate curls, for garnish (sidebar p. 130)	

Next page

BANANA CREAM PIE

Continued

1   Prepare the Pastry Cream, adding the nutmeg to the stand mixer in step 15, after the heavy cream has been whipped on Medium for 30 seconds.

2   Slice the bananas into 1-inch (2.5-cm) thick rounds. Toss with the orange and lemon juices to coat.

3   Let slices drain in a strainer or colander for 2 to 3 minutes.

4   Brush the inside of the empty pie shell with a thin coat of melted white chocolate.

5   Chill in the refrigerator until the chocolate cools and sets, about 5 minutes.

6   Remove the firm pastry cream from the refrigerator and whisk until smooth and fluffy. Layer the banana slices over the bottom of the prepared pie shell and top with spoonfuls of pastry cream. Make sure all of the bananas are completely covered and that the pastry cream meets the edge of the pie crust. Make decorative swirls or spikes in the pastry cream using a spatula or the back of a spoon.

7   Chill in the refrigerator for at least 1 hour. Garnish with white chocolate curls before serving.

The finished pie can be stored in the refrigerator for up to 3 days. Do not store at room temperature.

CHOCOLATE CURLS

At the pie shop, we top the Banana Cream Pie with white chocolate curls and the Chocolate Cream Pie with dark chocolate curls. You can make chocolate curls yourself by running a vegetable peeler over a block or bar of good-quality white or dark chocolate.

The trick is getting the chocolate at just the right temperature; chocolate that is too cold will break into shavings (actually, these make a pretty garnish too!), and chocolate that is too hot will come off in smooth strips but won't curl. You want to soften the chocolate without melting it, which you can do by either warming a wrapped bar of chocolate between your hands, or placing it, unwrapped, in the microwave for 1 to 2 seconds. White chocolate will soften much faster than dark chocolate.

You can store the curls in a covered container in the freezer until ready to use.

Coconut Cream Pie

Coconut cream pie is often overshadowed by its more

popular cousin, banana cream, and that's a shame. This is a wonderful pie, full of creamy rich coconut pastry cream piled on top of nutty coconut flakes. It's a comforting old-fashioned flavor and you've forgotten how much you love it!

Ingredients

Makes one 9-inch (22.5-cm) pie

1	**single-crust, blind-baked All-Butter Pie Dough shell (recipe p. 24, blind baking p. 34)**	
1 recipe	**Pastry Cream (recipe p. 126), substituting ingredients as noted**	
1¼ cups (296 mL)	**coconut milk**	312g
	Melted white chocolate, for coating the pie shell	
1 cup	**sweetened coconut flakes**	84g
¼ cup	**toasted sweetened coconut flakes (sidebar p. 105)**	21g

The finished pie can be stored in the refrigerator for up to 3 days. Do not store at room temperature.

1 Prepare the Pastry Cream, reducing the amount of sugar to ¾ cup (200g). Use 1¼ cups (296mL or 312g) of coconut milk to replace the same amount of whole milk (still using ½ cup [119mL or 121g] of the remaining 1¾ cups [415mL or 423.5mL] whole milk to soak the powdered gelatin).

2 Brush the inside of the empty pie shell with a thin coat of melted white chocolate. Chill in the refrigerator until the chocolate cools and sets, about 5 minutes.

3 Remove the pastry cream from the refrigerator and whisk until smooth and fluffy.

4 Spread 1 cup of the coconut flakes into the prepared pie shell. Top with spoonfuls of pastry cream. Make sure all of the coconut is completely covered and that the pastry cream meets the edge of the pie crust. Make decorative swirls or spikes in the pastry cream using a spatula or the back of a spoon.

5 Sprinkle the toasted coconut flakes across the top of the pie. Chill in the refrigerator for at least 1 hour before serving.

Caramel-Banana Cream Pie

For this pie, we make a caramel pastry cream and then drizzle even more caramel over the bananas in the bottom of the pie shell. The recipe may seem a bit involved at first, but once you master making the caramel, you'll have both a delicious variation on banana cream pie and extra caramel sauce for your ice cream! The black pepper in the caramel is the key to bringing all the flavors together. Don't skip it.

It's very important that you assemble all of the ingredients before beginning the recipe, including dividing out the whole milk. You will need 1½ cups (592mL or 605g) in step 6, and if you stop to measure out the milk at that point, the sugar will burn.

Ingredients

Makes one 9-inch (22.5-cm) pie

1	single-crust, blind-baked All-Butter Pie Dough shell (recipe p. 24, blind baking p. 34)	
1 sheet	leaf gelatin (silver strength)	2.5g
3 cups (711mL)	whole milk, divided	726g
1 Tablespoon	unflavored powdered gelatin	7g
1¼ cups plus 2 Tablespoons	granulated sugar, divided	276g
¼ cup	cornstarch	35g
3	large egg yolks	60g

1	large egg	50g
2 Tablespoons	unsalted butter	28g
1 Tablespoon	vanilla paste	15g
1 cup (237mL)	heavy cream	232g
3 Tablespoons (45mL)	Caramel Sauce (recipe follows)	
3	medium, ripe bananas	360g
2 Tablespoons	fresh orange juice	30g
1 Tablespoon	fresh lemon juice	15g

1 Place the leaf gelatin in a small bowl of ice water. Set aside to bloom for 10 minutes.

2 Pour ½ cup (119mL or 121g) of the milk into a small bowl. Sprinkle the powdered gelatin over the milk and let stand for 10 minutes.

3 Place 1¼ cups (250g) of the sugar in a medium, heavy saucepan.

4 Cook over medium-high heat, stirring occasionally, until the sugar melts and starts to turn brown. Carefully break up any remaining lumps of sugar.

5 Continue cooking until the melted sugar turns dark amber and just begins to smoke, no more than 30 seconds.

6 Immediately reduce the heat to medium and slowly stir in a small amount of the remaining whole milk. Be careful, as the sugar will steam and sputter.

7 Slowly pour in the rest of the whole milk in several additions, stirring after each addition until it is fully incorporated and the mixture is smooth.

8 Slowly pour in the milk-gelatin mixture, whisking constantly until the powdered gelatin is dissolved, about 1 minute.

9 Continue to cook over medium heat until the mixture is just below a boil and small bubbles are forming along the side of the saucepan. *About 4 minutes*

10 Meanwhile, place 2 tablespoons (25g) of the sugar and the cornstarch in a bowl and whisk to combine.

11 In a separate, heatproof bowl, combine the egg yolks and egg.

12 Whisk in the sugar and cornstarch.

13 Gradually whisk in the hot mixture.

14 Pour everything back into the saucepan and cook over medium heat, whisking constantly, until it starts to thicken and begins to boil. Whisk for 2 more minutes at a boil. Remove from the heat.

15 Remove the leaf gelatin from the ice water. Wring out the excess water, then whisk the gelatin into the pastry cream until it dissolves.

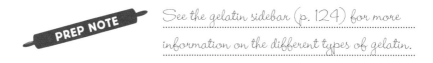

PREP NOTE *See the gelatin sidebar (p. 124) for more information on the different types of gelatin.*

Next page

CARAMEL–BANANA CREAM PIE

Continued

16 Whisk in the butter and vanilla paste.

17 Pour the pastry cream through a fine-mesh strainer into a heatproof bowl. Place a piece of plastic wrap directly onto the surface of the pastry cream and gently smooth with your fingers. This will prevent a skin from forming on top of the pastry cream.

18 Chill in the refrigerator until it is firm, about 2 hours. You can speed up this process by placing the pastry cream over an ice-water bath.

19 Pour the heavy cream into the bowl of a stand mixer fitted with the whisk attachment. Whip on Medium for 30 seconds, turn the mixer up to High and continue to mix until soft peaks form, about 1½ to 2 minutes.

20 Remove the firm pastry cream from the refrigerator. Remove the plastic wrap and set it aside.

21 Whisk the pastry cream until smooth, then gradually fold in the whipped cream until no streaks remain. Smooth the top of the pie filling and re-cover with the plastic wrap.

22 Chill the pastry cream in the refrigerator until it is set, about 1 hour.

23 While the pastry cream chills, prepare the Caramel Sauce. Set aside.

24 Slice the bananas into 1-inch (2.5-cm) thick rounds. Toss with the orange and lemon juices until coated. Let the slices drain in a strainer or colander for 2 to 3 minutes.

25 Remove the caramel pastry cream from the refrigerator and whisk until smooth and fluffy.

26 Spoon the Caramel Sauce into the bottom of the empty pie shell.

27 Layer the banana slices over the Caramel Sauce.

28 Top with spoonfuls of caramel pastry cream, making sure all of the bananas are completely covered and the pastry cream meets the edge of the pie crust. Make decorative swirls or spikes in the pastry cream using a spatula or the back of a spoon.

29 Chill in the refrigerator for at least 1 hour before serving.

The finished pie can be stored in the refrigerator for up to 3 days. Do not store at room temperature.

CARAMEL SAUCE
Makes about 1 cup (237mL or 232g)

This recipe makes more than you will need for the pie, so store the remainder in a covered jar in the refrigerator for a fruit dip or ice cream topping.

½ cup	**granulated sugar**	100g
½ cup (119mL)	**heavy cream, room temperature**	116g
Pinch	**freshly ground black pepper**	

1 Fill a medium heatproof bowl ¼ of the way up with ice. Add cold water just until the ice starts to float. Set aside.

2 Place a fine-mesh strainer over a medium heatproof bowl. Set aside.

3 Place the sugar in a 1-quart (948-mL), heavy saucepan. Cook over medium-high heat, without stirring, until the sugar melts around the edge of the saucepan, about 2 minutes.

4 Gently stir, then turn the heat down to medium and continue to cook until a puddle of melted sugar forms in the middle of the pan, about 3 to 4 more minutes. Stir until all the sugar is completely melted and has turned medium amber.

5 Turn the heat down to low. Immediately pour about 2 tablespoons of the cream into the melted sugar, stirring constantly. Be careful, as the sugar will steam and sputter. Add the rest of the cream in 4 to 5 additions, whisking constantly. The mixture will appear ropy at first, and then form a thick sauce.

6 Remove from the heat and gently dip the bottom of the saucepan into the bowl of ice water, making sure not to let any water spill into the caramel. Remove from the ice water. This will keep the sugar from cooking any further.

7 Pour through the strainer (there will be some hardened sugar that didn't melt) into the heatproof bowl. Place in the bowl of ice water, again taking care not to let any water get in the caramel. Add the black pepper and whisk occasionally until cool.

The remaining Caramel Sauce can be stored in the refrigerator, in a covered container, for several weeks.

Red Line Espresso Cream Pie

In Chicago, we are lucky to have a great local coffee roaster by the name of Metropolis Coffee Company, which also operates a café on the North Side. Located just one block from Chicago's Red Line El tracks, the café was one of our very first customers, offering our pies by the slice along with its own delicious coffee. The Redline Espresso that Metropolis roasts is aptly named—not only due to proximity, but also because the Red Line is the busiest train and one of only two lines that run 24 hours a day (the other one is the Blue Line).

We pour Metropolis coffee at the pie shop, but lack the space for an espresso machine—so we are forced to take our espresso in pie form! Substitute decaf espresso beans, if you must.

You will need to prepare the Espresso Milk and Espresso Cream at least six hours before you plan to make the pie.

Ingredients

Makes one 9-inch (22.5-cm) pie

1	single-crust, blind-baked All-Butter Pie Dough shell (recipe p. 24, blind baking p. 34)		1	large egg	50g
3 cups (711mL)	Espresso Milk (recipe follows)	726g	2 Tablespoons	unsalted butter	28g
2¼ teaspoons	powdered unflavored gelatin	5g	1 Tablespoon	vanilla paste	15g
1 cup plus 2 Tablespoons	granulated sugar, divided	226g		Melted bittersweet chocolate, for coating the pie shell	
¼ cup	cornstarch	35g	1 cup (237mL)	Espresso Cream (recipe follows)	242g
3	large egg yolks	60g		Roughly chopped chocolate-covered espresso beans, for garnish	

1   Strain the Espresso Milk into a 1-quart (948-mL) liquid measuring cup. You should have 3 cups (711mL); if you do not, add enough fresh whole milk to make up the difference.

2   Pour ½ cup (119mL or 121g) of the Espresso Milk into a small bowl. Sprinkle the powdered gelatin over the milk and let stand for 10 minutes.

3   Combine the milk-gelatin mixture with the remaining Espresso Milk in a medium, heavy saucepan.

4   Whisk over medium-high heat, until the powdered gelatin dissolves, about 1 minute.

5   Continue to heat, whisking occasionally, until the mixture comes to just below a boil and small bubbles are forming along the sides of the saucepan, about 4 minutes.

6   Meanwhile, place 1 cup (200g) of the sugar and the cornstarch in a bowl and whisk to combine.

7   In a separate, heatproof bowl, combine the egg yolks and egg.

8   Whisk in the sugar and cornstarch.

9   Gradually, in several additions, whisk in the hot milk mixture.

10 Pour everything back into the saucepan and whisk constantly over medium heat until the pastry cream begins to thicken and starts to boil, about 1½ to 2 minutes. Whisk at a boil for 2 more minutes.

11 Remove from the heat and whisk in the butter and vanilla paste.

12 Pour the pastry cream through a fine-mesh strainer into a heatproof bowl. Place a piece of plastic wrap directly onto the surface of the pastry cream and gently smooth with your fingers. This will prevent a skin from forming on top of the pastry cream.

13 Chill in the refrigerator until it is firm, about 2 hours. You can speed up this process by placing the pastry cream over an ice-water bath.

14 Brush the inside of the empty pie shell with a thin coat of melted chocolate. Place in the refrigerator until the chocolate cools and sets, about 5 minutes.

PREP NOTE See the gelatin sidebar (p. 124) for more information on the different types of gelatin.

Next page

RED LINE ESPRESSO CREAM PIE

Continued

15 Remove the firm espresso pastry cream from the refrigerator and whisk until smooth.

16 Spoon the pastry cream into the prepared pie shell and smooth the top with the back of the spoon or an offset spatula.

17 Place a piece of plastic wrap directly on the surface of the pie and chill in the refrigerator until set, about 1 hour.

18 Meanwhile, remove the Espresso Cream from the refrigerator and strain into the bowl of a stand mixer fitted with the whisk attachment. You should have 1 cup (237mL or 242g); if you do not, add enough fresh heavy cream to make up the difference. Whip on Medium-High for 30 seconds.

19 With the mixer running, slowly pour in the remaining 2 tablespoons of the sugar. Whip on High until soft peaks form.

20 Spoon the whipped cream onto the pie, making sure it covers the pastry cream and touches the edge of the crust, otherwise the pastry cream will dry out and form a skin. Swirl the whipped cream with the back of a spoon or an offset spatula.

21 Garnish with chocolate-covered espresso beans.

The finished pie can be stored in the refrigerator for up to 3 days. Do not store at room temperature.

ESPRESSO MILK
Makes about 3 cups (711mL or 726g)

½ cup	**espresso beans**	32g
1	**lemon**	
3¼ cups (830mL)	**whole milk**	787g

1   Place the espresso beans in a coffee grinder or food processor and pulse 3 to 4 times, until the beans resemble fine gravel.

2   Using a vegetable peeler, cut 2 1-inch (2.5-cm) strips of zest from the lemon.

3   Combine all the ingredients in a 2-quart (1.9-L) container and stir well.

4   Cover (if the container doesn't have a lid, plastic wrap will do) and chill in the refrigerator for 6 hours, up to overnight.

ESPRESSO CREAM
Makes about 1 cup (237mL or 232g)

⅓ cup	**espresso beans**	21g
2 cups (474 mL)	**heavy cream**	464g

1   Place the espresso beans in a coffee grinder or food processor and pulse 3 to 4 times, until the beans resemble fine gravel.

2   Combine the heavy cream and ground espresso beans in a 1-quart (948-mL) container.

3   Cover (if the container doesn't have a lid, plastic wrap will do) and chill in the refrigerator for 6 hours, up to overnight.

Chocolate Cream Pie

This is not a chocolate pie of the overexposed French silk variety. It is the classic, densely chocolaty pie your grandmother made (or would have made if she'd had access to single-bean Venezuelan chocolate). Topped with Lightly Sweetened Whipped Cream, it is just about perfect.

Ingredients

Makes one 9-inch (22.5-cm) pie

1	**single-crust, blind-baked All-Butter Pie Dough shell (recipe p. 24, blind baking p. 34)**	
2 cups (474mL)	**whole milk, divided**	484g
1 cup (237mL)	**heavy cream**	232g
3 Tablespoons	**cornstarch**	27g
2	**large eggs**	100g
½ cup	**granulated sugar**	100g
5 ounces	**50–60% semisweet chocolate, roughly chopped**	140g
5 ounces	**60–70% bittersweet chocolate, roughly chopped**	140g
4 Tablespoons	**unsalted butter**	56g
1 teaspoon	**vanilla paste**	5g
Pinch	**kosher salt**	
	Melted bittersweet chocolate, for coating the pie shell	
1 recipe	**Lightly Sweetened Whipped Cream (recipe p. 311)**	
	Dark chocolate curls or shavings, for garnish (sidebar p. 130)	

Next page

CHOCOLATE CREAM PIE

Continued

1   Combine 1½ cups (356mL or 438g) of the milk and the cream in a medium, heavy saucepan. Bring to a boil over medium-high heat, stirring occasionally so the milk does not scorch on the bottom of the pan.

2   Meanwhile, whisk the remaining ½ cup (119mL or 121g) of milk into the cornstarch to make a smooth slurry.

3   Place the eggs into a medium, deep heatproof bowl. Whisk in the sugar until well combined. Slowly pour in the slurry and whisk until smooth. Gradually whisk in the hot milk mixture, stirring until well combined.

4   Pour everything back into the saucepan and cook over medium heat, whisking constantly, until the mixture starts to thicken and just begins to boil. Whisk at a boil for 2 more minutes.

5   Remove the saucepan from the heat and add both of the chocolates and the butter. Whisk until everything is melted and well incorporated. Whisk in the vanilla paste and salt.

6   Pour the pastry cream through a fine-mesh strainer into a heatproof bowl. Place a piece of plastic wrap directly onto the surface of the pastry cream and gently smooth with your fingers. This will prevent a skin from forming on the top of the pastry cream.

7   Chill the pastry cream in the refrigerator until it is firm, about 2 hours. You can speed up this process by placing the bowl of pastry cream over an ice-water bath.

8   Brush the inside of the empty pie shell with melted bittersweet chocolate. Place in the refrigerator until the chocolate cools and sets, about 5 minutes.

9   Remove the pastry cream from the refrigerator and whisk vigorously until smooth and light. Scoop the pastry cream into the prepared pie shell, smoothing the top with a spoon or offset spatula. Place a piece of plastic wrap directly on top of the pie and chill in the refrigerator until firm, about 1 hour.

10 Remove the plastic wrap and top the pie with the Lightly Sweetened Whipped Cream, making sure the pastry cream is completely covered or it will dry out.

11 Garnish with chocolate curls or shavings.

The pastry cream can be made up to 1 day in advance. The finished pie can be stored in the refrigerator for up to 3 days. Do not store at room temperature.

CUSTARD PIES

True pie aficionados will tell you that custard pies are some of the best pies around. Their homely exterior hides a wonderfully silky texture and straightforward flavor. We sample lots of custard pies at the shop because we know that once you taste one, you'll be hooked.

Banana Custard Pie

Baker Erica created this pie—but she hates bananas!

Ingredients

Makes one 9-inch (22.5-cm) pie

1	**single-crust, blind-baked All-Butter Pie Dough shell** (recipe p. 24, blind baking p. 34)	
3	**ripe, medium, unpeeled bananas**	360g
¼ teaspoon	**ground nutmeg**	1g
2 cups (474mL)	**heavy cream**	464g
4	**large egg yolks**	80g
1	**large egg**	50g
⅔ cup	**granulated sugar**	133g
Pinch	**kosher salt**	
1 teaspoon	**vanilla paste**	5g

The baked pie can be stored in the refrigerator for up to 3 days. Do not leave at room temperature.

PREP NOTE

This is a great way to use up bananas that are getting too ripe. The riper the banana, the more banana flavor in the pie.

1. Preheat the oven to 350°F (180°C).

2. Place the bananas on a baking sheet and prick the peels with a fork. Sprinkle the nutmeg over the bananas, and then bake for 25 minutes, until they are dark brown and soft. The peels will start to shrivel. Set aside to cool slightly.

3. Place the cream in a small, heavy saucepan.

4. Scoop the banana pulp from the peels into a small bowl and measure out ⅔ cup (150g). Add the pulp to the cream and mash with a whisk. Cook over medium heat until mixture comes to just below a boil. Small bubbles will form along the side of the pan. Remove from the heat and let steep for 20 minutes.

5. Meanwhile, place the egg yolks and egg into a medium, heatproof bowl. Whisk in the sugar and salt. In small batches, pour the banana and cream mixture through a fine-mesh strainer and into the egg mixture. Mix well after each addition. Stir in the vanilla paste.

6. Pour the banana custard into the pie shell. Bake for 40 to 45 minutes, rotating 180 degrees after 20 minutes, until the edge of the filling is slightly puffed and the custard moves in 1 piece when the pie is gently shaken. Cool to room temperature, then chill in the refrigerator for at least 3 hours before slicing.

Coconut Custard Pie

If you could only have one pie in your recipe box, this
should be the one. The ingredients are few, the method is straightforward and quick, and it can be
made any time of year. Most importantly, it is delicious and comforting.

Ingredients

Makes one 9-inch (22.5-cm) pie

1	single-crust, blind-baked All-Butter Pie Dough shell (recipe p. 24, blind baking p. 34)	
⅔ cup	sweetened coconut flakes	57g
2⅓ cups (553mL)	heavy cream	541g
⅔ cup (158mL)	coconut milk	167g
4	large eggs	200g
¾ cup	granulated sugar	150g
½ teaspoon	kosher salt	1.5g
1 teaspoon	vanilla paste	5g
	Toasted sweetened coconut flakes (sidebar p. 105), for topping	

*The baked pie can be stored in the refrigerator for
up to 3 days. Do not leave at room temperature.*

1 Preheat the oven to 400°F (200°C).

2 Scatter the coconut flakes over the bottom of
the empty pie shell.

3 Combine the heavy cream and coconut milk
in a medium saucepan. Bring to a boil over
medium heat, whisking occasionally.

4 Meanwhile, whisk together the eggs, sugar,
and salt in a medium heatproof bowl until
well blended. Slowly pour in the hot coconut
milk mixture a little bit at a time, whisking
thoroughly after each addition. Add the vanilla
paste and whisk to combine.

5 Pour the pie filling through a fine-mesh
strainer into the pie shell.

6 Bake for 20 to 25 minutes, until the edge of the
filling closest to the crust is set and slightly
puffy. The middle of the pie should still be
quite loose. The custard filling should not appear set when it comes out of the oven. Cool at
room temperature for 5 minutes and recheck.
The pie should be completely set. If not, return
to the oven for 5 to 10 more minutes. Cool to
room temperature, then chill in the refrigerator for at least 3 hours before slicing. Top with
toasted coconut flakes before serving.

Dutch Apple Pie with Sour Cream Custard

"Dutch apple pie" usually refers to a pie with a traditional pie crust on the bottom, apple filling in the middle, and a crumble on top. For our version, we bake the apples in a sour cream custard and scatter a walnut streusel on top. We like it so much; we came up with a variation for every season.

Ingredients

Makes one 9-inch (22.5-cm) pie

1	single-crust, blind-baked All-Butter Pie Dough shell (recipe p. 24, blind baking p. 34)		⅛ teaspoon	kosher salt	
2 cups	apples, peeled and chopped into ½-inch-square (13-mm) pieces	263g	1 cup (237mL)	sour cream	242g
½ cup plus 2 Tablespoons	granulated sugar	126g	1	large egg	50g
2 Tablespoons	all-purpose flour	18g	1 teaspoon	vanilla paste	5g
			1 recipe	Walnut Streusel (recipe follows)	

The baked pie can be stored in the refrigerator for 2 to 3 days.

1   Preheat the oven to 300°F (150°C).

2   Spread the apple pieces over the bottom of the pie shell. Place on a baking sheet and set aside.

3   Place the sugar, flour, and salt in a small bowl and whisk until well combined.

4   Whisk together the sour cream, egg, and vanilla paste.

5   Add the dry ingredients and whisk until smooth. Pour into the prepared pie shell, over the apples. With a spatula, submerge any apples that float to the top.

6   Bake 20 to 25 minutes, until the edge of the filling is slightly puffed and the center is dry to the touch.

7   While the pie bakes, prepare the Walnut Streusel.

8   When the pie is ready, gently scatter the streusel over the top of the pie and bake 10 to 15 minutes more, until the streusel is crispy.

9   Cool to room temperature, then chill in the refrigerator for at least 1 hour before slicing.

WALNUT STREUSEL

Makes enough to top one pie

1 cup	**all-purpose flour**	142g	1 teaspoon	**ground cinnamon**	2g
¾ cup	**finely chopped walnuts**	75g	Pinch	**kosher salt**	
½ cup	**granulated sugar**	100g	6 Tablespoons	**unsalted butter, melted**	84g
½ cup	**firmly packed dark brown sugar**	120g			

1   Combine the flour, walnuts, granulated sugar, brown sugar, cinnamon, and salt in a medium bowl.

2   Pour in the melted butter and mix with your fingers until the mixture resembles coarse meal.

FRUIT VARIATIONS

The combination of fruit and tangy custard is just too good to let go, so we keep the Dutch pies with sour cream custard going year-round. Just replace the apples with any of the fruit variations below.

DUTCH BLUEBERRY VARIATION

Place 1¾ cups (263g) blueberries in a small bowl. Sort through them and pick out any stems and leaves. Zest a lemon over the blueberries, then toss them with 2 teaspoons (10g) of fresh lemon juice. Follow the rest of the recipe as directed.

DUTCH PEAR VARIATION

Use 1¾ cups (263g) pears that have been peeled, cored, and chopped into ½-inch (13-mm) pieces, then follow the rest of the recipe as directed. The pears for this variation need to be perfectly ripe. For that reason, we do not even offer this pie as a special order—we only make it when we have the perfect pears.

DUTCH CRANBERRY VARIATION

Place 2 cups (198g) fresh cranberries in the bowl of a food processor and pulse 2 to 3 times. Transfer them to a small bowl and zest an orange over them, then toss to combine. Follow the rest of the recipe as directed.

Pumpkin Pie

At the shop, pumpkin pie season starts on October 1 and runs full speed through New Year's Eve. Most folks wouldn't even think of celebrating the holidays without at least one. In the days leading up to Thanksgiving, when our ovens run nearly 24 hours a day, our whole block smells like pumpkin pie spice!

Ingredients

Makes one 9-inch (22.5-cm) pie

1	single-crust, blind-baked All-Butter Pie Dough shell (recipe p. 24, blind baking p. 34)		Pinch	kosher salt	
⅔ cup	firmly packed brown sugar	160g	2	large eggs	100g
⅓ cup	granulated sugar	66g	1 cup (237mL)	heavy cream	232g
1 Tablespoon	all-purpose flour	9g	⅓ cup (79mL)	whole milk	80g
1 teaspoon	pumpkin pie spice	3g	2 cups	canned pumpkin	486g
Pinch	freshly ground black pepper		2 Tablespoons	vanilla paste	30g

The pie filling can be stored in the refrigerator for up to 2 days before using. The baked pie can be stored in the refrigerator for up to 3 days. Do not leave at room temperature.

At the pie shop, we garnish the pumpkin pie with Pie Crust Cookies (p. 309).

Next page

PUMPKIN PIE

Continued

1   Preheat the oven to 350°F (180°C).

2   Place the pie shell on a baking sheet.

3   Combine the brown sugar, granulated sugar, flour, pumpkin pie spice, black pepper, and salt in a small bowl and mix with a whisk or your hands to break up the brown sugar and combine the ingredients. Set aside.

4   Place the eggs into a large bowl and break up the yolks with a whisk.

5   Add the cream and milk and whisk just to combine.

6   Add the pumpkin and vanilla paste and whisk until the batter is smooth.

7   Add the dry ingredients in 3 additions, mixing well after each one.

8   Pour the batter into the pie shell.

9   Bake for 1 hour to 1 hour and 20 minutes, until the filling is slightly puffed at the edge and the center is set. The center of the pie should be shiny but dry to the touch.

10 Remove from the oven and cover with a large mixing bowl or casserole dish. There should be at least 2 to 3 inches (5–7.5cm) of space between the pie and the top of the inverted bowl.

11 Prop up one side of the bowl with a knife or spoon to let the steam escape. This allows the pie to cool slowly and prevents cracks from forming on top of the pie.

12 Cool to room temperature, then chill in the refrigerator for at least 2 hours, up to overnight, before slicing.

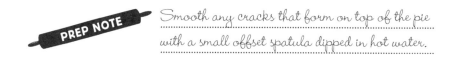

PREP NOTE *Smooth any cracks that form on top of the pie with a small offset spatula dipped in hot water.*

IN DEFENSE OF CANNED PUMPKIN

OK, I have a confession to make. I prefer canned (gasp!) instead of fresh pumpkin for making pumpkin pie. I was so excited the first time I made a pumpkin pie "from scratch," and so disappointed with the results! Even after I roasted, puréed, strained, and seasoned, the texture was stringy and watery and the flavor was faint. I found I had to sauté the pumpkin over low heat for 10 minutes or so to cook off the extra water and intensify the flavor. That was fine for a pie or two, but the results varied from pumpkin to pumpkin and each pie had to be seasoned to taste. Now I leave making pumpkin purée to the pros.

In the restaurants where I have worked, my best "pumpkin" desserts were often made with a mix of other types of winter squash from the farmers' market. Some of my favorite varieties are combined in the Three-Squash Pie. As it turns out, the line between pumpkin and squash is pretty fuzzy. While pumpkins are always squash, squash are rarely true pumpkins. And most of the ones we call pumpkins aren't pumpkins at all.

Here's the technical bit: a pumpkin is a squash of the Cucurbita *genetic family.* Cucurbita *has several species, or subcategories, and three of them contain the squash we commonly call pumpkins. They are* Cucurbita pepo, Cucurbita maxima *and* Cucurbita moschata. *All true pumpkins belong to* Cucurbita pepo *(as do pattypan squash and several varieties of zucchini). The definition has to do with the shape and woodiness of the pumpkin's stem, and nothing to do with its roundness, color, or suitability for a Jack-o-Lantern.*

Cucurbita moschata *is mostly squash that are tan and oblong, like the butternut squash and Dickinson pumpkin, a variety specially bred by Libby's (a food company) for their canned pumpkin. The Dickinson's pumpkin accounts for 85 percent of the canned pumpkin sold in the US—and it is not a pumpkin at all.*

Cucurbita maxima *is most of the fall and winter squashes you'll find at the farmers' market, but it also includes hybrids like Big Max and Atlantic Giant pumpkins. These are the two-ton behemoths featured on the front page of small-town newspapers every fall. The University of Texas School of Agriculture says these should really be called pumpkin-like squash.*

So in all likelihood, your favorite pumpkin pie is actually a squash pie, and Linus has been sitting out in that cold "pumpkin" patch waiting for the Great Pumpkin-Like Squash.

Caramel—Apple Cider Pie

Baker Molly developed this recipe late last winter to take

advantage of the last sweet ingredient still available from our farmers—wonderful apple cider. Inspired by an apple cider cream pie recipe that she saw on Lottie + Doof, one of our favorite food blogs, she cheerfully persevered through weeks of suggestions and "not-quite-theres" as we worked to get the tangy-to-sweet ratio just right!

Ingredients

Makes one 9-inch (22.5-cm) pie

1	single-crust, blind-baked All-Butter Pie Dough shell (recipe p. 24, blind baking p. 34)		4	large eggs	200g
2 cups (474mL)	apple cider	493g	1 Tablespoon	Calvados	18g
1 cup	granulated sugar	200g	1 Tablespoon	cider vinegar	11g
½ cup (119mL)	sour cream	121g	1 teaspoon	vanilla paste	5g
½ teaspoon	kosher salt	1.5g	¼ cup (59mL)	Caramel (recipe follows)	50g

1   Pour the apple cider into a 1-quart saucepan and bring to a boil over medium-high heat.

2   Reduce the heat and simmer until the cider is reduced to ½ cup (119mL or 120g), about 10 minutes. Set aside to cool.

3   Preheat the oven to 350°F (180°C).

4   Place the pie shell on a baking sheet.

5   Place the sugar, sour cream, and salt in a medium bowl and whisk to combine.

6   Crack the eggs into a small bowl and beat until just combined.

7   Whisk the eggs into the sugar mixture in 3 additions, mixing well after each one.

8   Stir the Calvados, vinegar, and vanilla paste into the apple cider. Pour this into the egg mixture and whisk until well combined.

9   Pour the batter into the pie shell and bake 40 to 45 minutes, until the edge of the filling is slightly puffed. Gently shake the pie. The custard should move as 1 piece. If the center of the pie jiggles by itself, return the pie to the oven for 5 to 10 more minutes. The top of the pie will be very shiny even when it is set.

10 Cool to room temperature.

11 Prepare the Caramel. Once it is cool, pour ¼ cup (59mL or 50g) over the baked, cooled pie. Spread with the back of a tablespoon or an offset spatula.

12 Chill in the refrigerator for at least 2 hours before serving.

The finished pie can be stored in the refrigerator for 2 to 3 days.

CARAMEL

½ cup plus 2 Tablespoons	**granulated sugar**	126g
½ cup (119mL)	**heavy cream, room temperature**	116g
⅛ teaspoon	**kosher salt**	

1   Fill a medium heatproof bowl ¼ of the way up with ice. Add cold water just until the ice starts to float. Set aside.

2   Place a fine-mesh strainer over a medium heatproof bowl. Set aside.

3   Place the sugar in a 1-quart (948-mL), heavy saucepan. Cook over medium-high heat, without stirring, until the sugar melts around the edge of the saucepan, about 2 minutes.

4   Gently stir, then turn the heat down to medium and continue to cook until a puddle of melted sugar forms in the middle of the pan, about 3 to 4 minutes. Stir until all the sugar is completely melted and has turned medium amber.

5   Turn the heat down to low. Immediately pour about 2 tablespoons of the cream into the melted sugar, stirring constantly. Be careful, as the sugar will steam and sputter.

6   Add the rest of the cream in 4 to 5 additions, whisking constantly. The mixture will appear ropy at first, and then form a thick sauce.

7   Remove from the heat and carefully dip the bottom of the saucepan into the bowl of ice water, making sure not to let any water spill into the caramel. Remove from the ice water. This will keep the sugar from cooking any further.

8   Add the salt and whisk until it dissolves.

9   Pour through the strainer (there will be some hardened sugar that didn't melt) into the heatproof bowl. Place in the bowl of ice water, again taking care not to let any water get in the caramel.

10 Whisk occasionally until cool.

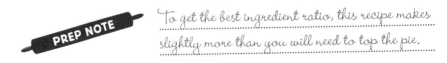

PREP NOTE To get the best ingredient ratio, this recipe makes slightly more than you will need to top the pie.

CURD PIES

Curd pies are made by cooking citrus juice, sugar, egg yolks, and butter together on the stove until the mixture thickens. The texture is wonderfully light and the flavor is intense. We use curds as the base for our Lemon and Passion Fruit Meringue pies. The Key Lime and Orange Cream pies in this chapter aren't true curds since they include sweetened condensed milk. We always include at least one of these pies on the day's menu at the shop. Our customers love the bright tropical flavors, especially in the dead of a Chicago winter.

Lemon Curd

We use Passion Fruit Curd to make three different pies at
Hoosier Mama—but Lemon Curd is the base for the iconic Lemon Meringue, so we have made Lemon the master recipe here. Instructions for how to switch it up to make Passion Fruit Curd follow.

Ingredients

Makes enough to fill one 9-inch (22.5-cm) pie

1 sheet	leaf gelatin (silver strength)	2.5g		1 cup	granulated sugar	200g
1 cup (237mL)	fresh lemon juice	250g		Pinch	kosher salt	
1¼ sticks	unsalted butter	140g		10	large egg yolks	200g

The finished curd can be stored in the refrigerator for up to 1 week. The passion fruit variation makes about 3½ to 4 cups (830–948mL or 882–1008g). The amount needed varies by pie, so sometimes you will have leftovers.

1   Place the leaf gelatin in a small bowl of ice water. Set aside to bloom for 10 minutes.

2   Combine the lemon juice, butter, sugar, and salt in a medium, heavy saucepan.

3   Place a fine-mesh strainer over the bowl of a stand mixer. Set the bowl close to the stove so you can strain the curd as soon as it is done cooking.

4   Place the saucepan over medium-high heat and cook until the sugar dissolves, the butter melts, and the mixture comes to a boil, about 3 minutes.

5   Meanwhile, place the egg yolks in a medium, heatproof bowl and whisk until well combined.

6   Slowly pour the hot lemon juice mixture over the yolks, whisking constantly. Return the mixture to the saucepan.

7   Cook over medium heat, whisking constantly, until the mixture thickens, about 2 minutes. Do not allow the mixture to boil. The curd is done when whisk tracks are visible for several seconds before disappearing, and the mixture easily coats the back of a spoon. Remove the curd from the heat.

8   Remove the leaf gelatin from the ice water. Wring out the excess water, then whisk the gelatin into the curd until it dissolves.

9   Pour the curd through the strainer.

10 Place the bowl back on the stand mixer fitted with the whisk attachment.

11 Whip on Low until the mixture begins to cool and thicken. Turn the mixer up to High and whip until the mixer bowl is cool to the touch.

PASSION FRUIT CURD VARIATION

Replace the lemon juice with 9 ounces by volume (270mL or 293g) of passion fruit purée. Bring the amount of granulated sugar down to ½ cup plus 2 tablespoons (125g). Follow the rest of the recipe as directed.

PREP NOTE   See the gelatin sidebar (p. 124) for more information on the different types of gelatin.

Lemon Meringue Pie

Most of our customers love this pie, but the ones who

don't really hate it! It has old-school lemon flavor, which means it is tart. If you like your lemon with a little pucker, this pie is for you. If not, try the Lemon Soufflé or Lemon Chess pies.

At the shop, we serve slices with a silver fork, since the citric acid can react with some flatware to cause a metallic taste.

Ingredients

Makes one 9-inch (22.5-cm) pie

1	**single-crust, blind-baked All-Butter Pie Dough shell (recipe p. 24, blind baking p. 34)**
	Melted white chocolate, for coating the pie shell
1 recipe	**Lemon Curd (recipe p. 156)**
1 recipe	**Creamy Meringue (recipe p. 308)**

The finished pie can be stored in the refrigerator for up to 3 days. Do not store at room temperature.

1 Brush the inside of the empty pie shell with a thin coat of melted white chocolate. Place in the refrigerator until the chocolate sets and hardens, about 5 minutes.

2 Spoon the Lemon Curd into the prepared pie shell and smooth the top with a spatula. If you are using curd that has been refrigerated, whip it in the bowl of a stand mixer fitted with the whisk attachment for 2 to 3 minutes first. Place a piece of plastic wrap directly on top of the curd. Chill in the refrigerator until the curd has set, about 1 hour.

3 Remove the pie from the refrigerator and carefully peel off the plastic wrap.

4 Prepare the Creamy Meringue. Spread it over the top of the pie, making sure that the meringue touches the edge of the pie shell all around to seal the curd underneath and prevent weeping. Use a spatula or the back of a spoon to make spikes and swirls in the meringue. Toast the meringue with a butane torch.

Passion Fruit Meringue Pie

Both wonderfully homey and wonderfully exotic!

Ingredients

Makes one 9-inch (22.5-cm) pie

1	**single-crust, blind-baked All-Butter Pie Dough shell (recipe p. 24, blind baking p. 34)**
	Melted white chocolate, for brushing pie shell
1 recipe (3½–4 cups)	**Passion Fruit Curd (recipe p. 157)**
1 recipe	**Creamy Meringue (recipe p. 308)**

1 Brush the inside of the empty pie shell with a thin layer of melted white chocolate. Place in the refrigerator until white chocolate sets and hardens, about 5 minutes.

2 Spoon the Passion Fruit Curd into the prepared pie shell and smooth the top with a spatula. If you are using curd that has been refrigerated, whip it in the bowl of a stand mixer fitted with the whisk attachment for 2 to 3 minutes first. Place a piece of plastic wrap directly on top of the curd. Chill in the refrigerator until the curd has set, about 1 hour.

3 Remove the pie from the refrigerator and carefully peel off the plastic wrap.

4 Prepare the Creamy Meringue. Spread it over the top of the pie, making sure that the meringue touches the edge of the pie shell all around to seal the curd underneath and prevent weeping. Use a spatula or the back of a spoon to make spikes and swirls in the meringue. Toast the meringue with a butane torch.

The finished pie can be stored in the refrigerator for up to 3 days. Do not store at room temperature

Strawberry and Passion Fruit Chiffon Pie

Make this pie in high summer, when strawberries are at their tastiest. We mix some freshly ground pepper with the cut strawberries to help them stand up to the passion fruit. How adamant are we that the pepper be ground fresh? We counted the number of cranks (15!) of the pepper mill per pie! Make the Passion Fruit Curd one day ahead so it is good and set.

Ingredients

Makes one 9-inch (22.5-cm) pie

1	single-crust, blind-baked All-Butter Pie Dough shell (recipe p. 24, blind baking p. 34)	
2½ cups	Passion Fruit Curd (recipe p. 157)	630g
1½ cups (356mL)	heavy cream	348g
2 Tablespoons	granulated sugar	26g
1 teaspoon	vanilla paste	5g
	Melted white chocolate, for coating the pie shell	
2 cups	Japanese-cut strawberries (sidebar p. 63)	226g
2 pinches	freshly ground black pepper	

Next page

STRAWBERRY AND PASSION FRUIT CHIFFON PIE
Continued

1   Place the Passion Fruit Curd in the bowl of a stand mixer fitted with the whisk attachment.

2   Whip on High for 30 seconds, until the curd is smooth. Transfer to another bowl and thoroughly wash the stand mixer bowl.

3   Combine the heavy cream, sugar, and vanilla paste in the bowl of the stand mixer still fitted with the whisk attachment.

4   Whip on Medium until soft peaks form when the whisk attachment is dipped into the cream and slowly pulled back out, about 1 minute and 30 seconds.

5   Gently fold the whipped cream mixture into the Passion Fruit Curd in 3 additions and smooth the top with a spatula.

6   Place a sheet of plastic wrap directly on top of the curd mixture and chill in the refrigerator until set, about 1 hour.

7   Meanwhile, brush the inside of the empty pie shell with a thin layer of melted white chocolate. Chill in the refrigerator until the chocolate sets and hardens, about 5 minutes.

8   Toss the strawberries with the black pepper. Layer the strawberries in the bottom of the prepared pie shell.

9   Remove the curd mixture from the refrigerator and whisk just until smooth. Mound on top of strawberries and smooth the top with a spatula or the back of a spoon.

This pie is best served the day it is made. The black pepper brings out the juice in the strawberries, which can puddle in the bottom of the pie after 1 or 2 days. The pie still tastes wonderful, but the slices are not as pretty. The finished pie can be stored in the refrigerator for up to 2 days.

Key Lime Pie

I never understood all the fuss about Key lime pie until I tracked down an actual Key lime. Key limes have a wonderfully floral flavor. They are tarter and more fragrant than the Persian limes you typically find in the grocery store. They are also much smaller, so juicing enough Key limes to make a pie is a daunting task, so much so that my assistant Erica thought she was being hazed when I gave her that job on her first day with us!

Today, most commercially grown Key limes come from Mexico or South America. A hurricane in 1926 wiped out most of the Florida Keys' lime groves. The few trees that remain are mostly in backyard gardens.

According to Florida lore, the pie was invented by shrimp fishermen in the Keys, who, while at sea, had lots of time but no ovens with which to bake pie. So they developed a recipe where the acid in the lime juice "cooks" the eggs and sweetened condensed milk, and thickens the filling, all without baking. Who knew fishermen made such great food scientists!

For safety and consistency, we briefly bake the pies at Hoosier Mama and suggest you do too. If you choose not to bake, be sure to whip the filling until it starts to thicken, then put it in the fridge to set overnight.

Next page

KEY LIME PIE

Continued

Ingredients

Makes one 9-inch (22.5-cm) pie

1	**Gingersnap Crumb Crust shell (recipe p. 45)**	
3	**large egg yolks**	60g
17–20	**Key limes, for zesting and juicing**	
1¼ cups (296mL)	**sweetened condensed milk**	400g
	Sweeter Whipped Cream (recipe p. 311) or Creamy Meringue (recipe p. 308), for topping	

.... STATE OF PIE ....

In 1965, Florida State Representative Bernie Papy, Jr., of Key West, introduced a bill that would impose a $100 fine on anyone advertising Key lime pie that was not made with real Florida Key limes. Sadly, the bill was defeated. In 2006, however, after ten years of sometimes-contentious debate between Key lime supporters and North Florida pecan growers—who advocated for pecan pie—the legislature (including the long-serving Rep. Papy) passed a bill that declared Key lime pie the official pie of the state of Florida.

Several other states have official pies, including Indiana, which made sugar cream its state pie in 2009, and Vermont, which brazenly declared apple pie its very own in 1999.

1 Preheat the oven to 350°F (180°C).

2 Place the egg yolks into the bowl of a stand mixer fitted with the whisk attachment. Zest 3 of the Key limes over the egg yolks, then set the limes aside to juice later. Whip the yolks on High, until they are thick and light in color, about 10 minutes.

3 While the yolks are whipping, juice the Key limes. Pour the juice through a fine-mesh strainer, then measure out ⅔ cup (158mL or 160g). Set the measured juice aside and discard the rest, or save for another use.

4 Add the sweetened condensed milk to the yolks and continue mixing on Medium until well combined. Turn the mixer down to Low and slowly pour in the Key lime juice. Continue mixing until the filling starts to thicken. *About 3 or 4 minutes*

5 Pour the filling into the pie shell and bake for 20 to 25 minutes, until the pie is just set and the center feels dry to the touch. Cool to room temperature, then chill in the refrigerator for at least 1 hour.

6 Top the pie with Sweeter Whipped Cream or Creamy Meringue. There is no need to thaw frozen pies before topping. Chill in the refrigerator for at least 30 minutes before serving.

Finished pies can be stored in the refrigerator for up to 3 days, and unfinished pies can be stored in the freezer for up to 1 week.

Orange Cream Pie

We call this our "Dreamsicle Pie." Enough said!

Ingredients

Makes one 9-inch (22.5-cm) pie

1	**Graham–Pecan Crumb Crust shell (recipe p. 46)**	
2 cups (474mL)	**fresh orange juice**	496g
1	**orange, for zesting**	
2 cups (474mL)	**sweetened condensed milk**	640g
5	**large egg yolks**	100g
1½ Tablespoons	**fresh Key lime juice**	23g
1 teaspoon	**vanilla paste**	5g
Pinch	**kosher salt**	
	Lightly Sweetened Whipped Cream (recipe p. 311), for topping	

1 Preheat the oven to 350°F (180°C).

2 In a saucepan, bring the orange juice to a boil over medium heat. Reduce the heat and simmer until the orange juice is reduced to ⅔ cup, about 8 to 10 minutes. Transfer to a medium bowl and zest the orange over the bowl. Stir in the sweetened condensed milk and mix until well combined.

3 Lightly beat the egg yolks in a small bowl. Whisk into the orange juice a little at a time. Stir in the Key lime juice, vanilla paste, and salt.

4 Pour the filling into the pie shell and bake for 15 minutes, until the center of pie is just set.

5 Cool to room temperature, then chill in the refrigerator for at least 2 hours, up to overnight. Top with Lightly Sweetened Whipped Cream.

The baked pie can be frozen for up to 1 week before topping with whipped cream. The finished pie can be stored in the refrigerator for up to 3 days.

PREP NOTE   *If you have a nut allergy, or just don't care for pecans, use a Gingersnap (p. 45), Chocolate (p. 46), or plain Graham Cracker (p. 46) pie shell instead.*

Lemon Soufflé Pie

This pie has bright lemon flavor and a light, ethereal

texture that melts in your mouth. It takes just a few minutes to mix, and even less time to bake. Just make sure the oven is preheated and the pie shell is waiting on a baking sheet, because once the egg whites are folded in, the pie must go directly into the oven.

Ingredients

Makes one 9-inch (22.5-cm) pie

1	single-crust, blind-baked All-Butter Pie Dough shell (recipe p. 24, blind baking p. 34)	
6	large egg yolks	120g
1½	lemons, for zesting	
½ cup plus 1 Tablespoon	granulated sugar	113g

¼ cup	fresh lemon juice	60g
Pinch	kosher salt	
3	large egg whites	60g

The baked pie can be stored in the refrigerator for up to 2 days.

1   Preheat the oven to 350°F (180°C).

2   Place the pie shell on a baking sheet and set aside.

3   Fill a medium saucepan halfway with water and bring to a simmer over medium-high heat.

4   Place the egg yolks in a medium, heatproof bowl. Zest the lemons over the egg yolks.

5   Rest the bowl on top of the simmering saucepan and whisk until the egg yolks are foamy. *About 1 minute*

6   Remove the bowl from the heat and whisk in the sugar, lemon juice, and salt.

7   Place the bowl back over the simmering water and cook, whisking constantly, until thickened, about 10 minutes. Remove from the heat and set aside.

8   Place the egg whites in the bowl of a stand mixer fitted with the whisk attachment. Whip the egg whites to soft peaks.

9   Fold ⅓ of the egg whites into the lemon filling and mix until most of the white streaks are gone. Fold in the rest of the egg whites and mix until no streaks are visible.

10 Gently pour the filling into the prepared pie shell and place it immediately into the oven.

11 Bake for 15 minutes without opening the oven door. The pie is done when it is slightly puffed and pale yellow. It may brown just a bit around the edge.

12 Cool to room temperature, then chill in the refrigerator for at least 1 hour before serving.

Desperation Pies

These pies are made on the farm in the middle of winter, when nothing's in the larder and the fruit is gone until spring. Or, as my former assistant Sam once put it, "How desperate would you have to be to find a bottle of vinegar in an empty pantry and say, 'Yeah, I can make pie out of that.'"

Hoosier Sugar Cream Pie

The recipe for sugar cream pie traveled across the prairie

in covered wagons with the earliest settlers of the Indiana Territories. According to pie lore, it was a great favorite of pioneering farm wives, who, to avoid washing utensils or a bowl, would throw the few staple ingredients in an unbaked pie shell and mix with their fingers before rushing back to their work in the fields.

At Hoosier Mama, we pre-bake the pie shell and use utensils, but the basic recipe—cream and sugar thickened with a little flour—remains unchanged. It is a homely pie by any standard and it languished in the pie case until we started handing out samples. Now it's a customer favorite.

The flavor is wonderful—somewhere between crème brûlée and melted caramel ice cream, depending on the exact recipe. Recipes are closely guarded and passed down from generation to generation, with each family claiming their recipe is best.

Our recipe, somewhat controversially, calls for both white and brown sugar. In the interest of family harmony, my mother-in-law's recipe, which has white sugar only, follows.

The baked pie can be stored in the refrigerator for 3 to 5 days.
Hoosier Mama Pie makers like to throw leftover Sugar Creams in the freezer and snack on the frozen slices.

Next page

HOOSIER SUGAR CREAM PIE

Continued

Ingredients

Makes one 9-inch (22.5-cm) pie

1	single-crust, blind-baked All-Butter Pie Dough shell (recipe p. 24, blind baking p. 34)	
½ cup	granulated sugar	100g
½ cup	dark brown sugar	120g
2 Tablespoons	all-purpose flour	18g
Pinch	kosher salt	
2 cups (474mL)	heavy cream	464g
1 teaspoon	vanilla paste	5g
	Confectioners' sugar, for dusting	

1 Preheat the oven to 400°F (200°C).

2 Place the pie shell on a baking sheet. Set aside.

3 Combine the granulated sugar, brown sugar, flour, and salt in a medium bowl. Mix with a whisk or your hands to break up any clumps and to combine ingredients.

4 Gently stir in the heavy cream with a wooden spoon or spatula. Do not overmix. Whipping the cream will prevent the pie from setting.

5 Stir in the vanilla paste.

6 Pour the filling into the prepared pie shell and bake for 20 minutes.

7 Rotate 180 degrees and bake for 20 to 25 more minutes, until large bubbles cover the surface. The pie will not appear to be set when it comes out of the oven.

8 Cool to room temperature, then chill in the refrigerator for at least 4 hours, up to overnight, before slicing. Dust with confectioners' sugar before serving.

My Mother-in-Law's Sugar Cream Pie

This is my mother-in-law Sandie Siegelin's sugar cream

pie recipe. It was passed down from her mother, Marteena Martin of Carbon, Indiana. For this pie, the filling is cooked on the stovetop and then poured into a blind-baked pie shell. The filling thickens and sets as it cools.

Makes one 9-inch (22.5-cm) pie

1	**single-crust, blind-baked All-Butter Pie Dough shell (recipe p. 24, blind baking p. 34)**	
¼ cup	**cornstarch**	34g
2 cups (474mL)	**whole milk**	484g
¾ cup	**granulated sugar**	150g
1 stick	**unsalted butter**	113g
1 teaspoon	**vanilla paste**	5g
¼ teaspoon	**ground nutmeg**	1g

The finished pie can be stored in the refrigerator for up to 3 days.

1 Place the cornstarch into a small bowl. Whisk in a few tablespoons of the milk to form a smooth, thin paste.

2 Transfer to a medium, heavy saucepan and add the remaining milk, the sugar, and the butter.

3 Cook over medium heat until thickened. *About 7 or 8 minutes*

4 Stir in the vanilla paste and nutmeg.

5 Pour the filling into the pie shell.

6 Cool to room temperature, then chill in the refrigerator 6 to 8 hours before slicing. The pie may appear wobbly, but should cut cleanly.

Buttermilk Pie

My mother used to drink buttermilk by the glass. While I wouldn't go that far, I do love this pie. It's rich and tangy and creamy and refreshing all at the same time! While it is a classic desperation pie that you can make on a cold winter day, it is equally welcome on a hot summer evening, topped with fresh berries.

Ingredients

Makes one 9-inch (22.5-cm) pie

1	**single-crust, blind-baked All-Butter Pie Dough shell (recipe p. 24, blind baking p. 34)**	
1 cup	**granulated sugar**	200g
6 Tablespoons	**unsalted butter**	84g
¼	**lemon, for zesting**	
2	**large egg yolks**	40g
3 Tablespoons	**all-purpose flour**	27g
¼–½ teaspoon	**ground nutmeg**	.5–1g
¼ teaspoon	**kosher salt**	1g
1 Tablespoon	**fresh lemon juice**	13g
1 cup (237mL)	**buttermilk**	242g
2	**large egg whites**	60g

1 Preheat the oven to 350°F (180°C).

2 Combine the sugar and butter in the bowl of a stand mixer fitted with the paddle attachment.

3 Zest the lemon over the ingredients in the bowl, and set the lemon aside to juice later. Cream together the butter, sugar, and lemon zest on Medium until light and fluffy, 2 to 3 minutes.

4 In a small bowl, whisk together the egg yolks and add to the mixer. Mix on Low until combined.

5 In another small bowl, whisk together the flour, nutmeg, and salt and add to the mixer. Mix on Medium until ingredients are thoroughly combined.

6 With the mixer on Low, slowly pour in the lemon juice, followed by the buttermilk. Scrape down the side and bottom of the bowl with a spatula.

7   In a separate bowl, whip the egg whites into soft peaks. Fold ⅓ of the whipped egg whites into the batter. Once combined, fold the remaining egg whites into the batter.

8   Gently pour the batter into the pie shell. Bake for 35 to 45 minutes, rotating 180 degrees after 20 minutes. The pie is done when a dark golden brown crust forms on top and the filling is set.

9   Cool for at least 2 hours before serving.

The baked pie can be stored in the refrigerator for up to 3 days.

Vinegar Chess Pie

Though all chess pies were originally considered

desperation pies, most of our variations, like chocolate, don't seem quite so desperate. So we created a whole Chess Pie section (p. 179), but left our Vinegar Chess Pie here along with its fellow "desperates."

We love this pie because it tastes so good yet sounds so terrible! In the beginning, we gave away a lot of samples to get folks to try it. Now our regulars like to take it to dinner parties to surprise their friends.

Ingredients

Makes one 9-inch (22.5-cm) pie

1	single-crust, napkin-fold All-Butter Pie Dough shell (recipe p. 24, napkin fold p. 36)	
	Pie Wash (p. 21), for brushing the pie shell	
1¼ cups	granulated sugar	250g
7 Tablespoons	unsalted butter	98g

Pinch	kosher salt	
1 Tablespoon	cornmeal	7g
3	large eggs	150g
1½ Tablespoons	apple cider vinegar	18g
1 teaspoon	vanilla paste	5g

1 Preheat the oven to 350°F (180°C).

2 Place the pie shell on a baking sheet and brush the rim with Pie Wash. Set aside.

3 Combine the sugar, butter, and salt in the bowl of a stand mixer.

4 Cream until light and fluffy, 2 to 3 minutes.

5 Add the cornmeal and mix until just combined.

6 Add the eggs one at a time, scraping down the side and bottom of the bowl after each addition.

7 Add the vinegar and vanilla paste and mix until just combined. The batter may curdle when the vinegar is added. The finished batter should be slightly lumpy.

8 Scrape down the side and bottom of the bowl and incorporate any unmixed butter.

9 Pour the batter into the pie shell and bake for 50 minutes to 1 hour, rotating 180 degrees every 20 minutes, until a dark golden brown crust forms on top and the filling is set.

10 Cool for at least 2 hours before serving. The pie will fall a bit as it cools.

The finished batter can be stored in the refrigerator for up to 2 days before using; it may separate as it cools, so whisk together before baking. The baked pie can be stored at room temperature for 3 to 5 days.

Oatmeal Pie

We adapted this recipe from one we found in *Farm Journal's Complete Pie Book*, a wonderful old cookbook from 1965 that's easy to find in used bookstores and vintage shops.

This recipe is dedicated to our customer, Jim, who we affectionately nicknamed "Oatmeal Pie Guy" for his singular obsession with this pie. He used to live around the corner from the pie shop, and we would text him whenever it came out of the oven. His lovely wife, Megan, graciously agreed to serve it instead of groom's cake at their rehearsal dinner. The pie tastes like a big chewy oatmeal cookie, or pecan pie with oats instead of pecans. Try it warm with a scoop of vanilla ice cream. It also makes a great breakfast pie!

Ingredients

Makes one 9-inch (22.5-cm) pie

1	single-crust, blind-baked All-Butter Pie Dough shell (recipe p. 24, blind baking p. 34)	
¼ cup	granulated sugar	50g
4 Tablespoons	unsalted butter	56g
½ teaspoon	ground cinnamon	1g
½ teaspoon	ground cloves	1g
¼ teaspoon	kosher salt	1g
1 cup (237mL)	grade B maple syrup	311g
3	large eggs	150g
1 cup	old-fashioned oats	90g

1 Preheat the oven to 350°F (180°C).

2 Combine the sugar and butter in the bowl of a stand mixer fitted with the paddle attachment. Cream on Medium until light and fluffy, about 2 minutes. Mix in the cinnamon, cloves, and salt. Pour in the maple syrup and mix until combined.

3 Add the eggs one at a time, scraping down the side and bottom of the bowl after each addition. Stir in the oats.

4 Pour the batter into the pie shell and bake for 45 minutes to 1 hour, until a knife inserted in the center of the pie comes out clean.

The baked pie can be stored at room temperature for up to 3 days.

Chess Pies

If you've never heard of chess pie, you probably don't live in the South, where this simple recipe has been a staple for nearly 200 years. A basic chess pie is just butter, sugar, eggs, and perhaps a little cornmeal—but there's nothing basic about the flavor. A crackly crust forms, hiding a rich, sweet, slightly gooey center.

Lemon Chess Pie

I first came across chess pie in Baltimore, where it has been popular on this side of the Atlantic since the arrival of the first English settlers who brought the recipe with them. *Martha Washington's Booke of Cookery*, which dates to 1749, contains a recipe that is very similar to chess pie, though it is not mentioned by name.

Chess is rare in the Northern states and "what is chess pie?" is probably the most frequently asked question in the pie shop. While we love sharing "new" pies with our customers, it is nice, every once in a while, to hear a Southern drawl and know no explanation is necessary.

Why is it called chess? No one knows for sure, but theories abound. My favorites are listed on p. 185, counting down to the most fun, but not necessarily the most accurate.

Lemon Chess Pie

Goes great with a cup of coffee or an espresso.

Ingredients

Makes one 9-inch (22.5-cm) pie

1	**single-crust, napkin-fold All-Butter Pie Dough shell (recipe p. 24, napkin fold p. 36)**	
	Pie Wash (p. 21), for brushing the pie shell	
1½ cups plus 2 Tablespoons	**granulated sugar**	326g
1 stick	**unsalted butter**	112g
Pinch	**kosher salt**	
1	**lemon, for zesting**	
2 Tablespoons	**cornmeal**	14g
1 Tablespoon	**all-purpose flour**	9g
4	**large eggs**	200g
¼ cup (59mL)	**whole milk**	61g
¼ cup (59mL)	**fresh lemon juice**	63g
1 recipe	**Sticky Blueberries (recipe follows)**	

1 Preheat the oven to 350°F (180°C).

2 Place the pie shell on a baking sheet and brush the rim with Pie Wash. Set aside.

3 Combine the sugar, butter, and salt in the bowl of a stand mixer fitted with the paddle attachment. Zest the lemon over the ingredients in the bowl. Set lemon aside to juice later. Cream together on Medium until light and fluffy, 2 to 3 minutes. Add the cornmeal and flour and continue to mix on Medium until the ingredients are just combined. Add the eggs one at a time, scraping down the side and bottom of the bowl after each addition.

4 With the mixer on Low, slowly pour in the milk. Add the lemon juice and mix until just combined. Don't be alarmed if the batter curdles when the lemon juice is added. Finished batter will be slightly lumpy.

5 Scrape down the side and bottom of the bowl and incorporate any unmixed butter. Pour the batter into the pie shell and bake for 50 minutes to 1 hour, rotating 180 degrees every 20 minutes, until a dark golden brown crust forms on top and the filling is set. Once cool, top with Sticky Blueberries.

The finished batter can be stored in the refrigerator for up to 2 days before using; it may separate as it cools so whisk together before baking. The baked pie can be stored at room temperature for 3 to 5 days.

STICKY BLUEBERRIES

Makes enough sticky blueberries to top one pie

In the summer, we like to top the Lemon Chess Pie with Sticky Blueberries. I learned this handy trick when I worked at Trio restaurant in Evanston, Illinois (which is now closed). Credit goes to Trio's founding pastry chef, Gale Gand.

If you are slicing the pie right away, it's best to do so before the berries are added.

1½ cups	**granulated sugar**	300g
1½ cups (356mL)	**water**	354g
2 cups	**blueberries**	300g

1 Place the sugar and water in a small saucepan and stir until combined.

2 Bring to a boil over medium-high heat, stirring occasionally.

3 While the sugar and water heat, sort the blueberries. Discard any bits of leaves, stems, or shriveled berries.

4 Place the blueberries in a colander set over a large bowl.

5 Pour the hot syrup over the berries. Shake the colander to make sure all the berries are covered. The leftover syrup may be reheated and used once more.

6 Let the berries cool until they are comfortable to touch, then pile them on top of the pie. The berries get stickier as the syrup cools, so if your berries roll off the pie, wait a few minutes and try again.

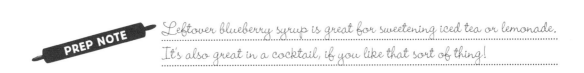

PREP NOTE *Leftover blueberry syrup is great for sweetening iced tea or lemonade. It's also great in a cocktail, if you like that sort of thing!*

Chocolate Chess Pie

One of our wholesale clients renamed this "Brownie Pie"

on its menu. It sold faster and took less explaining than the chess moniker. It does taste just like a

brownie in a pie shell. Children (and quite a few adults) go crazy for it!

Ingredients

Makes one 9-inch (22.5-cm) pie

1	single-crust, napkin-fold All-Butter Pie Dough shell (recipe p. 24, napkin fold p. 36)		4 ounces	70% bittersweet chocolate, chopped	113g
	Pie Wash (p. 21), for brushing the pie shell		4	large eggs	200g
1 stick	unsalted butter	112g	1½ Tablespoons	cornmeal	10g
1 cup	granulated sugar	200g	1 Tablespoon	vanilla paste	15g
			Pinch	kosher salt	

Next page

TOP FIVE EXPLANATIONS FOR THE NAME CHESS PIE

5. *The original recipe came from Chester, England.*

4. *It was originally called "chest pie," because it contains so much sugar that it can be safely stored at room temperature in a pie chest. Over the centuries, "chest" pie became "chess" pie.*

3. *The original recipe called for cheese curds; "chess" is a derivation of "cheese."*

2. *It is what Southern gentlemen ate when they retired to the drawing room after dinner to play chess.*

1. *It was such a staple in any Southern homemaker's dessert repertoire that if asked what she called it, she might have replied, "Oh I don't know, it's jess pie."*

CHOCOLATE CHESS PIE

Continued

1   Preheat the oven to 350°F (180°C).

2   Place the pie shell on a baking sheet and brush the rim with Pie Wash. Set aside.

3   Melt the butter in the top of a double boiler, or in a medium heatproof bowl set on top of a saucepan of simmering water.

4   Remove the butter from the heat and beat in the sugar until it is thoroughly incorporated. The mixture should look shiny, but not greasy. If the mixture appears greasy, continue to beat.

5   Melt the chocolate in a separate bowl in the same manner as the butter. Remove from the heat. Be sure to wipe any condensation off the bottom of the bowl, otherwise it may drip into your batter.

6   Stir the melted chocolate into the butter mixture.

7   Add the eggs one at a time, whisking to combine after each addition.

8   Add the cornmeal, vanilla paste, and salt and mix until thoroughly combined.

9   Scrape down the side and bottom of the bowl and incorporate any unmixed butter. Pour the batter into the pie shell.

10 Bake for 60 to 75 minutes, rotating 180 degrees every 20 minutes, until the top of the pie doesn't give when pressed firmly in the middle. The pie will rise up to 1 inch above the rim of the pie tin as it bakes, then fall slowly as it cools. The finished pie may be slightly concave.

The finished batter can be stored in the refrigerator for up to 2 days before using; it may separate as it cools so whisk it together before baking. The baked pie can be stored at room temperature for 3 to 5 days.

Bourbon Pecan Chess Pie

We developed this pie to represent New Orleans when

they played Indianapolis in Super Bowl XLIV. Hoosier Sugar Cream, of course, represented Indy. Customers voted with their forks by purchasing slices of pie that represented their favorite team. The Colts won our Super Bowl of Pie, but we still think this recipe is a winner!

The pie itself could be nicknamed the Big Easy. It can be mixed and in the oven in under 2 minutes (I had to time myself for a television demo once)!

Ingredients

Makes one 9-inch (22.5-cm) pie

1	single-crust, napkin-fold All-Butter Pie Dough shell (recipe p. 24, napkin fold p. 36)	
1¼ cups	granulated sugar	250g
7 Tablespoons	unsalted butter	98g
Pinch	kosher salt	
1 Tablespoon	cornmeal	7g
3	large eggs	150g
1½ Tablespoons	bourbon	21g
1 Tablespoon	vanilla paste	15g
	Pie Wash (p. 21), for brushing the pie	
	Roughly chopped Candied Pecans (recipe p. 307), for garnish	

1 Preheat the oven to 350°F (180°C).

2 Combine the sugar, butter, and salt in the bowl of a stand mixer fitted with the paddle attachment. Cream together until light and fluffy. *About 1 minute*

3 Stir in the cornmeal. Add the eggs one at a time, scraping down the side and bottom of the bowl after each addition. Stir in the bourbon and vanilla paste. Scrape down the side and bottom of the bowl and incorporate any unmixed butter.

4 Brush the top edge of the pie shell with Pie Wash. Pour the batter into the prepared pie shell and bake for 50 minutes to 1 hour, rotating 180 degrees every 20 minutes. The pie is done when a dark golden brown crust forms on top and the filling is set. Cool to room temperature before serving. Garnish with the Candied Pecans.

The baked pie can be stored at room temperature for 2 to 3 days.

Cranberry Chess Pie

Buttermilk and cranberries make this pie tart and creamy!

The filling can be stored in the refrigerator for up to 1 day before building the pie. The baked pie can be stored at room temperature for up to 2 days or in the refrigerator for 3 to 5 days.

Ingredients

Makes one 9-inch (22.5-cm) pie

1	**single-crust, napkin-fold All-Butter Pie Dough shell (recipe p. 24, napkin fold p. 36)**	
	Pie Wash (p. 21), for brushing the pie shell	
1¼ cups	**granulated sugar**	250g
1 stick	**unsalted butter**	112g
1	**orange, for zesting**	
3	**large eggs**	150g

7 Tablespoons	**all-purpose flour**	63g
1 Tablespoon	**cornmeal**	7g
Pinch	**kosher salt**	
1 cup (237mL)	**buttermilk**	242g
1 Tablespoon	**vanilla paste**	15g
2 cups	**coarsely chopped cranberries**	200g
	Confectioners' sugar, for dusting	

1 Preheat the oven to 350°F (180°C).

2 Place the pie shell on a baking sheet and brush the rim with Pie Wash. Set aside.

3 Combine the sugar and butter in the bowl of a stand mixer fitted with the paddle attachment. Zest the orange over the bowl and cream together until light and fluffy. Add the eggs one at a time, scraping down the side and bottom of the bowl after each addition.

4 Whisk the flour, cornmeal, and salt together in a small bowl.

5 Stir the buttermilk and vanilla paste together in a small bowl or pitcher.

6 Add ⅓ of the dry ingredients to the butter mixture and mix just to combine. With the stand mixer on Low, add half of the buttermilk mixture and mix just to combine. Add another ⅓ of the dry ingredients and mix just to combine.

7 With the mixer on Low, add the rest of the buttermilk mixture and mix just to combine. Add the final ⅓ of the dry ingredients and mix just to combine.

8 Scrape the side and bottom of the bowl and incorporate any unmixed butter. Gently fold in the cranberries. Pour the batter into the prepared pie shell and smooth the top with the back of a spoon or a spatula. Bake for 40 to 45 minutes, rotating 180 degrees every 20 minutes. The pie is done when the top is slightly puffed and has turned a light golden brown. Cool to room temperature.

9 Serve at room temperature or slightly chilled. Dust with confectioners' sugar before serving.

Over-the-Top Pies

At Hoosier Mama, we like to
celebrate the simplicity of pie, but
sometimes we get carried away. For
these pies, more is definitely more!
Inspired by everything from candy
bars to the King of Rock 'n' Roll,
these pies take a bit longer to make,
but I think you'll agree the result is
well worth the extra time.

Blackberry and Passion Fruit Chiffon Meringue Pie

Baker Molly developed this and the Strawberry and Passion Fruit Chiffon recipe after I lamented one day that we didn't have more uses for the spectacular Passion Fruit Curd. We did try to find a shorter name but settled on the most descriptive instead. Make the Passion Fruit Curd one day ahead so it is good and set.

Ingredients

Makes one 9-inch (22.5-cm) pie

1	**single-crust, blind-baked All-Butter Pie Dough shell (recipe p. 24, blind baking p. 34)**	
1¼ cups (296mL)	**Passion Fruit Curd (recipe p. 157)**	315g
¾ cup (178mL)	**heavy cream**	174g
½ teaspoon	**vanilla paste**	2.5g

	Melted white chocolate, for coating the shell	
1 cup	**blackberries, cut in half**	115g
8	**large blackberries, for garnish**	
1 recipe	**Creamy Meringue (recipe p. 308)**	

Next page

BLACKBERRY AND PASSION FRUIT CHIFFON MERINGUE PIE

Continued

1 Place the Passion Fruit Curd in the bowl of a stand mixer fitted with the whisk attachment. Whip on High for 30 seconds until it is smooth. Transfer to another bowl and thoroughly wash the stand mixer bowl.

2 Combine the heavy cream and vanilla paste in the bowl of the stand mixer still fitted with the whisk attachment. Whip on Medium until soft peaks form when the whip attachment is dipped into the cream and slowly pulled back out, about 1 minute.

3 Gently fold the whipped cream into the Passion Fruit Curd in 3 additions and smooth the top with a spatula. Place a sheet of plastic wrap directly on top of the curd mixture and chill in the refrigerator until set, about 1 hour.

4 Meanwhile, brush the inside of the empty pie shell with a thin coat of melted chocolate. Chill in the refrigerator until the chocolate sets and hardens, about 5 minutes.

5 Remove from the refrigerator and scatter the blackberry halves in the bottom of the prepared pie shell. Spoon the curd mixture over the blackberries, making sure all of the berries are covered. Place a sheet of plastic wrap directly on top of the curd.

6 Chill in the refrigerator until the curd has set, about 1 hour.

7 Remove the pie from the refrigerator and carefully peel off the plastic wrap. Arrange the remaining whole blackberries around the pie, close to the crimp.

8 Prepare the Creamy Meringue. Spread it over the top of the pie, stopping about 1 inch (2.5cm) from the outer crimp. Make sure the blackberries are still visible. Use a spatula or the back of a spoon to make spikes and swirls in the meringue.

9 Toast the meringue with a butane torch. Be careful not to torch the blackberries.

This pie is best served the day it is made. Because the meringue does not seal to the edges of the pie crust, it may weep after a day or two. The pie will still taste amazing, but it won't be as pretty. The finished pie can be stored in the refrigerator for up to 2 days.

Peanut Butter Pie with Chocolate Ganache

This pie is for my great neighbor, Glenn Sullivan, who

badgered me for months to develop a peanut butter recipe. It is rich and sweet with a gingersnap crust and chocolate ganache drizzle. Glenn is still one of the few people I know who can eat a whole slice in one sitting.

Ingredients

Makes one 9-inch (22.5-cm) pie

1	**Gingersnap Crumb Crust shell (recipe p. 45)**	
1 (8-ounce) package	**cream cheese, softened**	226g
6 Tablespoons	**unsalted butter, softened**	84g
¾ cup	**smooth peanut butter**	125g
2	**pasteurized egg yolks**	
1 (14-ounce) can	**sweetened condensed milk**	397g
1 teaspoon	**vanilla paste**	5g
1 recipe	**Chocolate Ganache (recipe p. 310)**	
⅓ cup	**roughly chopped salted dry roasted peanuts**	40g

1 Combine the cream cheese and butter in the bowl of a stand mixer fitted with the paddle attachment. Cream on Medium until smooth, about 3 minutes. Add the peanut butter and mix until well combined. Add the pasteurized egg yolks 1 at a time, beating well after each addition. Stir in the sweetened condensed milk and vanilla paste.

2 Spoon the filling into the pie shell. Smooth the top of the pie with an offset spatula or the back of a spoon. Chill in the refrigerator until set, about 30 minutes.

3 Drizzle the Chocolate Ganache over the top of the pie. Press the roughly chopped peanuts around the edge of the pie.

The finished pie can be stored in the refrigerator for up to 2 days. Do not freeze.

Because this pie is not baked, for food safety you must use pasteurized shell eggs for this recipe. According to the US Department of Agriculture, "in-shell pasteurized eggs may be used safely without cooking."

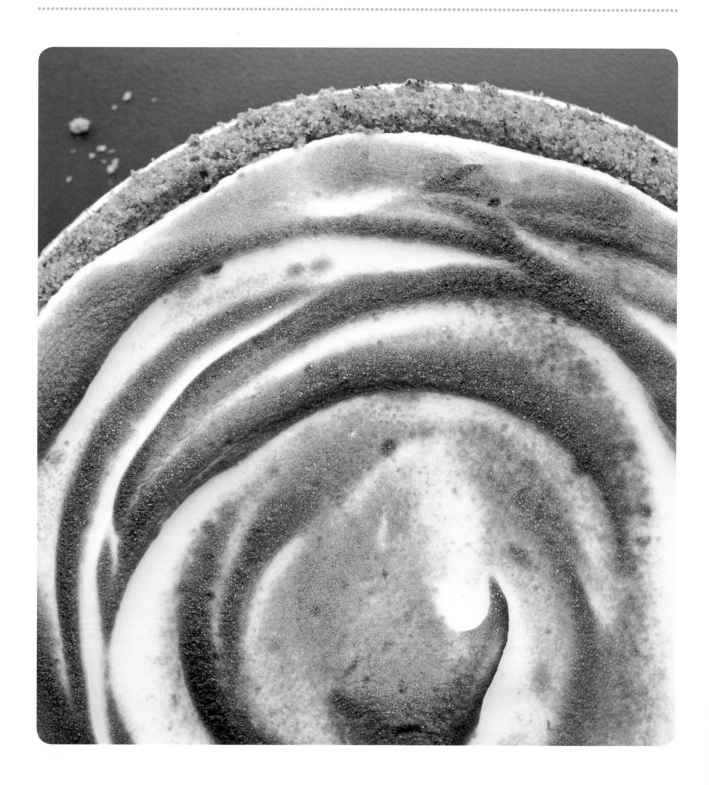

S'more Pie

A graham cracker shell seemed so ubiquitous—until we
realized we could use it to recreate the timeless campfire treat. This pie evokes the taste of s'mores
right down to the bits of burnt marshmallow.

Ingredients

Makes one 9-inch (22.5-cm) pie

1	**Graham Cracker Crumb Crust shell (recipe p. 46)**	
1 cup (237mL)	**whole milk, divided**	242g
1 cup (237mL)	**heavy cream, divided**	232g
1½ Tablespoons	**cornstarch**	13.5g
1	**large egg**	50g
¼ cup	**granulated sugar**	50g
5 ounces	**semisweet chocolate, roughly chopped**	142g

2 Tablespoons	**unsalted butter**	28g
½ teaspoon	**vanilla paste**	2.5g
Pinch	**kosher salt**	
½ recipe	**Chocolate Ganache (recipe p. 310)**	
½ recipe	**Creamy Meringue (recipe p. 308)**	

The chocolate pastry cream can be made up to 1 day in advance. The finished pie can be stored in the refrigerator for 2 to 3 days.

Next page

S'MORE PIE

Continued

1   Combine ¾ cup (178mL or 181g) of the milk and ½ cup (119mL or 116g) of the cream in a small, heavy saucepan. Bring to a boil over medium-high heat, stirring occasionally so the milk does not scorch on the bottom of the pan.

2   Meanwhile, whisk the remaining ¼ cup (59mL or 60g) of the milk into the cornstarch to make a slurry. Set aside.

3   Place the egg into a medium, deep heatproof bowl. Whisk in the sugar until well combined. Slowly pour in the slurry and whisk until smooth.

4   Gradually whisk in the hot milk mixture, stirring until well combined.

5   Pour the mixture back into the saucepan and cook over medium heat, whisking constantly, until it starts to thicken and just begins to boil. Whisk at a boil for 2 more minutes.

6   Remove the saucepan from the heat and add the chocolate and butter. Whisk until both are melted and well incorporated. Whisk in the vanilla paste and salt.

7   Pour the pastry cream through a fine-mesh strainer into a heatproof bowl. Place a piece of plastic wrap directly onto the surface of the pastry cream and gently smooth with your fingers. This will prevent a skin from forming on the top of the pastry cream. Chill in the refrigerator until it is firm, about 2 hours. You can speed this process by placing the bowl of pastry cream over an ice-water bath.

8   Prepare the Chocolate Ganache, then immediately pour it into the bottom of the empty pie shell. Place the shell in the refrigerator until the ganache is set, about 30 minutes.

9   Remove the chocolate pastry cream from the refrigerator and transfer to the bowl of a stand mixer fitted with the whisk attachment. Whip on Medium until it is light and fluffy. Remove from the stand mixer and set aside. Thoroughly wash the stand mixer bowl.

10 In the bowl of the stand mixer still fitted with the whisk attachment, whip the remaining ½ cup (119mL or 116g) of the cream to soft peaks. Gently fold the whipped cream into the pastry cream.

11 Remove the prepared pie shell from the refrigerator. Spoon the pastry cream into the shell, over the ganache. Gently smooth the top of the pie with an offset spatula, making sure the pastry cream touches the edge of the pie shell. Chill in the refrigerator until the pastry cream is set, about 1 hour.

12 Prepare the Creamy Meringue, but remove it from the stand mixer when it is still lukewarm. Pour it directly onto the center of the pie and, with the back of a serving spoon, spread it out from the center in concentric circles. Toast with a butane torch. Be sure to get a few spots "extra toasty," as if it got scorched in the campfire! The finished pie can be served immediately.

Joyous Almond Pie

This pie was inspired by a candy bar. See if you can guess which one!

You will need to make the Almond Milk and Almond Cream at least six hours ahead. Before making them, toast 2 full cups (382g) of almonds (see the toasting nuts sidebar on p. 105); that way you will have enough for the pie, plus some left over for garnish.

Ingredients

Makes one 9-inch (22.5-cm) pie

1	**Chocolate Wafer Crumb Crust shell (recipe p. 46)**	
½ sheet	**leaf gelatin (silver strength)**	1.25g
3 cups (711mL)	**Almond Milk, divided (recipe follows)**	721g
1 Tablespoon	**powdered gelatin**	7g
¾ cup	**granulated sugar**	150g
¼ cup	**cornstarch**	35g
3	**large egg yolks**	60g
1	**large egg**	50g
2 Tablespoons	**unsalted butter**	28g
1 Tablespoon	**vanilla paste**	15g

⅛ teaspoon plus pinch	**kosher salt, divided**	
1 cup (237mL)	**Almond Cream (recipe follows)**	232g
1 cup	**sweetened coconut flakes**	85g
3 Tablespoons (45mL)	**sweetened condensed milk**	59g
1 Tablespoon	**coconut milk**	
	Melted bittersweet chocolate, for coating the pie shell	
⅓ cup	**raw, unblanched almonds, toasted and roughly chopped, plus more for garnish**	64g

Next page

JOYOUS ALMOND PIE

Continued

1   Place the leaf gelatin in a small bowl of ice water. Set aside to bloom for 10 minutes.

2   Strain the Almond Milk into a 1-quart (948-mL) liquid measuring cup. You should have 3 cups (711mL or 721g) of milk; if you do not, add enough fresh whole milk to make up the difference.

3   Pour ½ cup (119mL or 120g) of the Almond Milk into a small bowl. Sprinkle the powdered gelatin over the milk and let stand for 10 minutes.

4   Combine the milk-gelatin mixture with the remaining 2½ cups (593mL or 600g) of the Almond Milk in a medium, heavy saucepan. Whisk over medium-high heat until the powdered gelatin dissolves, about 1 minute. Continue to heat, whisking occasionally, until the mixture is just below a boil and small bubbles are forming along the side of the saucepan, about 4 minutes.

5   Meanwhile, place the sugar and cornstarch in a bowl and whisk to combine.

6   Place the egg yolks and egg into a medium, heatproof bowl. Whisk in the sugar and cornstarch. Gradually, in several additions, whisk in the hot milk mixture.

7   Pour everything back into the saucepan and whisk constantly over medium heat, until the pastry cream begins to thicken and starts to boil, about 1½ to 2 minutes. Whisk at a boil for 2 more minutes. Remove from the heat.

8   Remove the leaf gelatin from the water. Wring out the excess water, then whisk the gelatin into the pastry cream until it dissolves. Whisk in the butter, vanilla paste, and ⅛ teaspoon of the salt.

9   Pour the pastry cream through a fine-mesh strainer into a heatproof bowl. Place a piece of plastic wrap directly onto the surface of the pastry cream and gently smooth the plastic with your fingers. This will prevent a skin from forming on the top of the pastry cream.

10   Chill the pastry cream in the refrigerator until it is firm, about 3 hours. You can speed this process by placing the pastry cream over an ice-water bath.

11   When the pastry cream is firm, strain the Almond Cream into a liquid measuring cup. You should have 1 cup (237mL or 232g) of almond cream; if you do not, add enough fresh heavy cream to make up the difference.

12 Pour the Almond Cream into the bowl of a stand mixer fitted with the whisk attachment. Whip on Medium speed for 30 seconds. Turn the mixer up to High and continue to whip cream until soft peaks form, about 1½ to 2 minutes.

13 Remove the firm pastry cream from the refrigerator. Remove the plastic wrap and set aside. Whisk the pastry cream until smooth. Gradually fold in the whipped cream, until no streaks of whipped cream remain. Smooth the top of the pie filling and replace the sheet of plastic wrap.

14 Chill the pastry cream in the refrigerator until set, about 1 hour.

15 Brush the inside of the empty pie shell with a thin coat of melted chocolate. Place the pie shell in the refrigerator until the chocolate cools and sets, about 5 minutes.

16 In the bowl of a stand mixer fitted with the paddle attachment, mix the coconut flakes, sweetened condensed milk, and coconut milk until thoroughly combined.

17 Pour the condensed milk mixture into the prepared pie shell and spread it out. Top with ⅓ cup (38g) of the almonds. Sprinkle with the pinch of salt.

18 Remove the almond pastry cream from the refrigerator and whisk until smooth and fluffy. Spoon on top of the pie. Make decorative swirls or spikes in the pastry cream using a spatula or the back of a spoon.

19 Garnish with the remaining roughly chopped almonds.

20 Chill in the refrigerator for at least 2 hours before slicing.

The finished pie can be stored in the refrigerator up to 3 days.

PREP NOTE See the gelatin sidebar (p. 124) for more information on the different types of gelatin.

ALMOND MILK
Makes about 3 cups (711mL or 721g)

4 cups (948mL)	**whole milk**	968g
1 cup	**raw unblanched almonds, toasted and roughly chopped**	191g

1 Combine the whole milk and chopped almonds in a medium, heavy saucepan.

2 Bring to a boil over medium heat.

3 Cool to room temperature, then pour into a covered container.

4 Chill in the refrigerator for at least 6 hours, up to overnight.

ALMOND CREAM
Makes about 1 cup (237mL or 232g)

2 cups (474mL)	**heavy cream**	464g
½ cup	**raw, unblanched almonds, toasted and roughly chopped**	95.5g

1 Combine the heavy cream and almonds in a small, heavy saucepan.

2 Bring to a boil over medium heat.

3 Cool to room temperature, then pour into a covered container.

4 Chill in the refrigerator for at least 6 hours, up to overnight.

Mexican Chocolate Pie (Pay de Chocolate Mexicano)

In the Mexican state of Oaxaca, indigenous groups have been making chocolate for centuries. They grind local cocoa beans with nuts, chilies, and spices, and form it into bars that are used to make traditional drinking chocolate.

When importing handmade Oaxacan chocolate directly from Mexico proved cost-prohibitive (imagine!), my assistant Kelsey decided to infuse the flavors into the chocolate herself. The result is a chocolate cream pie for grown-ups, with hints of ground cinnamon, almonds, and vanilla. Chiles de arbol and cayenne pepper give it a little kick.

The Almond Milk and Almond Chile Cream both call for well-toasted almonds; simply bake them at 300°F for 15 to 20 minutes (regular toasted almonds only need to be baked for 10 minutes). Make the milk and cream recipes at least six hours in advance.

PREP NOTE See the gelatin sidebar (p. 124) for more information on the different types of gelatin.

Next page

MEXICAN CHOCOLATE PIE (PAY DE CHOCOLATE MEXICANO)

Continued

Makes one 9-inch (22.5-cm) pie

1	**Chocolate Wafer Crumb Crust shell (recipe p. 46)**		5 ounces	**semisweet chocolate, chopped**	142g
¼ sheet	**leaf gelatin (silver strength)**	.62g	4 Tablespoons	**unsalted butter**	56g
2 cups (474mL)	**Almond Milk, divided (recipe follows)**	484g	1 teaspoon	**vanilla paste**	5g
1 cup (237mL)	**Almond Chile Cream (recipe follows)**	232g	½ teaspoon	**ground cinnamon**	1g
3 Tablespoons	**cornstarch**	27g	¼ teaspoon	**ground cayenne pepper**	1g
2	**large eggs**	100g	Pinch	**kosher salt**	
½ cup	**granulated sugar**	100g	1 cup (237mL)	**heavy cream**	232g
5 ounces	**bittersweet chocolate, chopped**	142g	⅓ cup plus 2 Tablespoons	**raw, unblanched almonds, toasted and finely chopped**	76g

1   Place the leaf gelatin in a small bowl of ice water. Set aside to bloom for 10 minutes.

2   Strain the Almond Milk into a 1-quart (948-mL) liquid measuring cup. You should have 2 cups (474mL or 484g); if you do not, add enough fresh whole milk to make up the difference.

3   Strain the Almond Chile Cream into a liquid measuring cup. You should have 1 cup (237mL or 232g); if you do not, add enough fresh heavy cream to make up the difference.

4   Combine 1½ cups (356mL or 363g) of the Almond Milk and the Almond Chile Cream in a medium, heavy saucepan.

5   Bring to a boil over medium-high heat, stirring occasionally so the milk does not scorch on the bottom of the pan.

6 Meanwhile, whisk the remaining ½ cup (119mL or 121g) of the Almond Milk into the cornstarch to make a smooth slurry. Set aside.

7 Crack the eggs into a medium, deep heatproof bowl. Whisk in the sugar until well combined.

8 Slowly pour the slurry into the egg mixture and whisk until smooth.

9 Slowly whisk in the hot milk mixture, stirring until well combined.

10 Pour everything back into the saucepan and whisk constantly over medium heat until the mixture starts to thicken and boil, about 1½ to 2 minutes. Whisk at a boil for 2 more minutes. Remove from the heat and add both of the chocolates and the butter. Whisk until everything is melted and well incorporated.

11 Remove the leaf gelatin from the ice water. Wring out any excess water, then whisk the gelatin into the pastry cream until it dissolves. Whisk in the vanilla paste, cinnamon, cayenne pepper, and salt.

12 Pour the pastry cream through a fine-mesh strainer into a heatproof bowl. Place a piece of plastic wrap directly onto the surface of the pastry cream and gently smooth with your fingers. This will prevent a skin from forming on the top of the pastry cream. Chill in the refrigerator until it is firm, about 2 hours. You can speed up this process by placing the bowl of pastry cream over an ice-water bath.

13 When the pastry cream is firm, pour the heavy cream into the bowl of a stand mixer fitted with the whisk attachment. Whip on Medium for 30 seconds. Turn the mixer up to High and continue to whip until soft peaks form, about 1½ to 2 minutes.

14 Remove the firm pastry cream from the refrigerator. Remove the plastic wrap and set it aside. Whisk the pastry cream until smooth, then gradually fold in the whipped cream until no streaks of whipped cream remain. Smooth the top of the pie filling and replace the sheet of plastic wrap. Chill in the refrigerator until it is set, about 1 hour.

15 Scatter ⅓ cup (76g) of the toasted almonds onto the bottom of the pie shell.

16 Remove the pastry cream from the refrigerator and whisk until smooth and fluffy. Spoon on top of the almonds. Make decorative swirls or spikes in the pastry cream using a spatula or the back of a spoon. Garnish with the remaining 2 tablespoons of roughly chopped almonds. Chill in the refrigerator for at least 2 hours before slicing.

The pastry cream can be made up to 1 day in advance. The finished pie can be stored in the refrigerator for up to 3 days.

ALMOND MILK
Makes about 2 cups (474mL or 484g)

2½ cups (593mL)	**whole milk**	605g
⅔ cup	**unblanched, raw almonds, well toasted and roughly chopped**	127g

1 Combine the whole milk and well-toasted almonds in a small, heavy saucepan.

2 Bring to a boil over medium heat. Set aside to cool to room temperature.

3 Pour into a covered container and chill in the refrigerator for at least 6 hours, up to overnight.

ALMOND CHILE CREAM
Makes about 1 cup (237mL or 232g)

2 cups (474mL)	**heavy cream**	464g
½ cup	**unblanched raw almonds, well toasted and very roughly chopped**	95.5g
6	**chiles de arbol**	4g

1 Combine the heavy cream and well-toasted almonds in a small, heavy saucepan.

2 Wearing gloves, crumble the chiles de arbol into the cream.

3 Bring the mixture to a boil over medium heat. Set aside to cool to room temperature.

4 Pour into a covered container and chill in the refrigerator for at least 6 hours, or up to overnight.

Fat Elvis Pie

This pie was inspired by the King's penchant for grilled peanut butter and banana sandwiches (some say he added bacon too). Originally we were going to call it simply "Elvis Pie," but once we tasted it, we knew the name needed an upgrade!

This pie calls for small amounts of chocolate pastry cream and Peanut Butter Pie (recipe p. 195) filling. The recipes here will give you just the right amount. If you would like to make the S'more and Fat Elvis pies at the same time, follow the pastry cream portion of the Chocolate Cream Pie recipe (p. 141), then use two cups of the pastry cream for S'mores and two cups for Elvis. You may have a tiny bit of pastry cream left over, but that problem is quickly solved with a spoon!

Next page

FAT ELVIS PIE

Continued

Ingredients

Makes one 9-inch (22.5-cm) pie

1	**Graham, Peanut, and Pretzel Crumb shell (recipe p. 46)**	
1 cup (237g)	**whole milk, divided**	242g
½ cup (119mL)	**heavy cream**	116g
1½ Tablespoons	**cornstarch**	13.5g
1	**large egg**	50g
¼ cup	**granulated sugar**	50g
2½ ounces	**semisweet chocolate, roughly chopped**	71g
2½ ounces	**bittersweet chocolate, roughly chopped**	71g
2 Tablespoons	**unsalted butter**	28g
1 teaspoon	**vanilla paste, divided**	5g
2 pinches	**kosher salt, divided**	
½ cup	**softened cream cheese**	68g
3 Tablespoons	**unsalted butter, softened**	42g

6 Tablespoons	**smooth peanut butter**	100g
1	**pasteurized egg yolk**	20g
½ cup plus 2 Tablespoons (134mL)	**sweetened condensed milk**	199g
2	**medium bananas, peeled and cut into 1-inch (2.5-cm) discs, bruises and mushy parts discarded**	240g
1 Tablespoon plus 1 teaspoon	**fresh orange juice**	20g
2 teaspoons	**fresh lemon juice**	10g
½ cup	**banana chips, crushed into ½- to 1-inch (13-mm to 2.5-cm) pieces**	43g
½ cup	**small knot-shaped pretzels, crushed into ½- to 1-inch (13-mm to 2.5-cm) pieces**	20g

The chocolate pastry cream can be made up to 1 day in advance. The finished pie can be stored in the refrigerator for up to 3 days.

CHOCOLATE PASTRY CREAM

1   Combine ¾ cup (178mL or 181g) of the milk and the heavy cream in a small, heavy saucepan.

2   Bring to a boil over medium-high heat, stirring occasionally so the milk does not scorch on the bottom of the pan.

3   Meanwhile, whisk the remaining ¼ cup (59mL or 60g) of the milk into the cornstarch to make a smooth slurry. Set aside.

4   Crack the egg into a medium, deep heatproof bowl. Whisk in the sugar until well combined.

5   Slowly pour the slurry into the egg mixture and whisk until smooth.

6   Gradually whisk in the hot milk mixture, stirring until well combined.

7   Pour everything back into the saucepan and cook over medium heat, whisking constantly, until it starts to thicken and just begins to boil, about 1½ to 2 minutes. Whisk at a boil for 2 more minutes.

8   Remove the saucepan from the heat and add both of the chocolates and the butter. Whisk until everything is melted and well incorporated.

9   Whisk in ½ teaspoon of the vanilla paste and 1 pinch of the salt.

10 Pour the pastry cream through a fine-mesh strainer into a heatproof bowl. Place a piece of plastic wrap directly onto the surface of the pastry cream and gently smooth with your fingers. This will prevent a skin from forming on the top of the pastry cream. Chill in the refrigerator until it is firm, about 2 hours. You can speed this process by placing the bowl of pastry cream over an ice-water bath.

PEANUT BUTTER PIE FILLING

1   Combine the cream cheese and softened butter in the bowl of a stand mixer fitted with the paddle attachment. Cream on Medium until smooth, about 3 minutes. Add the peanut butter and mix until well combined. Add the pasteurized egg yolk, beating well to combine. Stir in the sweetened condensed milk and the remaining ½ teaspoon vanilla paste. Set aside.

BANANA LAYER

1   Combine the bananas, orange juice and lemon juice in a small bowl. Toss bananas until they are well coated, then transfer the bananas to a strainer or colander and let drain for 2 to 3 minutes.

Next page

FAT ELVIS PIE

Continued

ASSEMBLE THE PIE

1 Spoon the chocolate pastry cream into the bottom of the pie shell. Using a serving spoon, make a well in the center of the pastry cream. Place the bananas in the well in a single layer on top of the pastry cream. Spoon the peanut butter filling on top of the bananas and gently smooth the top with an offset spatula or the back of a spoon. Sprinkle the remaining pinch of salt over the pie.

2 Place the pie in the refrigerator until set, about 20 minutes. Garnish right before serving by pressing the banana chip and pretzel pieces around the pie, just inside the crust's edge.

PREP NOTE The pretzels and banana chips get soggy in the refrigerator. If the pie will be eaten over 1 or 2 days, consider garnishing each slice "to order."

Turnovers

We love traditional pie because it can't be eaten on the go. (At least, not without a big mess or a traffic accident!) You have to sit down and savor a slice of pie—but sometimes you just don't have time for that. These little turnovers are fully portable and great for breakfast alongside a cup of coffee.

ASSEMBLING AND BAKING TURNOVERS

Cream Cheese Dough circles (recipe p. 50; amount varies, check individual turnover recipe)

2	**large egg whites, beaten**	40g

Coarse-grained sugar, for coating

1 Remove the Cream Cheese Dough circles from the refrigerator or freezer. Set aside until the circles are warm enough to be pliable.

2 Brush a thin line of beaten egg whites along the edge of the dough circle.

3 Place 2 to 3 tablespoons of filling in the center of the dough circle. Lift 3 points of the circle up until they meet in the middle. Pinch the points together to form a tri-cornered hat. Press along the 3 seams to seal.

4 Place the turnovers, 2 inches (5cm) apart, on a baking pan lined with parchment paper. Freeze for at least 1 hour.

5 Preheat the oven to 400°F (200°C).

6 Fill a shallow bowl or pie tin with coarse-grained sugar.

7 Remove the turnovers from the freezer.

8 Brush the 3 sides of each turnover with the beaten egg whites. With one hand, hold the turnover over the bowl of sugar. With the other hand, press the sugar onto each side of the turnover. Repeat until all the turnovers are well coated.

9 If the turnovers are still frozen, they may be baked immediately. If the turnovers have begun to thaw, return them to the freezer for 20 to 30 minutes, until fully frozen.

10 Bake for 25 to 30 minutes, until the turnovers are dark golden brown.

Unbaked turnovers can be stored in the freezer for up to 1 week. Baked turnovers can be stored at room temperature, in an airtight container, up to 2 days.

Forming turnovers; a sealed turnover.

TURNOVER FILLINGS

Once you have finished preparing each of these fillings, assemble and bake the turnovers according to the preceding instructions.

APPLE

Makes 12 turnovers

12	**Cream Cheese Dough circles (recipe p. 50)**	
2	**medium apples**	180g
¼ cup (59mL)	**Crème Fraîche (recipe p. 318)**	65g
¼ cup	**granulated sugar**	50g

1 Peel, core, and chop the apples into a ¼-inch (6-mm) dice (makes about 1½ cups). Place the diced apples in a small bowl.

2 Add the Crème Fraîche and sugar and mix until the apples are well coated.

PEAR-GINGER

Makes 12 turnovers

12	**Cream Cheese Dough circles (recipe p. 50)**	
2	**ripe pears**	190g
2 teaspoons	**minced candied ginger**	10g
¼ cup (59mL)	**Crème Fraîche (recipe p. 318)**	65g
¼ cup	**granulated sugar**	50g

1 Peel, core, and chop the pears into a ¼-inch (6-mm) dice and place in a small bowl. You will have about 1½ cups (165g) of diced pear.

2 Finely chop the candied ginger and add to the pears.

3 Add the Crème Fraîche and sugar and mix until the pears are well coated.

PEACH-JALAPENO

Makes about 8 turnovers

8	**Cream Cheese Dough circles (recipe p. 50)**	
3	**medium peaches**	120g
¼–½	**medium jalapeño pepper**	4–7g
1 teaspoon	**freshly squeezed lemon juice**	4g
1 Tablespoon	**granulated sugar**	13g
1 Tablespoon	**potato starch**	11g
Pinch	**kosher salt**	

 PREP NOTE *This recipe only works with ripe, juicy peaches.*

1 Preheat the oven to 400°F (200°C).

2 Peel, core, and chop the peaches into ¾-inch (18-mm) pieces (makes about 1 cup) and place in a small bowl.

3 Remove the stem, seeds, and veins from the jalapeño pepper. Mince the pepper (½ to 1 tablespoon) and add to the peaches. Add the lemon juice and mix well.

4 Combine the sugar, potato starch, and salt in another bowl and mix with a whisk until well blended.

5 Toss the peach mixture with the sugar mixture until the sugar starts to draw juice out of the peaches.

6 Transfer to a 9-inch (22.5-cm) pie tin or small baking dish and bake until the mixture thickens, about 10 to 15 minutes (time will vary depending on the juiciness of the peaches). Let the mixture cool to room temperature.

RASPBERRY

Makes about 12 turnovers

12	**Cream Cheese Dough circles (recipe p. 50)**	
2½ cups	**fresh raspberries, divided**	308g
1 teaspoon	**fresh lemon juice**	4g
¼ teaspoon	**vanilla paste**	1.25g
½ cup	**granulated sugar**	100g
1 Tablespoon	**cornstarch**	9g
½ teaspoon	**ground cinnamon**	1g
Pinch	**kosher salt**	

1 Preheat the oven to 400°F (200°C).

2 Combine 2 cups (246g) of the raspberries, the lemon juice, and the vanilla paste in a small bowl.

3 In a separate bowl, whisk together the sugar, cornstarch, cinnamon, and salt until well blended.

4 Combine the raspberry mixture with the sugar mixture and toss until the sugar starts to draw juice out of the berries.

5 Transfer the mixture to a 9-inch (22.5-cm) pie tin or small baking dish and bake for 10 minutes.

6 Remove from the oven and stir gently.

7 Return to the oven and bake until the mixture thickens, 10 to 12 minutes. Cool to room temperature.

8 Gently fold in the remaining ½ cup (62g) of fresh raspberries. If you have extra raspberries, add more to taste.

Savory Pies

As our tiny enterprise grew into a small enterprise and then grew some more, the work was shared and shared again. The shop has benefited from the talent, enthusiasm, and love of many pie makers and pie slingers.

In 2010 Allison Scott (then Allison Stout) took charge of our savory program. Since then, I don't think there has been a day when she was not thinking about her next savory pie creation. When she can't find sausage she likes, she makes her own. When a recipe calls for water, Allison adds beer, and when in doubt, she pickles something.

For the savory side of Hoosier Mama Pie Company I leave you in her capable, though spice-stained, hands.

—Paula

Seasonal Savory Pies

If pie is slow food, savory pies are even slower. These

recipes are not hard to follow, but you should not expect to throw a savory pie together in a hurry. Like all good pie, these take time. At the shop, we grind and hand mix our own spice blends, make sausage from scratch, and wait an hour for proper caramelized onions. Besides, savory pies taste best when the flavors are left to develop and marry in the fridge overnight. These steps guarantee that the experience of making the pie is as special as eating it.

Please don't feel hamstrung by the seasonality of these pies—this is merely a guide. Holed up in the dead of winter, when you've had it with butternut squash soup, try making the Corn Pudding Pie (p. 234) with frozen corn and Tomato Jam (p. 83). The Chicken Pot Pie (p. 262) might be just the comfort you need on a hot summer evening. Be inspired by what looks best at your local market. If you live near an ocean, make thickened clam chowder into a pie filling. If your family loves stewed black-eyed peas, try filling one of our cornmeal doughs with your grandmother's recipe.

A few great techniques can be the difference between a good pie and a great one. Two of our favorites are Roasted Garlic (p. 313) and Caramelized Onions (p. 312) We use them again and again in the recipes that follow.

ABOUT OUR SEASONAL SAVORY PIES

Because taste is subjective, we list base measurements for ingredients like cayenne pepper and lemon juice, but you should always taste your food along the way and adjust the seasoning based on your preference.

While you are cooking, save all the bits of vegetable scrap and leftover bones for stock. Store them in the freezer in a resealable plastic bag until you're ready to use them. See the homemade stock recipes (p. 323, p. 324, and p. 325) for more information.

If you can, always buy block cheese and shred it yourself. Pre-shredded cheese may save time, but is more expensive and likely contains unnecessary preservatives and additives to prevent clumping.

HOW TO CARE FOR YOUR SAVORY PIE

Overcome the urge to taste your pie as soon as it comes out of the oven. Let your savory pie sit for at least 15 minutes before slicing.

Refrigerate any pie leftovers immediately. Savory pies should be eaten within two days of baking. Always reheat leftover pie in an oven or toaster oven. Never use a microwave; it will destroy the crust's texture.

To prepare an unbaked pie for long-term storage, first freeze the pie for four hours, then wrap it tightly in plastic wrap and place it inside a large freezer bag, if it will fit. Pies can be stored like this for two weeks before baking, which comes in handy for our recipes like Pulled Pork Pie (p. 237), where the filling makes enough to fill three pie shells.

SPRING

Cellar vegetables left over from winter combine forces with the first green growth of the year to fill our transitional spring pies. We make do with what is on hand and wait for the call from our farmer friends to say that ramps are springing up in the forest and asparagus is on its way.

Cheddar Vegetable Pie

This pie is only as good as the Cheddar cheese you use.

Be sure to buy a cheese you would happily eat by itself. Tillamook Reserve, Cabot Extra Sharp, and Grafton Village One Year Aged Cheddar are all good and easy to find.

Ingredients

Makes one 9-inch (22.5-cm) pie

1	**double-crust All-Butter Pie Dough shell (recipe p. 24)**		1 teaspoon	**smoked ground paprika**	3g
1½ cups	**unpeeled red potatoes, chopped into 1-inch (2.5-cm) by ¼-inch pieces**	220g	2 pinches	**ground nutmeg**	
			½ cup	**all-purpose flour**	74g
1 cup	**carrots, peeled and chopped into 1-inch (2.5-cm) by ¼-inch pieces (about 2 medium carrots)**	150g	3 cups (711mL)	**warmed whole milk**	738g
			6 ounces	**sharp Cheddar cheese, shredded**	170g
1 cup	**chopped yellow onion (about ½ medium onion)**	128g	2 Tablespoons	**grainy Dijon mustard, such as Maille Old Style**	34g
2 Tablespoons plus 2 teaspoons	**olive oil, divided**	38g	2 teaspoons	**apple cider vinegar**	8g
			2 pinches	**granulated sugar**	1.5g
	Kosher salt and freshly ground black pepper, to taste		1 cup	**frozen peas**	140g
1½ cups	**broccoli florets**	90g	1	**large egg, beaten**	50g
1 stick	**unsalted butter**	112g			

1 Preheat the oven to 400°F (200°C).

2 Combine the potatoes, carrots, and onion in a small, ovenproof dish and toss with 2 tablespoons of the olive oil. Season to taste with salt and black pepper.

3 Roast the vegetables for 30 to 40 minutes, until the potatoes are almost cooked through but the carrots still have crunch.

4 Stir in the broccoli and 2 teaspoons of the olive oil. Roast an additional 15 to 20 minutes, or until the broccoli is crisp and starting to brown.

5 In a medium, heavy saucepan, melt the butter over low heat. Stir in the paprika and nutmeg and cook for 2 minutes to bloom spices. Turn the heat up to medium and whisk in flour. Cook the roux, stirring often, until the flour is a blonde color and smells slightly nutty, about 3 to 4 minutes.

6 Slowly pour the warmed milk into the roux, whisking constantly. Scrape the side and bottom of the pan where the flour has a tendency to clump. Whisk over medium heat until the sauce is thickened and coats the back of a spoon.

7 Reduce the heat to low and stir in the cheese until it is completely melted. Remove the pan from the heat and add the mustard, vinegar, and sugar. Season to taste with salt and black pepper.

8 Stir in the roasted vegetables and frozen peas. Cool to room temperature, then chill in the refrigerator for at least 2 hours, up to overnight.

9 Pour the cooled filling into the pie crust. Spread the mixture evenly into the shell with a spatula. Finish the pie according to the double-crust instructions (p. 39). Freeze for at least 1 hour.

10 Preheat the oven to 400°F (200°C).

11 Place the frozen pie on a baking sheet. Brush the beaten egg over the pie crust, taking care to get egg into all of the crimps and along the outside edge.

12 Bake from frozen for 50 to 60 minutes, rotating 180 degrees halfway through, until the crust is medium golden brown and the filling is heated through and bubbling out of the vents slightly. Toward the end of baking time, you may need to cover the edge of the pie with a crust guard or foil to prevent burning the crimped edge.

The Cheddar sauce in this recipe moonlights as a creamy base for baked macaroni and cheese at my house.

Mushroom–Spinach Pie

This pie is a favorite, among our vegetarian and meat-loving customers alike, for its surprising layers of complexity. Subtle goat cheese mixes with earthy thyme and spinach, pungent garlic, sweet onions, meaty mushrooms, and punches of cayenne pepper. The title might evoke a dull and dreary health-food item, but this pie stands up as a hearty, decadent meal.

For this recipe, it is important to cook the mushrooms in several batches. Crowding the pan will cause the mushrooms to steam instead of sauté, leading to a soggy pie.

Ingredients

Makes one 9-inch (22.5-cm) pie

1	double-crust All-Butter Pie Dough shell (recipe p. 24)	
¼ cup plus 2 teaspoons	olive oil, divided	64g
¾ cup	Caramelized Onions (recipe p. 312)	210g
4–5 cloves	garlic, minced	30g
	Kosher salt and freshly ground black pepper, to taste	
4 Tablespoons	unsalted butter, divided	56g
1 pound	mixed mushrooms, sliced (sidebar p. 228)	454g

10 ounces	spinach, stems removed, torn into bite-sized pieces	284g
4 ounces	goat cheese	113g
¼ cup (59mL)	Crème Fraîche (recipe p. 318)	65g
2 teaspoons	tomato paste	10g
1½ teaspoons	chopped fresh thyme	1.5g
¼ teaspoon	ground cayenne pepper, plus more to taste	1g
1	large egg, beaten	50g

1 Place 2 teaspoons of the olive oil and the Caramelized Onions in a large skillet over medium-low heat. Stir in the garlic and cook until the garlic is fragrant and cooked through, about 2 to 3 minutes. Spoon the mixture into a medium bowl and season to taste with salt and black pepper. Leave any remaining fat in the skillet.

2 Add 1 tablespoon of the butter and 1 tablespoon of the olive oil to the skillet and set over medium-high heat. Add about ⅓ of the mushrooms to the skillet and cook until they are brown on both sides, adding more butter and olive oil when necessary. *You might not use all of the oil and butter*

3 Transfer the cooked mushrooms to the bowl with the onion mixture and season to taste with salt and black pepper. Repeat steps 2 and 3, seasoning each batch, until all of the mushrooms are cooked.

4 Heat the pan over medium heat with any remaining fat, or if the pan is dry, add 1 tablespoon of the butter. Cook the spinach just until wilted, about 2 minutes. Remove from the pan with a slotted spoon and add to the mushroom mixture. Stir in the goat cheese, Crème Fraîche, tomato paste and thyme. Stir in the cayenne pepper, adding more to taste. Season to taste with salt and black pepper.

5 Chill in the refrigerator for at least 1 hour, or up to 2 days in an airtight container.

6 Pour the filling into the pie shell. Spread the mixture evenly with a spatula. Finish the pie according to the fork-crimp instructions (p. 41), then freeze for at least 1 hour.

7 Place the frozen pie on a baking sheet. Brush the beaten egg over the pie crust, taking care to get egg into all of the crimps and along the outside edge.

8 Preheat the oven to 400°F (200°C).

9 Bake from frozen for 50 to 60 minutes, rotating 180 degrees halfway through, until the crust is medium golden brown and the filling is heated through and bubbling out of the vents slightly. Toward the end of baking time, you may need to cover the edge of the pie with a crust guard or foil to prevent burning the crimped edge.

We use hearty winter spinach. If you are using a more delicate green like baby spinach, you can stir it into the mixture raw rather than wilt it. If you are using frozen spinach, thaw and squeeze the leaves to remove excess water before wilting. Drain thoroughly before adding to mushroom mixture.

PREP NOTE *Thinned with a little cream, the mushroom filling makes a beautiful pasta sauce.*

MUSHROOMS

At Hoosier Mama, we are lucky to have a great mushroom grower at the local farmers' market. River Valley Ranch, from Burlington, Wisconsin, grows or forages nearly a dozen varieties of mushrooms, from everyday buttons to morels and truffles. Below are some of our favorite kinds and how to use them. Most can easily be found at a gourmet grocer.

Shiitake Remove the stems, but save them to flavor a stock or soup later. Wipe the caps with a damp cloth to remove any dirt. Slice the caps thinly. Cook these first if you're using multiple mushrooms, as they are heartier and require a longer cooking time. Raw or undercooked shiitakes can sometimes cause shiitake dermatitis, a skin rash, so be sure to cook them thoroughly before eating.

Cremini Button, cremini, and portabella mushrooms are all the same common variety at various stages of growth. We use cremini mushrooms because they are firm and flavorful, but you can use whatever is on hand. Supermarket mushrooms are often very clean, so simply wipe them with a damp cloth. If quite dirty (common with a haul from the farmers' market) agitate them in a bowl of water for one minute, then let stand for a few more minutes. Dirt and sediment will fall to the bottom of the bowl and you can wipe any persistent remaining dirt from the mushrooms with a cloth. Leave the stems on and halve or quarter the mushrooms.

Oyster These delicate mushrooms can be intimidating—they look more like a musical instrument invented by Dr. Seuss than a vegetable—but they are quite easy to cook. Trim the bottom of the stem, especially of cultivated mushrooms, to remove any hay or wood. Starting at the top, tear thin, uniform strips from the mushroom all the way to the stem. Cook these mushrooms separately and test for doneness by tasting, because undercooked oyster mushrooms can be a bit rubbery in texture.

Colcannon Pie

Colcannon is a traditional Irish staple made of potatoes

and either kale or cabbage. My friend Abra Berens, owner of Bare Knuckle Farm and an accomplished cook, studied at the Ballymaloe Cookery School in County Cork. She taught me how to make colcannon. In a brilliant twist, she adds spicy pickled ramps as a garnish, and that little acidic crunch perfectly balances the otherwise heavy dish. When I was tinkering with the idea of a potato pie, it was too early for the fleeting ramp season, so I borrowed her technique and pickled some shallots and celery instead.

Ingredients

Makes one 9-inch (22.5-cm) pie

1	double-crust All-Butter Pie Dough shell (recipe p. 24)		2 Tablespoons	water	30g
¼ head	cabbage, shredded	227g	½ cup	Crème Fraiche (recipe p. 318)	130g
2 Tablespoons	olive oil	28g	3 Tablespoons (45mL)	buttermilk	45g
	Kosher salt and freshly ground black pepper, to taste		4 cups	Roasted Garlic Mashed Potatoes (recipe p. 317)	1000g
1 bunch	kale	170g	¼ cup	Celery and Shallot Pickles (recipe p. 322), or other pickle variety	
¼ cup (59mL)	hard cider, such as Ace	42g			
¼ cup (59mL)	apple cider vinegar	48g	1	large egg, beaten	50g
2 Tablespoons	maple syrup	41g			

Next page

COLCANNON PIE

Continued

1 Preheat the oven to 350°F (180°C).

2 Toss the cabbage with the olive oil and season to taste with salt and black pepper. Spread out on a baking sheet lined with parchment paper.

3 Roast, turning the pan and tossing the cabbage every 15 minutes, until the cabbage leaves are soft and starting to brown, about 25 to 30 minutes.

4 Meanwhile, wash the kale and remove and discard the center stems. Slice the kale finely, like the cabbage. Toss with the hard cider, vinegar, maple syrup, and water in an ovenproof baking dish. Season to taste with salt and black pepper.

5 Cover tightly with aluminum foil or a lid, then braise in the oven for 25 to 30 minutes, or until the kale is cooked through (you can put it in while the cabbage is still roasting). Halfway through, stir and add a bit more water and hard cider if the bottom of the baking dish is dry.

6 In a large bowl, stir the Crème Fraîche and buttermilk into the mashed potatoes.

7 Once cooled, combine the cabbage and kale, discarding any remaining liquid. Roughly chop the cooked leaves.

8 Finely chop the pickles. Fold the cabbage, kale, and pickles into the potatoes. Taste and adjust the seasonings. Pour the filling into the pie shell. Spread the mixture evenly into the shell with a spatula.

9 Finish according to the double-crust instructions (p. 39). Freeze for at least 1 hour.

10 Preheat the oven to 400°F (200°C).

11 Place the frozen pie on a baking sheet. Brush the beaten egg over the pie crust, taking care to get egg into all of the crimps and along the outside edge.

12 Bake from frozen for 50 to 60 minutes, rotating 180 degrees halfway through, until the crust is medium golden brown and the filling is heated through and bubbling out of the vents slightly. Toward the end of baking time, you may need to cover the edge of the pie with a crust guard or foil to prevent burning the crimped edge.

French Onion Soup Pie

If someone walks through the kitchen and comments on
how amazing it smells, chances are good butter and onions are in a hot pan. This pie celebrates
the simple onion. The bottom crust is supposed to get a little soggy, like the bottom of the crouton
that traditionally floats on top of a crock of French onion soup. Instead of a top crust, we shred pie
dough with a cheese grater, toss it with some Gruyère cheese, and scatter it on top. The edge of the
crust stays crisp, perfect for dipping into the filling.

Ingredients

Makes six 6-inch (15-cm) pies

6	**6-inch (15-cm) blind-baked All-Butter Pie Dough pie shells (recipe p. 24, sidebar p. 232)**	
16 cups	**thinly sliced onions (8 medium onions)**	2268g
3 cups	**peeled pearl onions**	255g
3 Tablespoons	**unsalted butter**	42g
3 Tablespoons (45mL)	**olive oil**	42g
1 Tablespoon	**sherry wine**	12g
5 cups (1.19L)	**Homemade Beef Stock (recipe p. 324)**	1200g

2 teaspoons	**chopped fresh thyme**	2g
2 Tablespoons	**Worcestershire sauce**	20g
2 Tablespoons	**stout beer, such as Guinness**	21g
1 teaspoon	**balsamic vinegar**	6g
	Kosher salt and freshly ground black pepper, to taste	
1	**9–10-ounce ball refrigerated All-Butter Pie Dough (recipe p. 24)**	255–284g
9 ounces	**Gruyère cheese, shredded**	255g

Next page

FRENCH ONION SOUP PIE

Continued

1 Caramelize the sliced and pearl onions with the butter and olive oil according to the Caramelized Onions recipe (recipe p. 312). Once the onions are caramelized, add the sherry to deglaze the pan. Increase the heat to high and stir in the beef stock and thyme. Bring to a boil, then reduce the heat to medium-low and simmer for 30 to 40 minutes, stirring occasionally. Remove from the heat and stir in the Worcestershire sauce, beer, and balsamic vinegar, and season to taste with salt and black pepper. Cool to room temperature and then chill in the refrigerator for at least 2 hours, preferably overnight.

2 Preheat the oven to 400°F (200°C).

3 Place the 6-inch (15-cm) pie shells on a parchment paper- or foil-lined baking sheet. Divide the onion soup mixture evenly among the shells, about 1 cup per shell.

4 Using a cheese grater or the grater attachment on a food processor, shred the ball of dough. This works best when the dough is very cold. If the dough starts to melt, put it in the freezer for 15 minutes and start again. Toss the shredded dough and Gruyère cheese together and distribute evenly on top of the 6 pies.

5 Bake for 25 to 35 minutes, until the dough on top is golden brown, the filling is bubbling, and all of the cheese is melted.

Blanching pearl onions makes them much easier to peel: put them in rapidly boiling water for about one minute, then immediately plunge them into ice water to halt the cooking process. Alternately, you could buy them frozen and avoid the peeling altogether. We would not judge you. Peeling pearl onions is one of the worst kitchen jobs.

SIX-INCH (15-CM) PIES

1. *Prepare the All-Butter Pie Dough. You will have 2 balls of dough; divide each into 3 equal pieces.*
2. *Roll out 1 piece to ⅛ inch (3mm) thick.*
3. *Cut out a 10-inch circle of dough using a 9-inch pie tin as your template.*
4. *Lightly coat a 6-inch (15-cm) pie tin with cooking spray and dust with flour.*
5. *Center the dough round over the pie tin and tap into place. Finish with a traditional single-crust crimp (p. 32).*
6. *Repeat steps 2–5 for each of the 6 pieces of dough. Blind bake as you would a 9-inch (22.5cm) pie (p. 34).*

SUMMER

Our summer savory pies are inspired by what we see at the market and what we want to eat after a hot day in the kitchen, like lighter veggie pies and pulled pork pies with pickles.

Corn Pudding Pie

The summer sweet corn and caramelized onions play off

the brightness of the sour cream and tomatoes. Taste the fresh corn kernels before using—peak-season corn can be very sweet, so you may only need to add a pinch of sugar, or you can leave it out of the recipe entirely. Early-season or frozen corn tends to be starchy or bland, so adding up to one teaspoon of sugar helps to balance the flavors of the finished pie.

Substitute frozen corn only when fresh corn isn't available. Do not thaw; just cook the corn a little longer, about 5 to 7 minutes, or until it is fragrant.

Ingredients

Makes one 9-inch (22.5-cm) pie

1	single-crust, blind-baked All-Butter Pie Dough shell (recipe p. 24, blind baking p. 34)		2	large eggs	100g
¾ cup	cherry or grape tomatoes	94g	½ cup (119mL)	sour cream	121g
2 teaspoons	extra virgin olive oil	10g	½ cup (119mL)	whole milk	121g
1 teaspoon	kosher salt, plus more to taste	3g	¼ cup (59mL)	heavy cream	60g
	Freshly ground black pepper, to taste		¼ cup	cornmeal	40g
3-4 Tablespoons	unsalted butter	42–56g	2 ounces (¼ cup)	shredded sharp Cheddar cheese	57g
½ cup	finely chopped yellow onion	64g		Granulated sugar, to taste (optional)	
1½ cups (2–3 ears)	fresh corn kernels	150g	1	large egg white	30g
			2 Tablespoons	Caramelized Onions (optional, recipe p. 312)	48g

1   Preheat the oven to 350°F (180°C).

2   Halve the tomatoes and toss with the olive oil. Season to taste with salt and black pepper. Roast on a baking sheet lined with parchment paper for 20 to 25 minutes, or until the tomato skins are shriveled. Set aside to cool.

3   In a small sauté pan, melt the butter over medium heat. Add the chopped yellow onion and cook, stirring frequently, until it is soft and translucent, about 3 to 5 minutes.

4   Stir in the corn and cook until the fragrance of corn overtakes the onion, about 2 to 3 minutes. Remove from the heat, season to taste with salt and black pepper, and set aside to cool.

5   In a medium bowl, beat the eggs, sour cream, milk, and cream with a whisk until just combined. Stir in the cornmeal, the Cheddar cheese, 1 teaspoon of the salt, the sugar (if the corn is starchy or bland), and the cooled corn mixture.

6   Place the pie shell on a baking sheet and heat in the oven for 2 to 3 minutes. Remove from the oven and brush a thin layer of the egg white on the bottom and side of the hot shell. Spread the cherry tomatoes (and Caramelized Onions, if using) on the bottom of the shell. Pour the corn mixture over the top.

7   Bake for 30 to 40 minutes, or until the filling is a light golden brown and the center is just set. Cool for 15 minutes before slicing.

This pie is equally delicious as a hot accompaniment to fried chicken or as a chilled dish at a beach picnic.

CRAB–CORN PUDDING VARIATION

Generous lump crabmeat elevates this corn pudding pie from a picnic side dish to an elegant centerpiece of the dinner table. Follow the instructions above, with the following exceptions: cook the chopped onion in 2 tablespoons bacon fat and 2 tablespoons unsalted butter, and replace the Cheddar with ¾ cup (227g) jumbo lump crabmeat and 2 teaspoons (3g) chopped chives.

PREP NOTE

Adding the egg white provides a barrier for the filling and helps to avoid a soggy crust.

Pulled Pork Pie

Hailing from Kansas City, I take barbecue seriously. I'm

not a regionalist—I love mustardy Carolina sauces, spicy Oklahoma hot links, dry-rubbed ribs from Memphis, and Texas beef brisket equally. But I set out to make a slice of pie that evokes the pulled pork sandwiches from my favorite restaurants and roadside stands growing up. Smoking the meat before braising is ideal, but that poses a bit of a dilemma in the 750-square-foot confines of the pie shop. Instead, we use smoked paprika in the rub, cook the meat slow and low, and add chipotles to the Kansas City-style sauce to mimic that intense smoke flavor. If you've got access to a smoker, by all means use it. Good barbecue is worth the wait.

While this recipe is long, the steps are simple and unfussy. At home, I braise the pork shoulder overnight. Most of your time will be spent trying not to sneak bites while your house fills with the intoxicating aroma of smoky pork. In true barbecue fashion, this recipe makes plenty to share. You can freeze the unbaked pies, tightly wrapped, for up to 2 weeks.

Next page

SMOKING INSTRUCTIONS

Hickory or Applewood are good wood chip choices.

1. *Set the smoker to 225°F (110°C).*
2. *Place a pan of water underneath the pork shoulder to provide some humidity and to catch any dripping fat. Smoke the shoulder for 2 to 3 hours.*
3. *Set in a pan with the braising liquid, fruits, and vegetables. Finish cooking the pork according to the recipe's instructions, but total cooking time might be shorter. Check the pork's internal temperature after 8 hours.*

PULLED PORK PIE

Continued

Makes 3–4 generous 9-inch (22.5-cm) pies, or 1–2 pies and lots of pulled pork sandwiches

3	**double-crust All-Butter Pie Dough shells (recipe p. 24)**		2 teaspoons	**mustard seeds**	4g
1	**8-pound boneless pork shoulder**	3629g	2 teaspoons	**coriander seeds**	5g
1 recipe	**Spice Rub (recipe follows)**		1	**bay leaf**	.25g
1	**medium yellow onion**	255g	2 (12-ounce [360-mL])	**bottles of summer beer, such as Boulevard Wheat or Shiner Ruby Redbird**	680g
1	**apple**	110g	½ cup (119mL)	**apple cider vinegar**	96g
1	**orange (use the same one from the Spice Rub)**	170g	¼ cup (59mL)	**molasses or maple syrup**	80g
1 head	**garlic**	50g	½ recipe	**Barbecue Sauce, plus more to taste (recipe p. 315)**	
2 sprigs	**thyme**	1g	1	**large egg, beaten, plus more as needed**	50g
2	**dried pasilla peppers**	4g			
2	**dried chiles de arbol**	1g			

It's important to bring the pork to room temperature before braising, because it will prevent the oven's temperature from suddenly dropping, and will result in a more evenly cooked piece of pork.

You can substitute two 4- to 5-pound (1.82–2.27kg) shoulders if you have trouble finding a larger one—but cooking time may vary.

The leftover braising liquid makes a hearty ramen broth or reduces nicely for a sauce. It also freezes beautifully.

1   Remove the pork shoulder from the refrigerator and pat it dry with paper towels. Place in the large bowl with the Spice Rub and begin massaging the rub into the meat, taking care to work it into all of the crevices and folds. Cover the bowl tightly with plastic wrap and chill the pork in the refrigerator overnight.

2   Bring the pork shoulder to room temperature by letting it sit in the bowl for 45 to 60 minutes. If you have access to a smoker, please use it now (sidebar p. 237).

3   Preheat the oven to 250°F (120°C).

4   While the meat is tempering, prepare the braising liquid: halve the onion and the apple and put them into a large Dutch oven or heavy, ovenproof roasting pan. Halve the orange you zested earlier for the Spice Rub and squeeze the juice into the pan, then put the orange halves into the pan as well. Carefully halve the garlic head horizontally (across its equator) and put it in the pan. Add the thyme, dried peppers, mustard and coriander seeds, and bay leaf. Pour in the beer, vinegar and molasses.

5   Set the pork shoulder into the pan, resting it on top of the vegetables and fruit, with the fattiest part of the meat facing up. Score the fat cap with cross-hatching marks about ½-inch (1.25-cm) deep. Massage any excess rub from the bowl into the top and sides of the meat. Cover the pan with heavy-duty foil and a tight-fitting lid. Place the pan on the center rack of the oven and braise for 9 to 12 hours, rotating 180 degrees every 2 hours, until the internal temperature of the pork shoulder registers 195°F (90°C) on an instant-read thermometer and the meat pulls apart easily.

6   Remove the pan from the oven and take off the lid and foil, making sure to remove any foil that is stuck to the meat or fat cap. Let cool in the braising liquid for 1 to 2 hours.

7   Carefully remove the shoulder from the pan with tongs and place in a large bowl. Once it is cool enough to touch, pull apart the meat into large pieces with your fingers. Discard any sinewy or rubbery pieces of fat and tendon from between layers of meat. Pull the pork apart into bite-sized pieces. Do not shred the pork with forks; this will break down the meat excessively, and the resulting pie will be pulpy and lack texture.

8   Pour the braising liquid through a mesh strainer and discard the vegetables and other solids. Let sit at room temperature until the fat separates and forms a layer at the top of the container, about 20 minutes. Skim at least ½ cup (119mL or 119g) of fat off the top of the liquid and add it to the pork in the roasting pan, adding more to taste. Discard the remaining fat. Add at least 2 cups (474mL or 474g) of the braising liquid to the pork in the bowl, adding more to taste, and reserve the rest of the liquid for another use.

9   Add the Barbecue Sauce to the pork. Wearing plastic gloves, gently mix the pork and barbecue sauce together with your hands. Taste and add more sauce as needed. Chill in the refrigerator for at least 1 hour.

Next page

PULLED PORK PIE

Continued

10 Fill the pie shells with mounds of pulled pork. I like each pie slice to have about the same amount of pork as a big pulled pork sandwich, but fill it as densely as you prefer. Finish the pie according to the double-crust instructions (p. 39). Freeze for at least 1 hour.

11 Preheat the oven to 400°F (200°C).

12 Place the frozen pie (or pies, if you are baking more than one) on a baking sheet. Brush the beaten egg over the pie crusts, taking care to get egg into all of the crimps and along the outside edges.

13 Bake from frozen for 60 to 75 minutes, rotating 180 degrees every 30 minutes, until the crusts are medium golden brown and the fillings are heated through and bubbling out of the vents slightly. Toward the end of baking time, you may need to cover the edges of the pies with crust guards or foil to prevent burning the crimped edges. Serve with Seasonal Pickles (p. 320) and more of the Barbecue Sauce (p. 315).

SPICE RUB

1 cup	**packed dark brown sugar**	240g
1 cup	**kosher salt**	144g
2 teaspoons	**freshly ground black pepper**	4.5g
2 teaspoons	**ground cinnamon**	3g
2 teaspoons	**chili powder**	4g
2 teaspoons	**smoked paprika**	6g
1 teaspoon	**ground cayenne pepper**	4g
1 teaspoon	**ground ginger**	2g
1	**orange**	170g

1 In a large bowl, combine all of the ingredients from the brown sugar through the ginger. Rub between your fingers to break up any clumps and stir with your hands until the mixture is uniform and sandy.

2 Zest the orange over the mixture and toss carefully to combine. Save the orange for use in the Pulled Pork Pie.

This rub can be made in advance and stored in an airtight container for up to 2 weeks.

Tomato Pie

During the few weeks each year that tomatoes are the best-tasting produce available, we use them in many creative ways at the pie shop. Besides our favorite staff meal of BLTs, we roast them, candy them, throw them in quiches, add them to hand pies, and feature them prominently in this supper pie. Little is done to gussy them up, because they taste so good on their own. We remove some of the water to concentrate the tomato flavor, then pair them with the always classic garlic and onion.

Ingredients

Makes one 9-inch (22.5-cm) pie

1	single-crust All-Butter Pie Dough shell (recipe p. 24)		5 cloves	garlic, minced	25g
10	All-Butter Pie Dough lattice strips (p. 42)		½ cup	finely chopped Caramelized Onions (recipe p. 312)	140g
6 pounds	ripe tomatoes	2722g	10	basil leaves, torn into ½-inch (13-mm) pieces	8g
½ cup (119mL)	olive oil	100g	1½ ounces	Parmesan cheese, shredded	43g
¼ cup (59mL)	balsamic vinegar	64g		Crust Dust (p. 21), for sprinkling	
	Kosher salt and freshly ground black pepper, to taste		1	large egg, beaten	50g
1 Tablespoon	unsalted butter	14g			

Next page

TOMATO PIE

Continued

1   Preheat the oven to 250°F (120°C).

2   Cut the tomatoes into halves. Hold them over a bowl and gently squeeze out the seeds and liquid. Save the tomato water for another use (see the Note following the recipe). Cut the tomatoes into 1- to 2-inch (2.5–5-cm) pieces.

3   Toss the tomatoes, olive oil, and vinegar together in a large bowl. Spread the tomatoes out in a single layer on 2 or more baking sheets lined with parchment paper. Drizzle any remaining oil and vinegar over the top. Season the tomatoes to taste with salt and black pepper, then roast in the oven for 60 to 75 minutes, checking occasionally, since cooking time can vary with the varieties of tomatoes you're using. The tomato skins should be shriveled and the tomato pieces should have decreased in size by about ⅓, indicating their loss of liquid. If the edges begin to darken or burn, turn the heat down. Once the tomatoes are done, turn off the oven but leave the tomatoes in the hot oven for 20 to 30 more minutes before removing and cooling to room temperature.

4   Melt the butter over medium-low heat in a small sauté pan. Stir in the garlic and reduce the heat to low. Continue cooking, stirring frequently, until the garlic is fragrant but not browned, about 2 to 3 minutes. Remove from the heat and let cool.

5   In a medium bowl, combine the roasted tomatoes, garlic mixture, Caramelized Onions, basil, and Parmesan cheese. Season to taste with salt and black pepper.

6   Sprinkle the Crust Dust into the empty pie shell. Using a slotted spoon, scoop the tomatoes into the pie shell and discard any remaining juices. Finish the pie according to lattice-top instructions (p. 42). Freeze for at least 1 hour.

7   Preheat the oven to 400°F (200°C).

8   Place the frozen pie on a baking sheet. Brush the beaten egg all over the lattice, taking care to get egg into all of the crimps and along the outside edge. Sprinkle salt and black pepper over the lattice and crimped edge.

9   Bake from frozen for 60 to 75 minutes, rotating 180 degrees every 30 minutes, until the crust is medium golden brown and the filling is heated and bubbling out from between lattice strips slightly. Toward the end of baking time, you may need to cover the edges of the pie with a crust guard or foil to prevent burning the crimped edge.

Reserved tomato water, drained of seeds and pulp, makes a flavorful addition to salad dressing or a cocktail. You can also substitute tomato water for plain water or stock when cooking rice, risotto, or quinoa.

TOMATO SAUCE VARIATION

Use this filling as the tomato sauce in the Chicago-Style Pie (p. 258). Omit the Parmesan, and combine the roasted tomatoes with the cooked garlic, Caramelized Onions, and basil. Pulse all of the ingredients in a blender or food processor, adding a little olive oil to thin out the sauce.

LEANING SHED FARM TOMATOES

Dave Dyrek

We use sweet and spicy peppers, cucumbers, and beans from Leaning Shed, but their heirloom tomatoes are the stars of the show at the Green City Market. At the peak of the season, over 40 heirloom varieties arrive in Chicago from Berrien Springs, Michigan, on Dave and Denise Dyrek's truck. Their tomatoes are so irresistible, I invariably end up eating a few right in their booth.

As a rule, meaty tomatoes like plum and Roma work best in this pie. Throwing in an assortment of bright and tangy heirlooms adds dimension and texture to the filling, but use the best ripe tomatoes available, regardless of variety.

Here are descriptions of a few of our favorite heirlooms:

- *Britain's Breakfast—meaty, with lots of flesh and few seeds*
- *San Marzano—intense, fleshy tomato, few seeds, balanced flavor*
- *Black Plum/Russian Black—earthy, sweet, and spicy*
- *Green Zebra—tangy, sharp, acidic kick*
- *Red Zebra—bright flavor, juicy*
- *Woodle Orange—meaty, little pulp and juice*

Chicken Tomatillo Pie

Everyday supper recipes sometimes transform into
delicious savory pies. Janice, our morning baker, brought in her recipe for chicken enchiladas
thinking they might make a nice addition to our savory lineup. She's been making them for years,
but they entered new territory when baked into the flavorful, crunchy cornmeal crust she developed.
Janice adds Cheddar cheese, spicy salsa verde, and cumin to the roasted dark-meat chicken in this
pie version of her enchiladas.

Ingredients

Makes one 9-inch (22.5-cm) pie

1	double-crust Peppery Cornmeal Dough shell (recipe p. 47)		1½ teaspoons	ground cumin	2.5g
2 pounds	chicken thighs, bone in, skin on (about 5 thighs)	907g	3 Tablespoons	all-purpose flour	27g
1 Tablespoon plus 2 teaspoons	olive oil, divided	30g	1½ cups	Homemade Chicken Stock (recipe p. 323)	360g
	Kosher salt and freshly ground black pepper, to taste		1 cup (327mL)	Salsa Verde (recipe follows), plus more for serving	184g
2 Tablespoons	unsalted butter	28g	6 ounces	Cheddar cheese, shredded	170g
¼ cup	small-diced onion	32g		Juice of 1 lime	
3	garlic cloves, minced	15g	1	large egg, beaten	50g

1   Preheat the oven to 400°F (200°C).

2   Place the chicken thighs in an ovenproof baking dish or small roasting pan. Drizzle with 2 teaspoons of the olive oil and season both sides with salt and black pepper.

3   Roast skin-side up for 25 minutes, or until an instant-read thermometer inserted into the thickest part of the meat registers 165°F (71°C).

4   In a medium saucepan, melt the butter and 1 tablespoon of the olive oil over medium heat. Add the onions and cook, stirring frequently, until they are soft and translucent, about 3 to 5 minutes.

5   Stir in the garlic and cumin and cook for 2 to 3 more minutes.

6   Whisk in the flour and cook for 3 to 4 more minutes.

7   Slowly add the chicken stock, whisking constantly. Cook, whisking often, until the mixture thickens, about 5 to 7 minutes. Remove from the heat and cool to room temperature.

8   Remove the chicken skin and discard (or have a delightful snack). Pull the chicken from the bones and roughly chop the meat.

9   Once the cumin gravy has cooled, stir in the chicken, Salsa Verde, and cheese. Taste and adjust the seasonings with salt, black pepper, and lime juice. Spoon into the pie shell. Spread the mixture evenly into the shell with a spatula.

10 Finish the pie according to the fork-crimp instructions (p. 41). Freeze for at least 1 hour.

11 Preheat the oven to 400°F (200°C).

12 Place the frozen pie on a baking sheet. Brush the beaten egg all over the pie crust, taking care to get egg into all of the crimps and along the outside edge.

13 Bake from frozen for 60 to 75 minutes, rotating 180 degrees every 30 minutes, until the crust is medium golden brown and the filling is heated through and bubbling out of the vents slightly. Toward the end of baking time, you may need to cover the edge of the pie with a crust guard or foil to prevent burning the crimped edge.

14 Serve with extra Salsa Verde.

SALSA VERDE

Makes 2¼ cups (533mL or 414g)

1 head	**garlic**	50g		2	**jalapeño peppers, stems removed**	100g
2–3 Tablespoons	**olive oil**	28–42g		3 Tablespoons	**chopped cilantro**	18g
1½ pounds	**tomatillos, halved**	680g			**Juice of 1 lime**	
½	**medium, yellow onion, chopped into 1-inch (2.5-cm) pieces**	128g			**Kosher salt and freshly ground black pepper, to taste**	

1 Preheat the oven to 400°F (200°C).

2 Cut the garlic head horizontally across its equator and place in a small, ovenproof baking dish. Cover with the olive oil and then wrap the entire dish tightly in foil.

3 Roast for 45 to 60 minutes, until the garlic is softened. Set aside to cool. Once the garlic is cool, squeeze the cloves from the papery skin. Put half of the garlic in the bowl of a food processor and reserve the remaining garlic for another use.

4 Place the tomatillos, onion, and jalapeño peppers on a baking sheet lined with parchment paper and roast for 30 to 40 minutes, until the tomatillos and jalapeño peppers have blistered and become a muted army-green color. Remove from the oven and let cool.

5 Place the garlic, tomatillos, and onion in the bowl of a food processor and pulse to combine the ingredients. Mix for 30 seconds to make a smooth salsa, or just pulse a few times to make a chunky salsa. Transfer the ingredients to a separate bowl and rinse out the food processor bowl.

6 Place the jalapeño peppers in the bowl of the food processor and pulse for 30 seconds to 1 minute, until they are finely chopped. Since the heat can vary from pepper to pepper, add the jalapeños to the tomatillo mixture a little at a time, tasting along the way to achieve the desired spice level.

7 Stir in the cilantro and lime juice and season to taste with salt and black pepper.

This salsa can be made with a blender or by hand. Chop the vegetables to the desired size and combine. Wash your hands thoroughly after handling the jalapeño peppers!

FALL

Delicious autumn! My very soul is wedded to it, and if I were a bird I would fly about the earth seeking the successive autumns. —George Eliot

Fall is my favorite pie season. It marks the return of heartier produce and cozier meals. It means darker beers, sweaters, football, and meat pies. And savory pies start to hold their own against their prettier, sweet counterparts.

Pork, Apple, and Sage Supper Pie

This is the first savory pie we ever made at Hoosier

Mama. After a year of making only sweet pies, we wanted to try something new. (And we needed a snack.) Angela Boggiano's excellent book, *Pie*, inspired us to dream up all kinds of savory pies.

Ask your butcher to recommend a flavorful breakfast sausage for the filling. Ours comes from C&D Family Farms, where farmers Crystal and Dan Nells are committed to humanely raising "healthy, natural, and happy hogs." Their pasture-raised pigs eat an all-natural feed free from antibiotics and hormones. We think the pork tastes better that way.

Ingredients

Makes one 9-inch (22.5-cm) pie

1	double-crust All-Butter Pie Dough shell (recipe p. 24)		¼ cup	whole-grain mustard, such as Maille Old Style	67g
2 Tablespoons	olive oil	28g	1 Tablespoon	finely chopped fresh sage (about 15 medium leaves)	2.5g
2 Tablespoons	unsalted butter	28g	1 Tablespoon	chopped Italian parsley	6g
2 cups	unpeeled red potatoes, chopped into bite-sized pieces	300g	1 pound	pork breakfast sausage, casings removed	454g
½ cup	Caramelized Onions (recipe p. 312)	140g		Freshly ground black pepper, to taste	
2	Granny Smith apples, peeled, cored, and chopped into bite-sized pieces	220g	1	large egg, beaten	50g
½ cup (119mL)	Crème Fraîche (recipe p. 318)	130g		*Next page*	

PORK, APPLE, AND SAGE SUPPER PIE
Continued

1 Heat the olive oil and butter in a heavy, large sauté pan over medium heat. Once the pan is hot, stir in the potatoes and Caramelized Onions. Cook, stirring occasionally, for about 10 to 12 minutes to brown the sides of the potatoes.

2 Turn the heat to low and cover the pan with a lid. Continue to cook, stirring occasionally, until the potatoes are fork tender, about 5 more minutes.

3 Transfer the contents of the pan to a medium bowl and add the apples, Crème Fraîche, mustard, sage, and parsley.

4 Place the same sauté pan over medium-high heat and crumble the pork sausage into it, breaking up any large pieces. Cook, stirring often, until the pork is well browned, about 12 to 15 minutes. Scrape up any browned bits from the bottom of the pan and pour, along with sausage, into the potato mixture.

5 Season to taste with black pepper, stir to combine, and taste the filling. Adjust the seasonings if necessary. Chill in the refrigerator for at least 1 hour.

6 Pour the filling evenly into the pie shell. Pat the filling down so that the apple and potato edges will not poke through the top crust.

7 Finish the pie according to the double-crust instructions (p. 39). Freeze for at least 1 hour.

8 Preheat the oven to 400°F (200°C).

9 Place the frozen pie on a baking sheet. Brush the beaten egg over the pie crust, taking care to get egg into all of the crimps and along the outside edge.

10 Bake from frozen for 60 to 75 minutes, rotating 180 degrees every 30 minutes, until the crust is medium golden brown and the filling is heated through and bubbling out of the vents slightly. Toward the end of baking time, you may need to cover the edge of the pie with a crust guard or foil to prevent burning the crimped edge.

Sausage can prove to be quite salty, decreasing the need for additional salt or eliminating the need altogether.

Serve as a brunch pie, or try it as a midnight snack straight from the fridge.

Shepherd's Pie

When you order shepherd's pie, you often get a pie made

of ground beef, which is actually a cottage pie. As far as we know, shepherds don't spend much time following cows around the pasture—that would be a cowboy pie! This is a true shepherd's pie, made with traditional ground lamb and topped with garlicky mashed potatoes—a rustic dish for a comforting weeknight meal.

It is important that the vegetables be chopped into roughly equal-sized pieces—about ¼ to ½ inch (6–13mm) thick—so that they cook uniformly.

Ingredients

Makes six 6-inch (15-cm) pies

4 Tablespoons	**unsalted butter**	56g		2½ cups (593mL)	**Homemade Beef Stock (recipe p. 324)**	600g
⅔ cup	**peeled and chopped carrots**	126g		1 cup	**frozen peas**	140g
⅔ cup	**chopped celery**	80g		2½ Tablespoons	**Worcestershire sauce**	25g
⅔ cup	**chopped onion**	85g			**Kosher salt and freshly ground black pepper, to taste**	
⅔ cup	**chopped shallots**	120g		1 recipe	**Roasted Garlic Mashed Potatoes (recipe p. 317)**	
2 pounds	**ground lamb**	907g		2 Tablespoons	**unsalted butter, melted**	28g
½ cup	**all-purpose flour**	74g				
½ teaspoon	**ground nutmeg**	2g				
½ teaspoon	**ground cayenne pepper**	2g				

Next page

SHEPHERD'S PIE

Continued

1   In a large (12-inch or 30-cm) skillet, melt the butter over medium-high heat. Stir in the chopped vegetables and cook, stirring occasionally, for 8 to 10 minutes, or until the onion and shallots are translucent. The celery and carrots should still be a bit crunchy. Transfer the vegetables and fat to a bowl.

2   Return the same skillet to the stove over medium-high heat. Crumble the ground lamb into the pan, breaking up any large pieces. Stir often, until the lamb is cooked through, about 10 to 12 minutes.

3   Pour the cooked lamb into a colander set over a bowl and let drain for 2 minutes. Pour ⅓ cup (79mL or 80g) of the drained fat back into the skillet along with the cooked lamb. Discard any remaining fat.

4   Place the skillet over medium heat and stir in the flour, nutmeg, and cayenne pepper. Cook, stirring constantly, for 3 to 4 minutes.

5   Slowly pour in the beef stock, ½ cup (119mL or 120g) at a time, stirring after each addition and pausing to let the mixture thicken slightly. Take care to scrape up any browned bits from the bottom or edges of the skillet.

6   Stir in the cooked vegetables, frozen peas, and Worcestershire sauce, and season to taste with salt and black pepper. Reduce the heat to low, cover, and simmer for 10 to 15 minutes.

7   Fill 6 6-inch pie tins or ramekins each with 1 cup (150g) of the lamb mixture. Place the tins on a baking sheet lined with parchment paper and top with the warm mashed potatoes, using a spoon for a rustic look or piping the potatoes with a pastry bag for a fancier presentation.

8   Preheat the oven to 400°F (200°C).

9   Drizzle the melted butter over the potatoes and bake the pies in the oven until they are golden brown, about 20 minutes.

The ramekins full of lamb can be stored in the freezer, tightly wrapped, for up to 2 weeks. Thaw overnight in the refrigerator before topping with the mashed potatoes, heating, and eating. The finished pies can be stored in the refrigerator for up to 2 days.

 PREP NOTE

The pies can be served without crisping in the oven; simply top with hot mashed potatoes and serve.

Frito–Chili Pie

For the uninitiated, Frito–Chili Pie is traditionally made

by ladling a mess of chili straight into a small bag of corn chips. This delicacy is big in Texas and throughout the southwestern United States; I grew up eating chili pies, both from the school cafeteria at lunch and from the snack shack at Friday-night high school football games. Hoosier Mama's version is an actual pie: we make a crumb crust with corn chips and cornmeal, then top with generous mounds of chili, cheese, sour cream, fresh oregano, and still more corn chips.

Next page

ROASTING PEPPERS

Roasting adds a smoky flavor and pleasant texture to peppers; skip the store-bought jars and do it yourself at home.

If you have a gas stove, put the pepper directly on the burner grate and scorch the skin over medium-high heat. Turn the pepper every few minutes with (heatproof!) tongs until it's blackened on all sides. Don't be alarmed if the stem catches on fire, but do be careful to keep towels and other flammable materials away from the stove. An oven broiler also works for roasting peppers: preheat the broiler, put a tray of peppers directly under the heat, and broil for 3 to 4 minutes. Carefully remove the pan and turn the peppers over with tongs, then broil on the other side for 3 to 4 more minutes.

Immediately put the hot peppers in a bowl, cover with plastic wrap, and let them steam for about 10 minutes. Once they are cool enough to touch, peel the burnt skins off the peppers. I like to use the plastic wrap from the bowl to scrape the skin off the slippery pepper. Discard the seeds, skin, and stem.

FRITO-CHILI PIE

Continued

Ingredients

Makes four 6-inch (15-cm) pies

⅔ cup	**dried kidney beans or 1 (15-ounce) can pinto beans**	110g
⅔ cup	**dried pinto beans or 1 (15-ounce) can pinto beans**	110g
4	**Frito® Crumb Crust shells (recipe p. 49)**	
2 Tablespoons	**unsalted butter**	28g
2 Tablespoons	**olive oil**	28g
1	**medium yellow onion, diced small**	255g
1	**large green bell pepper, diced small**	250g
1	**large red bell pepper, diced small**	250g
5 cloves	**garlic, minced**	25g
1 pound	**ground beef**	454g
1	**poblano pepper, roasted and diced small (see sidebar, p. 253)**	150g
1	**medium jalapeño pepper, finely chopped**	50g

2	**chipotle peppers in adobo sauce, finely chopped**	28g
1 Tablespoon	**chili powder**	6g
1 Tablespoon	**ground cumin**	6g
1 teaspoon	**finely chopped fresh Mexican oregano**	1.5g
½ teaspoon	**ground cayenne pepper**	2g
1 (28-ounce) can	**crushed tomatoes**	794g
6–8 ounces (177–236mL)	**light ale or wheat beer**	170–227g
	Juice of 1–2 limes, plus more to taste	
	Kosher salt and freshly ground black pepper, to taste	
	Shredded sharp Cheddar cheese, for topping	
	Sour cream, finely chopped Mexican oregano, and Fritos® corn chips, for topping	

PREP NOTE *Chipotle peppers in adobo sauce can be found in either the canned goods or the ethnic/international foods aisle of any major grocery store.*

1   If you are using canned beans, skip this step. If you are using dried beans, rinse and then soak them in water for 8 to 12 hours. Place in a pot with the soaking water, adding more water if necessary, so that the beans are covered with water by about 1 inch (2.5cm). Bring to a boil over high heat, then cover and reduce the heat to low and simmer until the beans are soft, about 1½ to 2 hours.

2   In a heavy, large sauté pan or Dutch oven, melt the butter and olive oil over medium-high heat.

3   Stir in the onion and cook, stirring occasionally, for 8 to 10 minutes, until the onion is translucent.

4   Add the bell peppers and garlic and reduce the heat to medium. Cook for an additional 5 minutes, until the garlic is fragrant but not browned.

5   Meanwhile, place a large skillet over medium-high heat and add the ground beef. Cook, stirring occasionally, until beef is browned and cooked through. Drain any excess fat and discard.

6   Add the poblano, jalapeño, and chipotle peppers, the chili powder, cumin, oregano, and cayenne pepper to the onion mixture. Stir to combine and cook for 3 to 4 minutes. If the pan dries out, add a few teaspoons of olive oil to prevent the ingredients from sticking.

7   Stir in the beef and crushed tomatoes.

8   Add the beans and ale and bring to a boil. Cover, reduce the heat to low, and simmer for 45 to 60 minutes, stirring occasionally and adding more ale if the pot dries out. Remove from the heat and season to taste with lime juice, salt, and black pepper.

9   Preheat the oven to 400°F (200°C).

10 Place the shells on a baking sheet lined with parchment paper. Spoon in the chili; there may be some chili left over.

11 Top each pie with the shredded Cheddar cheese and bake for 10 to 15 minutes, or until the cheese is completely melted.

12 Serve hot, topped with sour cream, finely chopped oregano, and corn chips.

For stubborn Texans: We know our chili is not traditional, slow-cooked, bean-free Texas chili, but we like it all the same.

Oktoberfest Pie

Oktoberfest Pie is a celebration of pork and beer. We start with generously spiced house-made Bratwurst (p. 330), but brats from your local butcher are a fine substitution—just make sure to remove any casings. We like the Oktoberfest beer from the Spoetzl Brewery in Shiner, Texas, but feel free to choose any brand you love to drink. Prost!

Ingredients

Makes one 9-inch (22.5-cm) pie

1	double-crust All-Butter Pie Dough shell (recipe p. 24)		1½ cups	sliced yellow onions	150g
1 pound	unpeeled Yukon gold potatoes, scrubbed	454g	1½ cups	sauerkraut, juices included	263g
	Kosher salt and freshly ground white pepper, to taste		1¾ teaspoons	caraway seeds, divided	2.5g
½ cup (119mL)	buttermilk	121g	1 cup (237mL)	Oktoberfest beer, such as Spoetzl's Shiner Bock	238g
¼ cup	coarse-grained mustard, such as Maille Old Style	67g	1 pound	Bratwurst (recipe p. 330)	454g
2 Tablespoons	olive oil	28g	2 Tablespoons	unsalted butter, melted	28g
2 Tablespoons	unsalted butter	28g	1	large egg, beaten	50g

1   Place the potatoes in a medium saucepan. Cover with cold water by 2 inches (5cm). Add a few large pinches of salt to the water and boil until the potatoes are fork tender.

2   Pour out the water and let the potatoes steam and cool for a few minutes. Smash them into bite-sized pieces with the back of a fork.   *Do not mash smooth*

3   Combine the potatoes, buttermilk, and mustard in a large bowl. Season to taste with salt and white pepper.

4   Place the olive oil and butter in a large, heavy skillet over medium heat. Stir in the sliced onions and sweat them, stirring occasionally, until they are translucent.

5   Add the sauerkraut, 1½ teaspoons of the caraway seeds, and the beer, and simmer, uncovered, over medium-low heat for 20 to 30 minutes. Remove from the heat and add to the potatoes.

6   Place the same skillet over medium-high heat and crumble the Bratwurst into the pan. Break up any large pieces, then cook through until browned, stirring often, about 10 to 12 minutes.

7   Add the Bratwurst to the onions and potatoes and stir to combine. Season to taste with salt and white pepper. Chill the filling in the refrigerator for at least 1 hour.

8   Spoon the filling into the pie shell. Press the mixture evenly into the shell and finish the pie according to the double-crust instructions (p. 39). Freeze for at least 1 hour.

9   Preheat the oven to 400°F (200°C).

10 Place the frozen pie on a baking sheet. Brush all over with the melted butter, then brush the beaten egg over the pie crust, taking care to get egg into all of the crimps and along the outside edge.

11 Sprinkle the top of the pie with ¼ teaspoon of the caraway seeds.

12 Bake from frozen for 55 to 65 minutes, rotating 180 degrees every 20 minutes, until the crust is medium golden brown and the filling is heated through and bubbling out of the vents slightly. Toward the end of baking time, you may need to cover the edge of the pie with a crust guard or foil to prevent burning the crimped edge.

At the shop, we top the pie with diamond-shaped dough cutouts and cut vents to look like the Bavarian flag, then brush it all with the beaten egg.

Chicago-Style Pie

Doesn't every city deserve to have its own pie? We think so.

This pie celebrates Chicago on several levels: we use locally raised pork for our sausage, honoring our city's history as hog butcher for the world; the treasured Green City Market's produce stands supply tomatoes for the sauce; the peppers are a nod to our city's favorite sandwich, Italian beef; and we make it all from scratch because we're used to hard work in this city of big shoulders. We even decorate the top of this pie like the Chicago flag, adding a row of four stars across the center and cutting two long vents above and below.

If you use store-bought Italian sausage, be sure to remove any casings before use.

Ingredients

Makes one 9-inch (22.5-cm) pie

1	**double-crust All-Butter Pie Dough shell (recipe p. 24)**	
2 Tablespoons	**unsalted butter**	28g
1 Tablespoon	**olive oil**	14g
1	**medium onion, sliced into ¼-inch pieces (makes about 2 cups)**	255g
4–5	**large bell peppers, various colors, cut into 1-inch by 1-inch (2.5-cm by 2.5-cm) pieces**	1000–1250g
5 cloves	**garlic, minced**	25g
	Kosher salt and freshly ground black pepper, to taste	
3 cups (711mL)	**Tomato Sauce (recipe p. 243)**	715g
1 pound	**cooked Italian Sausage (recipe p. 328)**	454g
1	**large egg, beaten**	50g

1 Place the butter and olive oil in a large, heavy skillet over medium heat.

2 Stir in the onions and sweat, stirring occasionally, until the onions become translucent, about 10 minutes.

3 Add the bell peppers and stir. Cook for about 5 more minutes, stirring occasionally.

4 Stir in the garlic and cook for 2 to 3 more minutes, until the garlic is fragrant but not browned. Season to taste with salt and black pepper.

5 Pour in the Tomato Sauce and Italian Sausage and stir to combine.

6 Bring to a simmer and cook for 8 to 10 minutes. Taste and adjust the seasonings.

7 Chill the filling in the refrigerator for at least 1 hour.

8 Pour the filling into the pie shell. Press the mixture evenly into the shell.

9 Finish the pie according to the double-crust instructions (p. 39). Freeze for at least 1 hour.

10 Preheat the oven to 400°F (200°C).

11 Place the frozen pie on a baking sheet. Brush the beaten egg over the pie crust, taking care to get egg into all of the crimps and along the outside edge.

12 Bake from frozen for 55 to 65 minutes, rotating 180 degrees every 20 minutes, until the crust is medium golden brown and the filling is heated through and bubbling through the vents slightly. Toward the end of baking time, you may need to cover the edge of the pie with a crust guard or foil to prevent burning the crimped edge.

Chicken Pot Pie

WINTER

Humans have eaten pie for almost as long as they have been cooking. What began as a necessity to preserve meat has evolved into a craving for the comfort of slow roasts and hearty braises tucked between layers of crust.

Chicken Pot Pie

This is a year-round favorite for customers and the pie

shop staff alike. When a blustery winter storm is forecast, regulars stock up to help sustain them through the snow. When the temperature gauge inside the shop read over 100 degrees last August, I was amazed that we still sold out of Chicken Pot Pie that day. If you're used to getting pies in a little box from the frozen foods section of the grocery store, prepare for a revelation.

Ingredients

Makes one 9-inch (22.5-cm) pie

1	**double-crust Thyme Dough shell (recipe p. 25)**		1	**small yellow onion, peeled and quartered**	150g
3–4	**small red potatoes, scrubbed and sliced into ¼-inch half moons**	160g	1	**medium carrot, roughly chopped**	75g
2	**medium carrots, peeled and sliced into ¼-inch half moons**	150g	1 stalk	**celery, roughly chopped, leaves and root removed**	61g
1	**small yellow onion, peeled and diced small**	150g	5 cloves	**garlic, smashed, skins removed**	25g
1 Tablespoon	**olive oil**	14g	1 Tablespoon	**tomato paste**	15g
	Kosher salt and freshly ground black pepper, to taste		2 Tablespoons	**cognac or sherry**	24g
2 Tablespoons	**vegetable oil**	20g	1¾ cups (415mL)	**white wine, such as a Pinot Grigio**	395g
2 pounds	**chicken thighs, bone in, skin on (about 5 thighs)**	907g	1	**fresh bay leaf**	.25g
			2 sprigs	**fresh thyme**	1g

1¾ cups (415mL)	**Homemade Chicken Stock (recipe p. 323)**	400g
4 Tablespoons	**unsalted butter**	56g
¼ teaspoon	**ground nutmeg**	1g
¼ cup	**all-purpose flour**	37g
2 Tablespoons	**Crème Fraîche (recipe p. 318)**	33g
2 Tablespoons	**whole milk**	30g

2 Tablespoons	**heavy cream**	29g
½ teaspoon	**granulated sugar, plus more to taste**	2.75g
1 teaspoon	**red wine vinegar, plus more to taste**	4g
1 cup	**frozen peas**	140g
1	**large egg, beaten**	50g

1 Preheat the oven to 400°F (200°C).

2 In a 9-inch (22.5-cm) square glass baking dish, toss the potatoes, half moons of carrots, and diced onion with the olive oil to coat. Season with salt and black pepper. Roast for 45 to 60 minutes, stirring every 15 minutes, until the potatoes are cooked through. Set aside.

3 Place the vegetable oil in a large, heavy, ovenproof saucepan or Dutch oven over medium-high heat.

4 Season the chicken thighs on both sides with salt and black pepper, then place skin-side down in the hot saucepan. Cook 4 minutes; if the chicken skin sticks to the bottom of the pan, cook 1 to 2 more minutes. Turn the thighs and cook 4 more minutes. Transfer the thighs to a plate.

5 In the still-hot saucepan, add the onion quarters, chopped carrot, chopped celery, garlic, and tomato paste. Deglaze the pan with the cognac, then add the white wine and scrape up any browned bits from the bottom of the pan. Add the bay leaf and thyme sprigs.

6 Bring the mixture to a boil and cook 6 to 8 minutes, or until the strong alcohol smell burns off completely.

7 Stir in the chicken stock. Bring the liquid to a simmer. Put the chicken back into the pan, nestling it under the liquid as much as possible. Cover with a tight-fitting lid and bake in the oven for 22 to 25 minutes. The chicken should reach a minimum internal temperature of 165°F (71°C) on an instant-read thermometer.

8 Remove from the oven and transfer just the thighs to a bowl.

Next page

CHICKEN POT PIE

Continued

9 Pour the wine mixture and the vegetables through a strainer into a separate bowl. Reserve the wine mixture. Discard the bay leaf, thyme, and vegetables (or save for stock).

10 In the same saucepan, make a roux by melting the butter over low heat. Stir in the nutmeg and cook for 2 more minutes to bloom the spice. Turn the heat up to medium, then whisk in the flour. Cook the roux, stirring often, until the roux is a blonde color and smells slightly nutty, about 3 to 4 minutes.

11 Slowly whisk the reserved wine mixture into the roux. Take care to scrape the side of the pan where the flour will tend to stick. Whisk constantly until thickened.

12 Remove from the heat and stir in the Crème Fraîche, milk, and heavy cream until combined.

13 Add the sugar and vinegar. Season to taste with salt and black pepper. Set aside.

14 Remove and discard the chicken skin and bones. Pull the meat apart into roughly bite-sized pieces.

15 In a bowl, combine the roasted vegetables, gravy, chicken, and frozen peas. Taste and season again if necessary. Chill in the refrigerator for at least 1 hour.

16 Once cool, pour into the pie shell. Spread the mixture evenly into the shell with a spatula.

17 Finish the pie according to the fork-crimp instructions (p. 41). Freeze for at least 1 hour.

18 Preheat the oven to 400°F (200°C).

19 Place the frozen pie on a baking sheet. Brush the beaten egg over the pie crust, taking care to get it into all of the crimps and along the outside edge.

20 Bake from frozen for 60 to 75 minutes, rotating 180 degrees every 30 minutes, until the crust is medium golden brown and the filling is heated through and bubbling out of the vents slightly. Toward the end of the baking time, you may need to cover the edge of the pie with a crust guard or foil to prevent burning the crimped edge.

We prefer to use organic or Amish chicken. It alleviates our concerns about the environment and animal welfare, and we have found that conventionally raised chicken just doesn't taste very good.

Extra-Stout Beef Pie

We rely on Rob Levitt and his team at the Butcher & Larder, our neighborhood butcher shop, for a steady supply of beef, pork, and lamb. They are dedicated to whole-animal butchery (which means they make use of all parts of the animal), selling both traditional and unique cuts. Before opening the Butcher & Larder, Rob and his wife Allie, an amazing pastry chef, ran the popular and critically acclaimed restaurant mado, so we sometimes turn to them for cooking advice too.

At Hoosier Mama, we primarily use beef chuck, but ask your butcher about good cuts for slow braising and you might be introduced to something new entirely. To find a butcher in your neighborhood, check the Butcher's Guild map listed in the Resources section of this book (p. 336).

 **PREP NOTE** The stout's sharp bitterness cooks off during the long braise. It helps to re-introduce that flavor (see step 8) after cooking so it remains prominent in the pie.

Next page

EXTRA-STOUT BEEF PIE

Continued

Ingredients

Makes one 9-inch (22.5-cm) pie

1	double-crust All-Butter Pie Dough shell (recipe p. 24)	
1 pound	beef chuck, cut into bite-sized pieces	454g
	Kosher salt and freshly ground black pepper	
3–4 Tablespoons (45–60mL)	vegetable oil	42–56g
¼ cup	all-purpose flour	37g
⅓ cup	finely chopped shallots (about 2 small shallots)	75g
2 cloves	garlic, minced	10g
1 Tablespoon	tomato paste	15g
1	12-ounce (360-mL) bottle strong, dark stout beer, such as Guinness Extra Stout, divided	355g

1 cup (237mL)	Homemade Beef Stock (recipe p. 324)	240g
¼ cup (59mL)	light- or medium-roast brewed coffee	60g
1½ cups	quartered button mushrooms	85g
1 cup	pearl onions, peeled	85g
2	small, unpeeled red potatoes, chopped	85g
1	medium carrot, peeled, and chopped	85g
½ sprig	fresh rosemary	5g
1½ Tablespoons	Worcestershire sauce	15g
1	large egg, beaten	50g

You may use whatever coffee you've got on hand, but a light- or medium-roast coffee has more acidity than dark roast. If you go with a darker roast, add a splash of balsamic or sherry vinegar to brighten the flavors.

1   Temper the beef by taking it out of the refrigerator about 30 minutes before you start cooking, so the pan's temperature won't drop dramatically from adding cold beef, and so the beef will cook more evenly.

2   Preheat the oven to 250°F (120°C).

3   Season the beef with salt and black pepper. Place 2 tablespoons of the vegetable oil in a large, heavy ovenproof saucepan or Dutch oven over medium-high heat.

4   Toss the beef in the flour to coat, shaking off any excess flour. Working in batches to avoid crowding the pan, brown the beef on all sides in the saucepan. If necessary, add more vegetable oil, 1 tablespoon at a time, to coat the bottom of the pan. Move all the browned beef to a bowl.

5   Reduce the heat to low. Add 1 more tablespoon of the vegetable oil, the shallots, the garlic, the tomato paste, and any leftover flour. Cook for 2 minutes, stirring constantly. Stir in 9 ounces (270mL or 266g) of the beer, the beef stock, and the coffee. Scrape up any brown bits from the bottom of the pan.

6   Add the browned beef, mushrooms, onions, potatoes, and carrot. Season with salt and black pepper and stir to combine. The vegetables and beef will not be completely submerged in the liquid. Increase the heat to medium-high and bring the contents of the pan to a simmer. Cover with a tight lid or heavy-duty aluminum foil.

7   Put the pan in the middle rack of the oven. Cook for about 2 hours and 30 minutes, stirring every hour or so. The beef should be tender but not falling apart and the vegetables should be cooked through but not soggy. The sauce should be thin. Remove from the oven and add the rosemary, tucking it under the liquid. Let the filling come to room temperature and then chill overnight in the refrigerator.

8   Remove and discard the rosemary. Add the Worcestershire sauce and the remaining beer. Season the filling to taste with salt and black pepper. Pour half the filling into the pie shell. Add the remaining filling a bit at a time to avoid overfilling the pie. There may be some filling leftover. Finish according to the double-crust instructions (p. 39). Freeze for at least 1 hour.

9   Preheat the oven to 400°F (200°C).

10 Place the frozen pie on a baking sheet. Brush the beaten egg over the pie crust, taking care to get egg into all of the crimps and along the outside edge.

11 Bake from frozen for 1 hour to 1 hour and 15 minutes, rotating 180 degrees every 30 minutes, until the crust is medium golden brown and the filling is heated through and bubbling out of the vents slightly. Toward the end of baking time, you may need to cover the edge of the pie with a crust guard or foil to prevent burning the crimped edge.

Curried Winter Vegetable Pie

I hate recipes that call for ¼ cup of an obscure fresh
ingredient. What on earth are you supposed to do with the remainder? We avoid that issue in this
recipe by using whole vegetables, but we also create a new and delicious problem: there are a few
roasted vegetables left over that cannot quite fit in the pie. These veggies quickly become a salad
when tossed with a light vinaigrette; fried up with some corned beef, they make a nice breakfast
hash to pair with poached eggs. Problem solved.

The key to this recipe is chopping all of the vegetables roughly the same size so that they cook
uniformly (it is fine if there are irregular shapes—carrots do not grow into rectangles). Dicing them
into ½- to ¾-inch (13–19-mm) bite-sized pieces works nicely.

CURRY POWDER

We love the sweet Indian curry powder from Chicago's Spice House for our Curried Winter Veg-
etable Pie. The powder has warm and sweet flavor notes, but is not aggressively spicy. It pairs
well with the root vegetables and is brightened by the citrus we add at the end of the recipe. Feel
free to use your favorite curry powder instead, or use the ingredients listed here as a jumping-off
point to try blending your own with the freshest spices you can find.

The Spice House mixes the following spices by hand for their sweet curry powder:

• *turmeric*	• *coriander*	• *cumin*	• *ginger*
• *nutmeg*	• *fennel*	• *cinnamon*	• *fenugreek*
• *white pepper*	• *arrowroot*	• *cardamom*	• *cloves*
• *black pepper*	• *red pepper*		

Ingredients

Makes one 9-inch (22.5-cm) pie

1	**double-crust All-Butter Pie Dough shell (recipe p. 24)**	
1	**celery root, peeled and chopped (about 2 cups)**	255g
3 Tablespoons	**olive oil, divided**	42g
	Kosher salt and freshly ground black pepper, to taste	
1	**large sweet potato, peeled and chopped**	454g
4	**medium carrots, peeled and chopped**	454g
1–2	**medium turnips, trimmed and chopped**	255g
1	**medium yellow onion, chopped**	255g
1 cup (237mL)	**Homemade Vegetable Stock (recipe p. 325)**	240g

1 cup (237mL)	**whole milk**	246g
4 Tablespoons	**unsalted butter**	56g
1 Tablespoon	**sweet curry powder, plus more to taste (sidebar p. 268)**	4.5g
¼ teaspoon	**ground mace**	.75g
¼ teaspoon	**ground cayenne pepper**	1g
¼ cup	**all-purpose flour**	37g
2 Tablespoons	**orange juice**	24g
2 Tablespoons	**fresh lemon juice (about ½ lemon)**	24g
2 teaspoons	**granulated sugar**	9g
2 teaspoons	**chopped Italian parsley**	4g
½ cup	**dried currants**	57g
1	**large egg, beaten**	50g

At the pie shop we serve slices with a little dish of pickled vegetable or fruit chutney, such as our Apple-Shallot Chutney (p. 314).

Next page

CURRIED WINTER VEGETABLE PIE

Continued

1   Preheat the oven to 400°F (200°C).

2   In a large roasting pan, toss the celery root with 1 tablespoon of the olive oil and season to taste with salt and black pepper. Roast in the oven for 20 minutes.

3   Remove from the oven and stir in the sweet potatoes, carrots, turnips, and onion, along with 2 table-spoon of the olive oil. Season with salt and black pepper. Roast for another 45 to 55 minutes, stirring every 20 minutes, until the vegetables are fork tender.

4   Meanwhile, combine the Homemade Vegetable Stock and milk in a saucepan over high heat. Stir occasionally, until hot to the touch but not boiling, about 5 to 7 minutes.

5   While the stock mixture heats, melt the butter over medium heat in a large skillet. Stir in the curry powder, mace, and cayenne pepper, and cook for 2 minutes to bloom the spices. Whisk in the flour. Cook the roux, stirring often, until the flour is a blonde color and smells slightly nutty, about 3 to 4 minutes.

6   Slowly whisk the hot vegetable stock mixture into the roux. Scrape the side and bottom of the pan, where the flour has a tendency to clump. Whisk over medium heat, until the sauce is thickened and coats the back of a spoon. Remove from the heat and stir in the orange juice, lemon juice, sugar, and parsley. Season to taste with salt and black pepper. Combine this curry sauce with 4 cups (600g) of the roasted vegetables and the currants. Chill in the refrigerator for at least 1 hour.

7   Once cool, pour the filling into the pie shell. Spread the mixture evenly with a spatula. Finish the pie according to the double-crust instructions (p. 39). Freeze for at least 1 hour.

8   Preheat the oven to 400°F (200°C).

9   Place the frozen pie on a baking sheet. Brush the beaten egg all over the pie crust, taking care to get egg into all of the crimps along the outside edge.

10   Bake from frozen for 50 to 60 minutes, rotating 180 degrees every 30 minutes, until the crust is medium golden brown and the filling is heated through and bubbling out of the vents slightly. Toward the end of baking time, you may need to cover the edges of the pie with a crust guard or foil to prevent burning the crimped edge.

Ham and Bean Pie

I fell in love with the soup at my Grandma Georgia's

house, where enormous pots of it would bubble for hours on the stove. She was tasked with feeding my dad when he was a growing boy, so she sympathized with my mom, who would find entire apple pies and pizzas missing after my after-school "snacks." Beans were an inexpensive way to make a stick-to-your-ribs meal that could go a long way toward feeding my voracious appetite, so this became a once-a-week staple in our house. We never used a recipe, just threw odd bits from the crisper drawer in with the pork (sometimes bacon or just a ham hock) and beans. If you don't have pork stock on hand, water works just fine.

This makes a big batch, so there will be some leftover filling, which you are obligated to eat with cornbread. You can freeze the unbaked pies, tightly wrapped, for up to 2 weeks.

Next page

HAM AND BEAN PIE

Continued

Makes two 9-inch (22.5-cm) pies

2	**double-crust Honey Cornmeal Dough shells (recipe p. 48)**	
1 pound	**dried white beans, such as Rancho Gordo flageolet**	454g
1	**leek**	113g
1 Tablespoon	**whole coriander seeds**	5g
4 ounces	**thick-cut bacon, diced**	113g
2–3 Tablespoons	**olive oil**	28–42g
1	**medium onion, diced small**	255g
2	**medium carrots, diced small**	170g
1 stalk	**celery, diced small**	113g
5 cloves	**garlic, minced**	25g
2 cups (474mL)	**pork stock**	440g
6 ounces	**chopped ham pieces**	170g
1	**smoked ham hock**	454g
	Kosher salt and freshly ground black pepper, to taste	
1 Tablespoon	**sherry vinegar**	12g
1 teaspoon	**chopped fresh thyme**	1g
1	**large egg, beaten**	50g

We use Rancho Gordo beans (see Resources, p. 336) because they are fresh. Grocery store beans (or the ones in the back of your cabinet) are often old and will take longer to cook.

1 Rinse the beans under cold running water. Place them in a large bowl covered with water by 2 inches (5cm). Soak the beans for 8 to 12 hours, checking on them every few hours to add water if necessary. When ready to prepare the pie, drain the beans and reserve the water.

2 Remove and discard the woody green tops from the leeks and chop the white and light green parts into ¼-inch (6-mm) half moons. Put the leek pieces in a large bowl of cold water. Agitate the water and leeks with your hands for 20 to 30 seconds, then let sit for about 10 minutes. Any dirt and sand should fall to the bottom of the bowl. Gently remove the leeks and dry with a salad spinner or towel.

3 Toast the whole coriander seeds in a small dry skillet over medium-high heat, shaking the pan often, until the seeds are fragrant but not smoking, about 1 to 2 minutes. If they begin to smoke, remove the seeds from the skillet immediately. Crush the coriander seeds with a mortar and pestle or in a coffee grinder.

4 In a large, heavy pot, cook the bacon over medium-low heat to render the fat. Add the olive oil and stir in the onion and leeks. Cook, stirring occasionally, for 8 to 10 minutes, or until the onion is translucent. Add the carrots, celery, garlic, and coriander and cook for an additional 5 minutes, until the garlic is fragrant, but not browned.

5 Add the beans and the pork stock to the pot of softened vegetables. If necessary, add some of the soaking water to the pot to cover the beans by 1 to 2 inches (2.5–5cm). Stir in the chopped ham and nestle the ham hock under the liquid. Bring to a boil. Reduce the heat to low and simmer, covered, until the beans are soft, about 2 hours, but it can vary from 1 hour to as long as 4 hours. Stir every 30 minutes or so and add more water to the pot if needed to keep the beans covered. Once the beans are soft, season with salt and black pepper. Stir and let simmer with the lid off for 5 to 10 minutes so the beans absorb the seasoning. Season again to taste. Remove the pot from the heat and discard the ham hock. Stir in the sherry vinegar and thyme. Let the ham and beans cool to room temperature, then chill them in the refrigerator for at least 1 hour, preferably overnight.

6 Fill the pie shells with ham and beans, spreading the mixture evenly into each. Do not be alarmed if there is filling left over. Finish according to the fork-crimp instructions (p. 41). Freeze for at least 1 hour.

7 Preheat the oven to 400°F (200°C).

8 Place the frozen pie (or pies, if you are baking both at once) on a baking sheet. Brush the beaten egg over the pie crust, taking care to get egg into all of the nooks and crannies.

9 Bake from frozen for 60 to 75 minutes, rotating 180 degrees every 30 minutes, until the crust is medium golden brown and the filling is heated through and bubbling out of the vents slightly. Toward the end of baking time, you may need to cover the edges of the pie with a crust guard or foil to prevent burning the crimped edge.

Quiches

Too often, quiche is written off as girlie food, something "real men" wouldn't eat. At Hoosier Mama we make Chicago-style quiches full of bacon, sausage, and healthy amounts of cheese. Our veggie quiches are no cream puffs either. We have hearty recipes for every season, so don't even think of confining them to the brunch table.

ASSEMBLING AND BAKING QUICHES

There are three components to these quiches: the pie shell, the Quiche Base, and the individual filling recipes. You can prepare the base and the filling first, then assemble and bake the quiche; or you can make the base and the filling in between steps 2 and 3 below.

Ingredients

1–2	**single-crust, blind-baked All-Butter Pie Dough shells (recipe p. 24, blind baking p. 34)**	
1	**large egg white, beaten**	20g
1 recipe	**Quiche Base (recipe p. 277)**	

1 Preheat the oven to 350°F (180°C).

2 Place the pie shells (or shell, if you aren't making 2) on a sheet tray and heat in the oven for 2 to 3 minutes. Remove from the oven and brush a thin layer of egg white on the bottoms and sides of the hot shells.

3 Scatter in whatever filling you are using, distributing the ingredients evenly.

4 Pour ½ of the Quiche Base into each of the prepared shells, pressing the fillings with a fork to submerge them.

5 Bake for 45 to 55 minutes, rotating 180 degrees halfway through, until the top of the quiches are light golden brown. When you shake the pie tin, the filling should not be loose in the center; rather it should move as a wave. A skewer inserted into the center of a quiche will come out clean.

6 Cool for at least 15 minutes before serving.

The baked quiche can be stored in the refrigerator for up to 2 days.

 *Brushing an egg white onto the pie shells provides a barrier for the filling and avoids a soggy crust.*

Quiche Base

At the shop, we are used to making dozens of quiches at a time, both to send to cafés and for our own customers. This recipe scales down nicely to make two pies, but making only one at a time proved problematic. After several rounds of testing, we kept impractically ending up with half an egg on our ingredients list. If you would prefer to halve this recipe to make only one quiche, using four eggs will result in a very creamy pie, which half of our staff preferred. Five eggs will give you a thicker and quite eggy pie. I am in the eggy camp, but we suggest you just make two perfect quiches. Share the second with a neighbor or leave it in your office's break room for a staff treat.

The proceeding filling recipes make enough for one, so you can try different flavors. If you would like two of the same type of quiche, double the recipe for the filling.

Ingredients

Makes enough for two 9-inch (22.5-cm) quiches

1½ cups (356mL)	**whole milk**	363g	1 teaspoon	**kosher salt**	3g
1 cup (237mL)	**Crème Fraîche (recipe p. 318)**	260g	1 teaspoon	**freshly ground black pepper**	2g
½ cup (119mL)	**heavy cream**	116g	¼ teaspoon	**ground cayenne pepper**	1g
9	**large eggs**	513g			

Next page

QUICHE BASE

Continued

1   Combine the milk, Crème Fraîche, and heavy cream in a medium bowl and whisk gently together until the Crème Fraîche is fully incorporated. Take care not to whisk too vigorously, which can add air into the cream and may result in a floppy, souffléed custard.

2   In a large bowl, whisk together the eggs.

3   Add the milk mixture, salt, black pepper, and cayenne pepper and whisk to combine. Strain into a clean bowl or pitcher.

The unbaked base can be stored in the refrigerator, in an airtight container, for up to 1 day.

Spinach-Gruyère Quiche with Caramelized Onions

Ingredients

Makes one 9-inch (22.5-cm) quiche

2 teaspoons	**unsalted butter**	9g
3 ounces	**spinach, washed, stems removed, and torn into bite-sized pieces**	85g
¼ cup	**Caramelized Onions (recipe p. 312)**	70g
3 ounces	**Gruyère cheese, shredded**	85g

1 Melt the butter in a skillet over high heat and add the spinach. Toss to coat in the butter and cook for about 1 to 2 minutes, or until the spinach is just wilted. Drain the excess butter.

2 Arrange the Caramelized Onions and spinach in the bottom of shell.

3 Top with the Gruyère.

4 Finish according to the quiche instructions (p. 276).

We use hearty winter spinach for this quiche. If you're using the more delicate baby spinach or another green, you can add it to the quiche raw, rather than wilting it first.

Roasted Butternut Squash and Goat Cheese Quiche

Roasted butternut squash is a sweet contrast to tangy,

fluffy goat cheese. This quiche makes a perfect centerpiece for an autumn brunch.

Ingredients

Makes one 9-inch (22.5-cm) quiche

1	**medium butternut squash,** peeled, seeded, and cut into bite-sized pieces	907g
1–2 Tablespoons	**olive oil**	
	Kosher salt and freshly ground black pepper, to taste	
2 ounces	**goat cheese**	57g
4 leaves	**sage, finely chopped**	1g
⅛ cup	**softened onions (sidebar p. 284)**	20g

1 Preheat the oven to 325°F (160°C).

2 Toss together the squash and olive oil and season with salt and black pepper.

3 Roast on a baking sheet lined with parchment paper for 30 to 40 minutes, or until the squash is fork tender.

4 Place the goat cheese and the sage in a bowl and stir to combine.

5 Layer the bottom of the pie shell with the onion and 1 cup (245g) of the roasted squash. Save the remaining roasted squash for another use.

6 Top with the goat cheese mixture.

7 Finish according to the quiche instructions (p. 276).

Stirring together the sage and the goat cheese will ensure even distribution of the sage, which would otherwise float to the top of the egg mixture.

Asparagus–Ricotta Quiche

This was the first original recipe I developed at Hoosier

Mama. It was featured as a special on our Mother's Day menu and became a late spring hit. The initial asparagus deliveries of the season perk up everyone in the kitchen, and signal the end of root-vegetable dominance and the promise of more bright green vegetation on its way. Lemon may be an unexpected quiche addition, but it brightens the asparagus and lends tang to the ricotta.

Ingredients

Makes one 9-inch (22.5-cm) quiche

6–8	**asparagus spears, ends trimmed, cut into 1½-inch (4-cm) pieces**	227g
1–2 teaspoons	**olive oil**	5–10g
	Kosher salt and freshly ground black pepper, to taste	
½ cup	**Lemon Ricotta (recipe p. 319)**	125g
1 Tablespoon	**finely chopped garlic chives**	4g
½	**lemon, for zesting**	

1 Preheat the oven to 350°F (180°C).

2 Toss the asparagus pieces in olive oil, salt, and black pepper and roast on a baking sheet lined with parchment paper for 15 minutes, or until al dente.

3 Combine the Lemon Ricotta and garlic chives.

4 Scatter the asparagus and ricotta miture in the bottom of the pie shell.

5 Zest the lemon over the filling.

6 Finish according to the quiche instructions (p. 276).

Sausage, Escarole, and Smoked Mozzarella Quiche

Juli, the baker who dreamed up this combination, tested several kinds of Italian sausage before we finally decided to make it in-house to fit our specifications exactly. The sausage we make is spicy and salty, playing nicely off the bitter escarole, sweet onions, and smoky cheese to form this balanced quiche.

Ingredients

Makes one 9-inch (22.5-cm) quiche

¼ cup	**Caramelized Onions (p. 312)**	70g
¼ pound	**Italian Sausage (recipe p. 328), cooked and crumbled**	113g
2 ounces	**smoked mozzarella, pulled apart into bite-sized pieces**	57g
2	**escarole leaves, cut into chiffonade (see note)**	30g

1 Spread the onions and sausage on the bottom of the prepared shell.

2 Layer on the cheese and then top with the escarole.

3 Finish according to the quiche instructions (p. 276).

Chiffonade is a technique for cutting leafy herbs and vegetables such as lettuce or basil. Stack the leaves, roll them together tightly, and cut into strips. The escarole here is best cut into ½-inch (13-mm) strips.

Leek, Apple, and Cheddar Quiche

Tired of our quiche routine by mid-winter, we set out to brainstorm new flavors. Anthony, a savory baker, was inspired by the classic pairing of apples and Cheddar (and favorite pie shop snack), so he put together this quiche. It sounds like a curious combination, so sometimes we have to talk customers into trying it, but they inevitably agree that this quiche is stunningly good.

Ingredients

Makes one 9-inch (22.5-cm) quiche

½ cup	**sliced leeks**	52g
1 teaspoon	**unsalted butter**	4g
1 teaspoon	**olive oil**	4g
1	**firm, tart apple, such as Granny Smith, peeled and chopped**	110g
	Kosher salt and freshly ground black pepper, to taste	
¼ cup	**Caramelized Onions (recipe p. 312)**	70g
3 ounces	**sharp Cheddar cheese, shredded**	85g

1 Place the leeks in a large bowl of cold water. Agitate the water and leeks with your hands for 20 to 30 seconds. Let the leeks sit in the bowl for about 10 minutes. Any dirt and sand should fall to the bottom of the bowl. Gently remove and dry in a salad spinner or with a towel.

2 In a small sauté pan, melt the butter and olive oil over medium heat. Add the leeks and cook, stirring often, for 2 to 3 minutes. Cover the pan and continue to cook until the leeks are completely softened, about 10 minutes.

3 Add the chopped apple and cook 1 to 2 more minutes. Remove from the heat and season to taste with salt and black pepper.

4 Once cooled, spread the leeks, apple, and Caramelized Onions over the bottom of the pie shell.

5 Top with the Cheddar cheese.

6 Finish according to the quiche instructions (p. 276).

Ham and Brie Quiche

Cheese and ham and eggs: a classic combination for a croque madame, a diner omelet, or a quiche. We add chives and freshly ground mustard seeds to brighten flavors.

Ingredients

Makes one 9-inch (22.5-cm) quiche

⅛ cup	**softened onions** (sidebar p. 284)	20g
4 ounces	**thinly sliced ham**	113g
2–3 ounces	**Brie, rind removed and thinly sliced**	85g
1 Tablespoon	**finely chopped fresh chives**	4g
½ teaspoon	**freshly ground mustard seeds**	1g

1 Layer the bottom of the pie shell with the onion, ham, and Brie.

2 Whisk the chives and ground mustard into the Quiche Base before pouring it into the pie shell.

3 Finish according to the quiche instructions (p. 276).

········· **SOFTENING ONIONS** ·········

Softening is the process of sautéeing onions in butter and vegetable oil. The ratio below makes about ½ cup (80g), more than you will need for any one recipe, but they are great to have on hand to use in a variety of dishes.

1 teaspoon	**unsalted butter**	4g
2 teaspoons	**vegetable oil**	6g
1 cup	**small-diced onion**	127g

1 *In a small skillet, heat the butter and vegetable oil over medium heat. Add the onion and cook, stirring frequently, until they are soft and translucent, about 8 to 10 minutes.*

EVERYDAY QUICHE VARIATIONS

Follow the quiche instructions on page 276, and use these variations as your filling.

Each makes one 9-inch (22.5-cm) quiche

QUICHE LUANN

⅛ cup	**softened onions** (sidebar p. 284)	20g
5 slices	**thick-cut bacon, cooked crisp and cut into 1-inch (2.5-cm) pieces**	142g
3 ounces	**Cheddar cheese, shredded**	85g

MUSHROOM-GRUYÈRE QUICHE

2 Tablespoons	**unsalted butter**	28g
⅓ pound	**cremini or white button mushrooms, sliced**	151g
	Kosher salt and freshly ground black pepper, to taste	
⅛ cup	**softened onions** (sidebar p. 284)	20g
3 ounces	**Gruyère cheese, shredded**	85g

1 Melt the butter in a sauté pan over medium-high heat and sauté the mushrooms, taking care not to crowd the pan.

2 Once browned, remove them from the pan and drain any excess butter. Season to taste with salt and black pepper before building the quiche.

BROCCOLI-CHEDDAR QUICHE

⅛ cup	**softened onions** (sidebar p. 284)	20g
3 ounces	**sharp Cheddar cheese, shredded**	85g
1 cup	**small broccoli florets**	60g

1 After the Quiche Base is poured into the pie shell, add the broccoli florets and arrange them with the stems down and the florets facing up.

TOMATO QUICHE

¾ cup	**cherry tomatoes, halved or quartered depending on the size**	94g
2 ounces	**goat cheese**	57g
⅛ cup	**softened onions (sidebar p. 284)**	20g
4–6	**basil leaves, cut into chiffonade**	6g–8g

BACON, ARUGULA, AND TOMATO QUICHE

¾ cup	**cherry tomatoes, halved**	94g
1 handful	**arugula leaves**	15g
5 slices	**thick-cut bacon, cooked crisp and cut into 1-inch (2.5-cm) pieces**	142g

BACON AND BLUE CHEESE QUICHE

¼ cup	**Caramelized Onions (recipe p. 312)**	70g
1½ ounces	**crumbled blue cheese**	43g
5 slices	**thick-cut bacon, cooked crisp and cut into 1-inch (2.5-cm) pieces**	142g

SAUSAGE AND PEPPERS QUICHE

⅛ cup	**softened onions (sidebar p. 284)**	20g
¼ pound	**Italian Sausage, cooked (recipe p. 328)**	113g
½ cup	**sautéed bell pepper slices**	100g
1½ ounces	**Parmesan cheese, shredded**	143g

BROWN BUTTER ZUCCHINI AND SQUASH QUICHE

⅛ cup	**softened onions (sidebar p. 284)**	20g
½ cup	**zucchini and squash slices, cooked in 2 Tablespoons brown butter (sidebar p. 295)**	100g
2 ounces	**goat cheese**	57g

Hand Pies

Hand pies are perfect for exploring culinary inspiration without having to commit to a large pie or a whole meal. Tuck in Thanksgiving leftovers, try out a wild ingredient, or riff on a favorite recipe for the filling. Their size makes them perfect for exploring sweet and savory flavor combinations. I even served hundreds at my wedding as hors d'oeuvres!

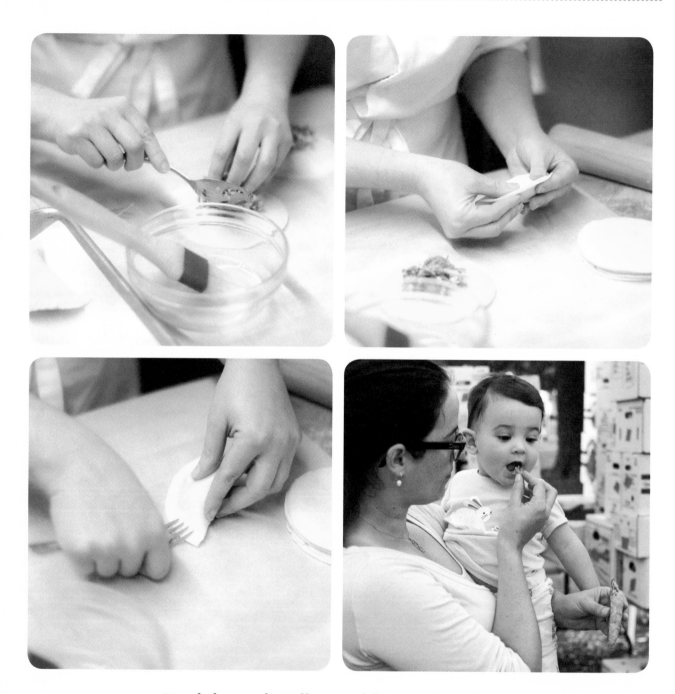

Top, left to right: Filling and forming hand pies.
Bottom, left to right: Crimping hand pies; Allie Leavitt of the
Butcher & Larder enjoys a hand pie with her daughter Avery.

ASSEMBLING AND BAKING HAND PIES

Cream Cheese Dough circles (recipe p. 50; amount varies, check individual hand pie recipe)

2	**large egg whites**	40g

1 Place a piece of parchment paper on your work surface. Line a baking sheet with parchment paper and set it nearby. Put the egg whites in a shallow bowl and gather a tablespoon, a fork, and a pastry brush if you have one on hand. Place a bowl of filling on the counter next to the parchment paper.

2 Remove 4 or 5 dough rounds from the refrigerator and place them on your parchment paper-lined work surface. If the rounds are stiff, warm them between your hands for a few seconds. If they warm up too quickly, return them to the refrigerator to cool and assemble fewer rounds at a time.

3 Using your finger or a pastry brush, apply the egg whites to the edge of each round. Place 2 heaping tablespoons of filling in the center of each round. Fold the dough in half over the filling, to form a half-moon shape. Pinch the edge together with your fingers and then seal the edge by crimping with the tines of a fork or the rounded bottom of a spoon.

4 Place the hand pies on the prepared baking sheet and begin the process again with 4 to 5 more refrigerated rounds. Freeze the baking sheet of hand pies for at least 1 hour.

5 Preheat the oven to 400°F (200°C).

6 Place the filled hand pies on a baking sheet lined with parchment paper at least 2 inches apart. Bake for 22 to 30 minutes, rotating 180 degrees halfway through. The crust should be light golden brown. For ground meat hand pies, an instant-read thermometer inserted into the middle of the filling should reach at least 160°F (70°C).

The unbaked hand pies can be stored in the freezer, in an airtight container, for up to 1 month.

Work in a cool area of your kitchen, during a cool time of day. Avoid working right next to the oven while roasting a chicken, for instance.

Sausage Hand Pies

While I was on my honeymoon in the UK, bakers were marching in the streets to protest a new tax on hot take-away snacks like pasties and sausage rolls that had been imposed by the Chancellor of the Exchequer. The issue became known as "Pasty-gate," wherein working-class "common" tastes were seen as shouldering the economic burden while the posh Chancellor slashed taxes for the upper class and could not recall the last time he had even eaten a pasty. Pity for him, because they are delicious. I joined the protest by buying a pastry-encrusted snack from every vendor I passed.

Ingredients

Makes about 20 hand pies

1 pound	**pork breakfast sausage, casings removed**	454g
1	**small onion, minced (about ¾ cup)**	135g
3 ounces	**Parmesan cheese, grated (about ¾ cup packed)**	85g
2 Tablespoons	**chopped Italian parsley**	12g
3–6	**sage leaves, very finely chopped**	1g
	Freshly ground black pepper, to taste	

1 Combine the sausage, onion, cheese, parsley and sage in a medium bowl and season with black pepper. Gently mix together with your hands until just combined. Take care not to overwork the mixture, which will result in tough, chewy meat.

2 In a small skillet, cook 1 tablespoon of the filling. Taste and adjust the seasoning.

3 Finish according to the hand-pie instructions (p. 291).

Sausage and cheese can prove quite salty, decreasing the need for additional salt or eliminating the need altogether.

Lamb Hand Pies

A hint of sweetness from apricots, orange zest, and

"Christmas" spices (such as cloves and cinnamon) elevate this otherwise simple ground-lamb pie. Lamb and apricots could become as classic a combination as pork chops and applesauce.

Ingredients

Makes 12–15 hand pies

3 ounces	**dried apricots, finely chopped**	85g
¼ cup (59mL)	**fresh orange juice, plus more to taste**	48g
2 Tablespoons	**olive oil**	28g
⅓ cup	**minced shallots**	75g
3	**garlic cloves, minced**	15g
1 pound	**ground lamb**	454g
	Zest of ½ orange	
¼ cup	**Ras El Hanout (recipe p. 316)**	20g
	Kosher salt and freshly ground black pepper, to taste	
	Ground cayenne pepper, to taste (optional)	

1. Soak the apricots in the orange juice for at least 2 hours, preferably overnight.

2. Place the olive oil in a small skillet over medium-low heat and sauté the shallots until softened, about 5 minutes. Stir in the garlic and reduce the heat to low. Continue cooking, stirring frequently, until the garlic is fragrant but not browned, 2 to 3 minutes. Set aside to cool.

3. Combine the lamb, the apricots and orange juice mixture, the cooled shallot mixture, orange zest, and Ras El Hanout. Season with salt and black pepper.

4. Place a small piece of lamb in the same skillet used to sauté the shallots. Cook, taste, and adjust the seasoning. You may add more Ras El Hanout or a few pinches of cayenne pepper to intensify the spiciness. Additional teaspoonfuls of orange juice will provide an acidic kick.

5. Finish according to the hand-pie instructions (p. 291).

Sweet Potato Hand Pies

Patiently roasting sweet potatoes at a low temperature develops a deep, caramelized flavor that can be lost when boiling or hurrying the potatoes along with higher temperatures. Browned butter provides a toasted, almost nutty flavor that, when layered with the mildly spicy curry powder, adds a savory balance to the finished bite. These hand pies make a great football tailgating snack or an untraditional starter for a Thanksgiving gathering.

Ingredients

Makes about 24 hand pies

4 pounds	**sweet potatoes, halved lengthwise**	1814g
2 Tablespoons	**olive oil**	28g
3 sticks	**unsalted butter**	336g
¼ cup	**Indian sweet yellow curry powder**	18g
1 Tablespoon	**kosher salt**	9g
2 teaspoons	**freshly ground black pepper**	4g

1 Preheat the oven to 300°F (149°C).

2 Brush the cut sides of the sweet potatoes with the oil and place them cut-side down on a baking sheet lined with parchment paper. Roast for 45 to 60 minutes, or until very tender. When the sweet potatoes are cool to the touch, remove the skins.

3 Meanwhile, brown the butter (sidebar p. 295). Once browned, remove from the heat and stir in the curry powder to bloom the spices. Stir in the salt and black pepper.

4 In a medium bowl, mash together the sweet potatoes and brown butter mixture with a fork until well combined. The mixture will be somewhat chunky. Taste and adjust the seasonings if necessary.

5 Finish according to the hand-pie instructions (p. 291).

BROWN BUTTER

Browning butter always elicits an enthusiastic reaction from the kitchen staff: "What are you cooking?" "What is that smell?" "When can we try some?" In a finished dish, people often have trouble pinning down the flavor, but they can tell that something is different and special.

Slowly cooking the butter causes the water to evaporate and the butterfat and milk solids to separate. The milk solids toast and turn brown, creating a deep and nutty flavor that works beautifully in both sweet and savory dishes. Just don't walk away from the stove, as the butter will inevitably burn. You can use a nonstick pan, but a lighter-colored pan, such as stainless steel or enameled cast iron, will allow you to track the progress of the butter's color with ease. Use a wide, heavy pan to allow for even cooking. Keep a bowl nearby so you can pour the butter out of the pan as soon as it is done to avoid burning the milk solids. Stir with a wooden spoon or a heatproof spatula, which will allow you to safely scrape up all of the toasted solids from the bottom of the pan.

You can use any amount of unsalted butter, but it's easiest to make with 1 pound (4 sticks or 448g).

Cube the butter and melt it over low heat, stirring occasionally. Once the butter is melted, increase the heat to medium-low. Stir often, scraping the milk solids from the bottom and watching for color change. The top of the butter will foam up. Once the flecks of milk solids on the bottom of the pan start to turn brown, stir the butter slowly and constantly. Aim for a golden to chocolate brown color for the solids. When ready, remove the brown butter from the heat and immediately pour into the waiting bowl.

Do not let the milk solids turn black. If the butter burns, it will taste acerbic and unpleasant. Throw it away and start over. Use the browned butter right away or store it in the refrigerator it for up to one week. Gently warm it over low heat to bring it back to a liquid state before using.

Corn and Chorizo Hand Pies

Hoosier Mama shares its little stretch of Chicago Avenue with several Mexican restaurants. Taco counters, sit-down restaurants—we've become connoisseurs of them all. We know where to order the best breakfast tacos and hash browns for the early crew, who makes the best gorditas, and on which corner to find our favorite elote vendor. This hand pie proudly reflects the flavors of our neighborhood.

Ingredients

Makes 20–24 hand pies

1 pound	**raw Mexican Chorizo (recipe p. 331)**	454g
4 cups	**fresh corn kernels**	400g
2 teaspoons	**kosher salt**	6g
2 teaspoons	**sweet paprika**	6g
1 teaspoon	**freshly ground black pepper**	2g
3	**limes, for zesting**	

1 Place the Mexican Chorizo, corn, salt, paprika, and black pepper in a bowl. Zest the limes over the bowl.

2 Using your hands, gently mix together all of the ingredients until just combined. Take care not to overwork the mixture, which will result in tough, chewy filling.

3 Finish according to the hand-pie instructions (p. 291).

When fresh corn is not in season, frozen corn may be substituted. If using frozen corn, rinse in warm water, drain completely, and pat dry with paper towels to remove excess water before mixing with remaining ingredients.

Corned Beef Hand Pies

At first we made these hand pies just as a St. Patrick's Day special, but after customers fervently argued for the pies' regular appearance on the menu, we now offer them throughout the spring. Using high-quality corned beef is key—find a quality producer in your area, or make your own. When cubing the beef, do not discard the extra fat you find around the edges of the meat; mix it into the filling, as it contains all of the concentrated flavors of the spices used in the brining process.

Ingredients

Makes about 24 hand pies

2 cups	**sliced, unpeeled red potatoes**	292g
3	**medium carrots, peeled and thinly sliced (about 2 cups)**	378g
2 Tablespoons plus 2 teaspoons	**olive oil, divided**	38g
	Kosher salt and freshly ground black pepper, to taste	
¼ head	**cabbage, sliced into ½-inch (13-mm) ribbons**	227g
2 slices	**bacon**	56g
1 pound	**corned beef, cubed**	57g
⅓ cup (79mL)	**Crème Fraîche (recipe p. 318)**	87g
¼ cup	**coarse-grained mustard, such as Maille Old Style, plus more to taste**	67g

1 Preheat the oven to 400°F (200°C).

2 Toss the potatoes and carrots in 2 tablespoons of the olive oil to coat, and season with salt and black pepper. Roast in an ovenproof pan for 45 to 60 minutes, until the potatoes are cooked through.

3 Place the cabbage on a baking sheet lined with parchment paper. Drizzle with 2 teaspoons of the olive oil and then cover with the raw bacon slices. Roast for 30 to 40 minutes, or until the cabbage has softened and browned on the edges. Cool and then chop the bacon and cabbage into bite-sized pieces.

4 In a medium bowl, combine all the ingredients and season to taste with salt and black pepper.

5 Finish according to the hand-pie instructions (p. 291).

Summer Harvest Hand Pies

Cleaning out the refrigerator can inspire a great dish.

I assembled a quick staff meal one afternoon by roasting all of the leftover produce on hand, then tossing it with herbs and lemon. We had a healthy and light lunch and decided on the spot that it could only be improved by folding it into a pie.

Ingredients

Makes about 24 hand pies

2	**medium zucchini, diced small**	260g
2	**medium yellow squash, diced small**	260g
2 teaspoons	**kosher salt, plus more to taste**	6g
1 pound	**cherry or grape tomatoes, halved**	454g
¼ cup (59mL)	**olive oil**	56g
2 ears	**sweet corn kernels**	150g
2 teaspoons	**chopped fresh oregano**	2g
2 teaspoons	**chopped fresh basil**	4g
1 teaspoon	**chopped fresh thyme**	1g
2 teaspoons	**fresh lemon juice, plus more to taste**	8g
	Freshly ground black pepper, to taste	

1 Place the zucchini and squash in a bowl and sprinkle liberally with 2 teaspoons of the salt; toss to coat. Set aside for 25 minutes, then place the zucchini and squash into a colander, drain the excess liquid, and pat dry with paper towels.

2 Preheat the oven to 350°F (180°C).

3 Toss the zucchini, yellow squash, and tomatoes in the olive oil. Roast for 20 to 25 minutes. Cool to room temperature.

4 In a large bowl, combine the zucchini, squash, tomatoes, and corn. Stir in the chopped herbs and the 2 teaspoons lemon juice and toss to combine. Season to taste with salt, black pepper, and additional lemon juice.

5 Finish according to the hand-pie instructions (p. 291).

Mashed Potato Hand Pies

An ideal use for leftover potatoes, you can add practically

any of your favorite ingredients to this delicious snack. We have been known to throw in roasted broccoli, pickled jalapeño peppers, or crumbled sausage. As this recipe lends itself to experimentation, feel free to put your own spin on it.

Ingredients

Makes 20–24 hand pies

2½ cups	**mashed potatoes**	625g
6 slices	**bacon, cooked crisp and crumbled**	170g
¼ cup (59mL)	**sour cream**	61g
2 ounces	**Cheddar cheese, shredded**	57g
20 sprigs	**chives, finely chopped**	
	Kosher salt and freshly ground black pepper, to taste	

1 Fold all of the ingredients together. Season to taste with salt and black pepper.

2 Finish according to the hand-pie instructions (p. 291).

Ratatouille Hand Pies

Inspired by Julia Child's method, we cook all of the vegetables separately for our version of ratatouille. The textural integrity of each individual component is maintained, and in the refrigerator overnight, the flavors meet diplomatically in a summit of glorious summer flavors. We depart from the classic method by roasting the vegetables, which intensifies their flavor and eliminates excess liquid. Flaky hand pies make an excellent vehicle for this celebration of the season's bounty.

Ingredients

Makes about 20 hand pies

1	medium zucchini, diced small (about 1 cup)	130g	½ cup	Caramelized Onions, finely chopped (recipe p. 312)	140g
1	medium yellow squash, diced small (about 1 cup)	130g	2 Tablespoons	Roasted Garlic (recipe p. 313)	25g
2 teaspoons	kosher salt, divided, plus more to taste	6g	2 teaspoons	chopped fresh basil	4g
1	medium eggplant, diced small (about 2 cups)	200g	2 teaspoons	chopped Italian parsley	4g
2 cups	cherry tomatoes	250g	1 teaspoon	chopped fresh tarragon	1g
1½ cups (356mL)	olive oil, divided	112g	½ teaspoon	chopped fresh thyme	.5g
	Freshly ground black pepper, to taste		1 Tablespoon	balsamic vinegar, plus more to taste	26g

1   Place the zucchini and squash in a bowl and toss with 1 teaspoon of the salt.

2   In a separate bowl, toss the eggplant and the remaining 1 teaspoon of salt. Let the vegetables stand for 30 minutes.

3   Preheat the oven to 350°F (180°C).

4   Drain the zucchini and squash and pat dry with paper towels. Rinse the eggplant in cold water and pat dry with paper towels.

5   Place the tomatoes and eggplant into 2 separate ovenproof pans (such as 9-inch [22.5-cm] square baking dishes, or on small baking sheets lined with parchment paper). Place the zucchini and squash into a third ovenproof pan.

6   Toss each pan of vegetables with 2 tablespoons of the olive oil and season to taste with salt and black pepper.

7   Arrange the vegetables into 1 tight layer in the center of each pan—it is OK if the vegetables overlap.

8   Roast until the vegetables are cooked through, 20 to 35 minutes. The tomatoes will cook quickly; check for doneness after 20 or 25 minutes. If the eggplant and squash look shriveled and dry, add more olive oil and stir the vegetables, then place back in the oven.

9   Once cooled, gently fold the vegetables together with the rest of the ingredients except for the balsamic vinegar.

10 Add a few more teaspoons of olive oil if the mixture seems dry.

11 Add the balsamic vinegar and season to taste with salt, black pepper, and more balsamic vinegar as needed.

12 Transfer to an airtight container and chill overnight in the refrigerator.

13 Finish according to the hand-pie instructions (p. 291).

Spinach-Feta Hand Pies

This is our version of spanakopita, a Greek snack made of spinach or other greens, onions, and salty cheese. Traditionally, the filling is surrounded by layers of folded phyllo dough and cut into triangles, but we bake ours using the flaky Cream Cheese Dough (p. 50). The cider-plumped raisins add sweetness, and we tie all the flavors together with a hint of nutmeg.

Ingredients

Makes 20–24 hand pies

1 cup (237mL)	apple cider	246.5g
1½ cups	raisins, chopped	227g
1 Tablespoon	unsalted butter	14g
1 Tablespoon	olive oil	14g
8 ounces	minced red onion, such as Tropea	227g
12 cloves	garlic, minced	60g
2 pounds	spinach, stems removed, and roughly torn into bite-sized pieces	907g
10 ounces	crumbled feta cheese	284g
¼ teaspoon plus pinch	ground nutmeg	1g
	Kosher salt and freshly ground black pepper, to taste	

1 In a small saucepan, bring the apple cider to a simmer. Add the raisins, then remove the pan from the heat and cover. Let the raisins soak for 15 minutes. Strain the raisins and discard any excess cider.

2 Heat the butter and olive oil in a large, heavy pan (like a Dutch oven) over medium-high heat. Once the pan is hot, stir in the onions and reduce the heat to medium. Cook, stirring occasionally, until the onions are translucent, about 8 to 10 minutes. Add the garlic and continue to cook until the garlic is fragrant, but not browned, about 2 to 3 minutes. Pile in the spinach. Cook, stirring occasionally, until the spinach is wilted, about 5 minutes.

3 Cool slightly and then stir in the raisins, feta, and nutmeg. Season to taste with salt and black pepper.

4 Finish according to the hand-pie instructions (p. 291).

Subrecipes

Chocolate Wafers

These are the wafers we use to make our Chocolate Wafer Crumb Crust (p. 46). We adapted it from a recipe we found on the excellent cooking blog Smitten Kitchen (smittenkitchen.com), where it was adapted from *Pure Dessert*, by Alice Medrich. The cookies are perfect—tender, crunchy, and super chocolaty. You can substitute with store-bought chocolate cookies, but once you taste these wafers, I don't think you will want to!

The recipe makes enough cookies for one Chocolate Wafer shell plus a little extra, which is good since you'll want to make some extra cookies for yourself!

Ingredients

Makes about 2½ cups (475g) of wafer crumbs, or 2 cups (380g) of wafer crumbs and some cookies

FOR THE WAFERS

1½ cups	**all-purpose flour**	222g
1 cup plus 2 Tablespoons	**granulated sugar**	226g
¾ cup	**cocoa powder**	71g
¼ teaspoon	**kosher salt**	1g
¼ teaspoon	**baking soda**	2g
1¾ sticks	**unsalted butter, cut into ½-inch (13-mm) cubes**	196g

3 Tablespoons (45mL)	**whole milk**	45g
1 teaspoon	**vanilla paste**	5g

FOR ROLLING

1 cup	**all-purpose flour**	148g
¼ cup	**cocoa powder**	24g

1 Combine the flour, sugar, cocoa powder, salt, and baking soda in the bowl of a food processor and pulse 2 to 3 times to combine.

2 Add the butter cubes and pulse 8 to 10 times, until the mixture resembles coarse meal.

3 In a separate bowl, combine the milk and vanilla paste. Pour the mixture into the food processor while it is running and process for 18 seconds.

4 Turn the dough out onto a work surface and knead together.

5 Divide the dough into 4 balls. Flatten each into a disc that is approximately 1 inch (2.5cm) thick. Wrap in plastic wrap and rest in the refrigerator overnight.

6 Preheat the oven to 400°F (200°C).

7 To prepare the rolling surface, mix together the flour and cocoa powder in a small bowl, then use it to dust the work surface.

8 Roll the dough into 4 sheets that are each ⅛ inch (3mm) thick.

9 Transfer the dough to 4 separate baking sheets and prick all over with a fork.

10 Bake for 15 to 20 minutes, until dough appears dry. Remove from the oven and set aside to cool completely.

The unbaked, unrolled wafer discs can be stored in the refrigerator up to 3 days. Once it has rested, the dough may be frozen for up to 2 weeks.

Pecan or Walnut Crumble

Use pecans in this recipe to top the Peach–Raspberry Pie (p. 84), and use walnuts for the Pear, Apple, and Cranberry Pie (p. 108).

Ingredients

Makes enough to top one 9-inch pie

1 cup	**all-purpose flour**	148g
½ cup	**granulated sugar**	100g
2 Tablespoons	**dark brown sugar**	30g
½ cup	**toasted walnuts or pecans (sidebar p. 105)**	50g
6 Tablespoons	**unsalted butter, cut into 1-inch (2.5-cm) cubes**	84g
Pinch	**kosher salt**	

1 Combine all of the ingredients in the bowl of a stand mixer fitted with the paddle attachment.

2 Mix on Low until the mixture resembles fine crumbs. Increase the speed to Medium and mix until gravel-sized pieces form.

3 Chill in the refrigerator for at least 30 minutes before using to top a pie.

The crumble can be stored in the refrigerator for 1 week.

Candied Pecans

This recipe makes much more than you need to top one
pie. Making any less is impractical and the nuts can be stored for up to two weeks at room temperature in an airtight container. They taste great on their own too!

Makes 1 cup (82g)

¼ cup	**granulated sugar**	50g
1 Tablespoon	**water**	15g
1 cup	**toasted pecans (sidebar p. 105)**	125g
1 teaspoon	**unsalted butter**	4g
Pinch	**kosher salt**	

1 Combine the sugar and water in a small, heavy saucepan. Bring to a boil over medium heat, stirring just until the sugar is dissolved.

2 When the boiling starts to slow down and large bubbles cover the surface of the liquid, remove the pan from the heat and stir in the pecans. Keep stirring until the sugar seizes and small white crystals form on the pecans, about 30 seconds.

3 Turn the heat to low and return the pan to the heat. Stir the pecans until the sugar melts and coats the pecans, about 3 minutes. The sugar will turn a dark amber color.

4 Transfer the pecans to a heatproof bowl. Stir in the butter and salt and mix until the pecans are cool to the touch.

The finished pecans can be stored in an airtight container for up to 2 weeks.

Creamy Meringue

Once you master this meringue—and it's not hard—you'll

look for any excuse to make it. Sweet and creamy, it's perfect with tart citrus curd and bitter dark-chocolate desserts. The key is gently heating the egg whites and sugar over a hot-water bath before whipping them. The heat dissolves the sugar and "cooks" the raw egg whites to a safe temperature. Use it to top cupcakes and frost layer cakes. In addition to great flavor, meringue adds lots of visual drama for very little effort. It's even more fun if you have a torch to toast the edges. For safety reasons, home cooks should limit themselves to the small butane variety, available at most kitchen goods stores.

Makes enough to top one pie

⅔ cup (158mL)	**egg whites**	160g
1 cup	**granulated sugar**	200g

1 Fill a 1-quart (948-mL) saucepan halfway with water and bring to a simmer over medium-high heat.

2 Combine the egg whites and granulated sugar in a medium stainless steel bowl and whisk to incorporate the sugar and break up the whites. Rest the bowl on top of the pot of simmering water and whisk constantly, until the egg whites reach 165°F (74°C) on an instant-read thermometer.

3 Pour into the bowl of a stand mixer and whip on High until the mixing bowl is cool to the touch.

4 Use immediately. Meringue will become harder to spread as it sits out.

Pie Crust Cookies

When I was little and making pies with my mom, we

passed the time the pie was in the oven by rolling cookies out of leftover pie dough. At the pie shop, we make Pie Crust Cookies to decorate the pumpkin pies and to pass out to customers waiting in line.

These simple little cookies are so popular that we started selling them by the bagful at the farmers' market.

Ingredients

Yield depends on amount of scrap dough

	Scrap pie dough	
1 cup	**granulated sugar**	200g
2 Tablespoons	**pumpkin pie spice or ground cinnamon**	13g
	Pie Wash (p. 21), for brushing the cookies	

The cookies can be stored in an airtight container for 2 to 3 days.

1 Preheat the oven to 400°F (200°C).

2 Combine the sugar and pumpkin pie spice (or cinnamon) in a small bowl. Mix with your fingers or a whisk until thoroughly combined.

3 Roll out the scrap pie dough between ⅛ and ¼ inch (3–6mm) thick. Cut the dough into any shape you like. (At the shop we use an oak-leaf cutter that is approximately 3 inches [7.5cm] tall by 2 inches [5cm] wide). To prevent the cookies from puffing in the oven, make a simple cut or two in each cookie using a paring knife, or you can prick the dough all over with a fork.

4 Place the cookies on a baking sheet so the edges do not touch. Brush with Pie Wash and sprinkle generously with the sugar mixture.

5 Bake until the cookies are dark golden brown on top and golden brown on the bottom. This will take anywhere between 5 and 20 minutes, depending on the size of the cookies. The cookies will crisp as they cool.

Chocolate Ganache

Use this ingredient ratio for the Jeffersonville Pie (p. 106)

and the Peanut Butter Pie with Chocolate Ganache (p. 195). For the S'more Pie (p. 197), halve the ingredients and don't bother with the parchment cone.

Ingredients

Makes about 1 cup (237mL)

4½ ounces	**bittersweet chocolate, roughly chopped**	127g
½ cup (119mL)	**heavy cream**	116g

1 Place the bittersweet chocolate in a small, heatproof bowl.

2 Bring the cream to a boil over medium heat. Pour over the chocolate through a fine-mesh strainer. Let stand for 30 seconds. Whisk the cream and chocolate until smooth.

3 Drizzle the ganache over the pie with a parchment cone (see sidebar).

MAKING A PARCHMENT CONE

1. Cut a 16x12-inch (40x30-cm) piece of parchment paper in half diagonally to make 2 triangles.
   Hold 1 triangle in front of you, with the longest side facing up and the center point facing down.
2. Take the right corner of the triangle between the thumb and index finger of your right hand. Turn the corner over, and pull it down until it lines up with the center point of the triangle.
3. Take the left corner of the triangle between the thumb and index finger of your left hand. Bring the corner around the front of the parchment cone and line it up behind the center point of the triangle.
4. Turn the cone over so the tip of the cone is facing down.
5. Fold the 3 aligned corners down into the cone to secure it. There are several good online videos that illustrate this process.
6. Pour an inch of ganache into the cone.
7. Roll the top edge of the cone down until it lines up with the top of the ganache.
8. Snip a small hole in the bottom point of the cone. The hole should be small enough that the ganache will only start to pour out when you squeeze the cone.
9. To stripe the pie, hold the cone just outside the pie's edge so that your stripes are even and you don't have one big dot where you started the striping. Squeeze, stripe, and finish outside of the pie, again so you don't have a big dot of chocolate. It helps to have parchment paper under the pie to catch the excess.

Lightly Sweetened Whipped Cream

This is our go-to whipped cream recipe—we use it to finish

our cream pies, and we offer it as an accompaniment to all of our other sweet pies, from rhubarb to pumpkin to mincemeat. Its mild sweetness allows the flavor of each pie to shine through.

If you have access to cream from a small, local dairy, this is the place to use it! Just remember: the higher the butterfat, the quicker the cream whips. Unhomogenized cream whips fine, but make sure you shake it well before pouring it out of the container.

Ingredients

Makes enough to top one 9-inch pie

1½ cups (356mL)	**heavy cream**	348g
3 Tablespoons	**granulated sugar**	39g

1 Pour the cream into the bowl of a stand mixer fitted with the whisk attachment. Whip the cream on Medium-High for 30 seconds.

2 With the mixer still running, slowly pour in the sugar. Increase the speed to High and whip until soft peaks form, about 2 minutes.

Whipped cream be stored in the refrigerator for 1 to 2 days. If the cream deflates or separates, simply whisk it back together by hand.

SWEETER WHIPPED CREAM VARIATION

Increase the amount of sugar to 6 tablespoons (78g) and follow the rest of the recipe as directed.

Caramelizing onions is time-consuming, but very simple.

Luckily, you don't have to hover over the stove the entire time. You can make it a day ahead, or, ideally, make a large batch and freeze what you don't use right away. You will be thankful to have this ingredient at the ready.

Ingredients

Makes 2½–3 cups (700–840g)

8	**medium yellow onions (about 16 cups sliced)**	2268g
1 stick	**unsalted butter**	112g
¼ cup (59mL)	**olive oil**	56g

The onions can be stored in the refrigerator, in an airtight container, for up to 1 week. Freezing the onions in ½- or 1-cup (140-280g) servings in freezer bags is quite convenient and they will keep for 6 to 8 weeks.

1 Peel the onions and cut into ¼-inch (6-mm) thick slices.

2 Heat the butter and olive oil in a large, heavy pan (like a Dutch oven) over medium-low heat.

3 Once the butter is melted, stir in the sliced onions to coat them in the fat. Don't worry about crowding the pan; the onions will cook down eventually. Cover the pan and continue to cook until the onions are uniformly translucent and soft, about 15 to 20 minutes.

4 Remove the lid and turn the heat up to medium. Continue cooking about 1 hour, stirring every 10 minutes or so. The goal is to brown the onions evenly, so if the onions begin to burn, adjust the heat to medium-low or low and add a few splashes of water to slow the cooking process. Stir more often and add a few teaspoons of olive oil if the onions begin to stick.

5 The onions are ready when they turn a uniform deep mahogany brown and have a rich, sweet flavor. Sometimes this takes a bit longer than 1 hour. *Judge by the color rather than the clock*

Roasted Garlic

Paula always says she can tell I'm in the kitchen when she smells garlic roasting. I learned this trick from my Grandma Adele, who knows garlic smells better than any potpourri or scented candle. She is always cooking and I have never known her to cook without garlic.

Roasted garlic is a great addition to pasta sauces, pizzas, or just spread across a hunk of good bread.

Ingredients

Makes 1 cup (200g)

8 heads	**garlic**	200g
½ cup (119mL)	**olive oil**	112g

1 Preheat the oven to 400°F (200°C).

2 Cut the garlic heads in half crosswise (across the equator) and place in a small, ovenproof dish. Drizzle with the olive oil and then wrap the entire dish tightly in foil. Roast for 50 to 60 minutes, until the garlic is completely softened. Cool to room temperature.

3 Squeeze the garlic cloves from their papery skin. Discard the skin and reserve the olive oil for another use. Smash the garlic cloves with a fork or purée in a food processor. Refrigerate right away.

Garlic stored in the refrigerator will keep up to 1 week. Beyond that it must be discarded, since garlic in oil has been linked with botulism (the danger arises when garlic stored in oil reaches a temperature of 40°F [4°C] and above).

Freezing small blocks in an ice cube tray is an easy way to divide the roasted garlic for future use. Once frozen, keep it in an airtight container or freezer bag. Stored in the freezer, roasted garlic can be stored safely for months.

The reserved olive oil can be used for salad dressings or cooking right away. Refrigerated, the garlic-infused oil will keep up to 1 week.

Apple-Shallot Chutney

Think of chutney as a kind of thick savory jam. It is

traditionally served with curries. This is one of our favorites to serve with the Curried Winter Vegetable Pie (p. 268). If you have a mesh tea ball infuser or a disposable tea bag, put the cloves inside that; otherwise, tie them up in cheesecloth. This allows the clove flavor to infuse into the dish, and makes it easy to safely remove and discard the cloves at the end.

Ingredients

Makes about ¾ cup (178mL or 170g)

1	tart apple, diced small (about 1 cup)	110g		1½ Tablespoons	granulated sugar, plus more to taste	25g
1 cup	sliced shallots	225g			Kosher salt, to taste	
¼ cup (59mL)	apple cider	60g		5–6	whole cloves	10g
¼ cup (59mL)	cider vinegar	48g				

1   Combine the sugar, apples, shallots, apple cider, cider vinegar, and two pinches of salt in a small saucepan. Nestle the cloves in the tea ball infuser and place it under the apples and shallots.

2   Bring to a boil over medium-high heat. Reduce the heat to low and simmer, stirring occasionally, for 15 to 20 minutes, until the apples and shallots are very soft and there is very little liquid remaining.

3   Season to taste with salt and sugar.

Barbecue Sauce

Ingredients

Makes about 1½ cups (356mL or 340g)

2 Tablespoons	**olive oil**	14g
2 Tablespoons	**unsalted butter**	28g
½ cup	**small-dice yellow onion**	64g
3 cloves	**garlic, minced**	15g
3 Tablespoons	**finely chopped chipotle chilies in adobo sauce**	30g
1 teaspoon	**smoked paprika**	3g
1 teaspoon	**chili powder**	2g
¾ teaspoon	**ground cayenne pepper, plus more to taste**	3g
¾ cup (178mL)	**sweet tea, such as Good Earth Sweet and Spicy Tea**	178g
¾ cup (178mL)	**apple cider vinegar**	144g
2	**6-ounce cans tomato paste**	340g
¼ cup (59mL)	**molasses**	78g
2 Tablespoons	**brown sugar**	30g
1 teaspoon	**kosher salt**	3g
¼ teaspoon	**freshly ground black pepper**	.5g

1 Place the olive oil and butter in a heavy sauté pan over medium-high heat. Once the pan is hot, stir in the onion and reduce the heat to medium. When the onion is translucent, add the minced garlic. Cook until the garlic is fragrant, but not browned. Add the chipotle chilies, paprika, chili powder, and cayenne pepper and stir. Cook, stirring constantly, for 2 minutes to bloom the spices.

2 Reduce the heat to low. Add the sweet tea, vinegar, tomato paste, molasses, brown sugar, salt, and black pepper to the pan. Cook, stirring often to prevent scorching on the bottom and avoid making a spattering mess on the stove, about 30 minutes.

3 Taste the sauce and adjust the seasonings. Your first impression should be sweet, followed by the bright acidity of the cider vinegar, with the heat from the cayenne pepper and chipotle chilies creeping up after the bite. Additions of brown sugar, molasses, and vinegar can be made 1 teaspoon at a time, while salt and cayenne pepper should be added in pinches to delicately change the balance of flavors.

Instead of sweet tea, a mix of equal parts bourbon and water are a nice variation.

 Chipotle chilies in adobo sauce can be found in either the canned goods or the ethnic/international foods aisle of any major grocery store.

Ras El Hanout

Originally from Morocco, ras el hanout is a spice mix

commonly used throughout North Africa. Families and merchants combine their best spices into this savory blend to season meat, vegetables, and rice. While there are some universal elements, each version inevitably has a special flavor specific to the neighborhood or what is growing in the garden. We throw in coffee.

Ingredients

Makes ½ cup (48g)

2 Tablespoons	**coriander seeds**	8g
2 Tablespoons	**cumin seeds**	10g
1 Tablespoon	**mustard seeds**	9g
1½ teaspoons	**garam masala**	3g
1½ teaspoons	**smoked paprika**	4.5g
1½ teaspoons	**ground cinnamon**	3g
1½ teaspoons	**freshly ground black pepper**	3g
¾ teaspoon	**ground ginger**	1.5g
¾ teaspoon	**ground cloves (or 5–6 whole cloves)**	2g
5–6	**chiles de arbol**	3g
1½ teaspoons	**ground medium-roast coffee**	7g

1 Place all of the spices and the chiles de arbol in a large, dry skillet. Toast over medium-high heat until fragrant but not smoking, shaking the pan often, about 2 to 3 minutes. If the spices begin to smoke, remove the spices from the pan immediately.

2 Remove and discard any chile stems; shake out and discard about half the seeds. You may leave all the seeds, but it will be spicy. Combine the chiles, spices, and coffee in a spice or coffee grinder and pulse until finely ground. Work in small batches if necessary.

Ras El Hanout can be stored at room temperature, in an airtight container, for up to 2 months. It will lose intensity of flavor over time.

Poured into a nice jar, this spice blend can serve as a thoughtful host or hostess gift. It can be used to flavor meatballs or hamburgers, as a rub on the outside of steak, lamb, oily fish like salmon, or combined with oil and citrus juice to marinate grilled vegetables.

Roasted Garlic Mashed Potatoes

Ingredients

Makes about 14 cups (3kg), or enough to top six 6-inch (15-cm) Shepherd's Pies (p. 251) with some left over

8 pounds	**potatoes, peeled and chopped into 1½-inch cubes (3¾-cm) (Yukon gold or russet are best)**	3629g
	Kosher salt	
1 cup (237mL)	**Crème Fraîche (recipe p. 318)**	260g
1 stick	**unsalted butter**	112g
¼–1 cup (59–237mL)	**whole milk**	61–242g
1 recipe	**Roasted Garlic (recipe p. 313)**	

1 Place the potatoes in a large pot and cover with cold water by 2 inches (5cm). Add a few large pinches of salt. Bring to a boil over high heat, then reduce the heat.

2 Continue to boil the potatoes at medium-high heat until they are fork tender, about 15 to 20 minutes. Transfer the potatoes to a colander and set aside, until the water is drained.

3 Add the Crème Fraîche and butter to the still warm pot and warm over medium heat until the butter is melted.

4 Using a food mill, process the warm potatoes over the pot and stir them together with the butter and Crème Fraîche. If you don't have a food mill, break them up with a potato masher or a hand mixer before combining with the Crème Fraîche and butter. If the potatoes are too thick, add the whole milk a few table-spoons at a time until you reach the desired consistency.

5 Fold the Roasted Garlic into the potatoes. Season to taste with salt.

Use the mashed potatoes within 2 days of making.

Crème Fraîche

Noting that Francophile home cooks had trouble finding

crème fraîche in American supermarkets, Julia Child included this delicious ingredient in her book, *Mastering the Art of French Cooking*. Some will argue that you can just substitute sour cream, but a side-by-side tasting reveals key differences. Crème fraîche has a higher fat content, and is bright without being too sharp or sour. It is also more versatile, since it will resist curdling when used as a thickener in hot soups and sauces. While the product is popping up more regularly in specialty grocers, it remains expensive. Save a few pennies or just have fun with this kitchen chemistry project.

Ingredients

Makes 2 cups (474mL or 464g)

2 cups (474mL)	**heavy cream**	464g
2 Tablespoons	**buttermilk**	30g

1 Combine the ingredients in a nonreactive container with a lid, like a glass canning jar.

2 Cover loosely and let stand at room temperature until it thickens, about 12 hours. It will get thicker and more tart the longer it is left at room temperature.

Can be stored in the refrigerator for up to 2 weeks.

Room temperature may affect the speed at which your ingredients thicken. Child's original recipe included heating the ingredients to lukewarm (not over 85°F [29°C]) to get the process started. Keeping the jar no cooler than 70°F (21°C) will help the lactic acid to form. If you have a drafty kitchen, an empty, turned-off oven is usually warmer than the rest of the room.

Lemon Ricotta

Ingredients

Makes about 2 cups (500g)

1 gallon (3.8L)	**whole milk**	3872g
2 cups (474mL)	**heavy cream**	464g
½–1 cup (119–237mL)	**apple cider or white wine vinegar**	96–192g
	Kosher salt and freshly ground black pepper, to taste	
	Zest and juice of 3 lemons, to taste	

PREP NOTE — *Remaining whey can be used as a substitute for water in bread making.*

1. Slowly bring the milk and heavy cream to a boil in a large, heavy, nonreactive saucepan, whisking occasionally to prevent burning on the bottom.

2. Once the liquid reaches a rolling boil, remove the pan from the heat and slowly stir in ¼ cup (59mL or 48g) of the vinegar.

3. Wait 2 minutes and stir in ¼ cup (59mL or 48g) more vinegar. Solids (curds) should begin to separate from the translucent whey. If you don't see thickened curds, gently stir in more vinegar ¼ cup (59mL or 48g) at a time, pausing for 2 minutes after each addition.

4. Pour the ricotta through a fine-mesh strainer that has cheesecloth draped over it. Let stand for at least 20 minutes to drain, up to 1 hour for thicker ricotta.

5. Fluff up the ricotta with a fork and season to taste with salt, black pepper, lemon zest, and lemon juice.

Lemon juice can be substituted for the vinegar, but decrease both the lemon zest and lemon juice in order to control the acidity.

Seasonal Pickles

These are quick pickles so they do not require any special
processing or canning. The basic requirements for all of our pickles are the same: vinegar with a
minimum of 5 percent acidity, a sweet ingredient like sugar or honey, some kosher salt, and water.
After that, all of the spices, aromatics, and produce are optional. We change vegetables (and sometimes fruits) based on the season, offering ramp and asparagus pickles in the springtime, carrots
and green beans later, and beets and peppers throughout the fall. This is an ethic I grew up with,
barefoot with the dirt of my grandparents' Missouri garden between my toes, snacking on the raw
green beans when I was supposed to be harvesting them.

Ingredients

Makes 1 quart (948L or 960g)

1½ cups (356mL)	**white wine vinegar or champagne vinegar**	288g	1 teaspoon	**crushed red pepper flakes or 3 chiles de arbol**	2g
1 cup (237mL)	**water**	237g	1	**fresh bay leaf**	.25g
¼ cup	**granulated sugar**	50g	5	**garlic cloves, thinly sliced**	25g
2 Tablespoons	**kosher salt**	18g	1	**shallot, thinly sliced**	38g
1 Tablespoon	**whole coriander seeds**	4g	1 pound	**green beans or asparagus, trimmed**	454g
1 teaspoon	**mustard seeds**	2g			

1 Heat the vinegar, water, sugar, and salt until all of the solids have dissolved, about 8 to 10 minutes. Bring to a simmer and keep the mixture warm.

2 Place the coriander, mustard, crushed red pepper or chiles de arbol, and bay leaf in a loose-leaf tea bag. Tie the top of the bag and place it in the bottom of a glass jar or other nonreactive container.

3 Add the garlic and shallot to the bottom of each jar.

4 Pack the jar with the green beans or asparagus.

5 Pour the warm liquid over the vegetables to cover.

6 Cool to room temperature, then cover tightly and refrigerate. The pickles taste best after being refrigerated for 1 or 2 days.

7 Serve with the Pulled Pork Pie (p. 237), or chop finely and add to a potato salad.

The pickles can be stored in the refrigerator for up to 10 days, and should not be consumed beyond 10 days.

At Hoosier Mama, we pack all of the spices into loose-leaf tea bags so that they don't stick to the pickles when you pull one out to eat, but the spices can go directly into the jars if you prefer.

Celery and Shallot Pickles

Ingredients

Makes 1 quart (948L or 960g)

1¼ cups (296mL)	**white wine vinegar**	240g
¾ cup (178mL)	**water**	177g
6 Tablespoons	**granulated sugar**	78g
2 Tablespoons	**kosher salt**	18g
2 Tablespoons	**whole coriander seeds**	8g
4–6	**chiles de arbol**	3g
1	**bay leaf**	.25g
5	**celery stalks, thinly sliced**	305g
1 cup	**thinly sliced shallots**	225g

1. In a medium saucepan, combine the vinegar, water, sugar, and salt. Cook over medium heat, stirring occasionally, until the sugar and salt dissolve completely.

2. Pack the coriander seeds, chiles, and bay leaf in a loose-leaf tea bag or a bit of cheesecloth.

3. While the liquid is still hot, put the bagged spices into the pan. Cool to room temperature.

4. Place the celery and shallots in a nonreactive container, like a glass jar or plastic container.

5. Pour the liquid over the vegetables, then cover and chill in the refrigerator for 24 to 48 hours.

The pickles can be stored in the refrigerator for 7 to 10 days.

If you have any extra pickling liquid, experiment with different fruits and vegetables you have around. This recipe makes delicious currant and raisin pickles that are perfect for salads, slaws, and snacks.

Homemade Chicken Stock

I make chicken stock every time I roast a chicken, but I also save and freeze random chicken scraps and bones from weeknight dinners. I simply combine these chicken scraps with some aromatics and simmer on the stove for a couple of hours.

Stock is forgiving and so if you're out of garlic, don't run to the store. If you have leeks, but no onions, throw them in the pot instead. Improvise.

Ingredients

Makes 1 quart (948L or 960g)

1	**chicken carcass**	
1–1½ pounds	**chicken bones and scraps (including skin)**	454–680g
2	**medium carrots, roughly chopped**	150g
2	**medium celery stalks, roughly chopped**	122g
1	**medium onion, roughly chopped**	255g
1 head	**garlic, halved**	50g
1 teaspoon	**whole black peppercorns**	2.75g
2 sprigs	**fresh thyme**	1g
1	**fresh bay leaf**	.25g
8 cups (1.9L)	**cold water**	1900g

1 Add all of the ingredients to a large stockpot. Cover with the cold water.

2 Bring to a boil over medium-high heat. Reduce the heat to low and cook, barely simmering with a few bubbles rising to the top, for 2 to 3 hours.

3 Remove from the heat. Pour the stock through a mesh strainer into a bowl or plastic container. Place the container of stock in an ice-water bath, then cover with plastic wrap or a lid and transfer to refrigerator to cool completely.

4 Skim fat off the top of the stock, if desired.

Store in the refrigerator for up to 1 week, and in the freezer for up to 2 months. Always reheat to a simmer before using.

This makes a rustic stock, so small quantities of chicken fat and bits of vegetables might remain. If you desire a more refined, clear stock, strain through cloth (I use plain white handkerchiefs rather than cheesecloth, because they are reusable) and then skim any fat once the stock has completely cooled in the refrigerator.

Homemade Beef Stock

Save leftover beef bones, preferably with a little meat, for
stock. Ask your butcher for marrow and other bones to supplement if you do not have enough, and
add a shank or an inexpensive cut of meat with bones.

Ingredients

Makes 1 quart (948L or 960g)

2 Tablespoons	**vegetable oil**	20g
2 pounds	**beef bones with meat**	907g
8 cups (1.9L)	**cold water, plus more as needed**	1900g
2	**medium carrots, roughly chopped**	150g
2	**medium celery stalks, roughly chopped**	122g
1	**medium onion, roughly chopped**	255g
1 head	**garlic, halved**	50g
1 teaspoon	**whole black peppercorns**	2.75g
2 sprigs	**fresh thyme**	1g
1	**fresh bay leaf**	.25g

*Store in the refrigerator for up to 1 week, and in the
freezer for up to 2 months. Always reheat to a simmer before using.*

1 Preheat the oven to 400°F (200°C).

2 Rub a roasting pan with the vegetable oil and
add the beef bones and meat to the pan. Roast
for 1 hour, rotating 180 degrees after 30 minutes.

3 Remove the pan from the oven and transfer the
bones and meat to large stockpot. Cover with
the cold water. Bring to a boil over medium-
high heat. Reduce the heat to low and cook,
barely simmering with a few bubbles rising to
the top, for 2 hours.

4 Add the carrots, celery, onion, garlic, peppercorns, thyme, and bay leaf to the pot. Add
hot water to the pot, if necessary, to cover
the bones and aromatics. Increase the heat
to medium-low and simmer gently for 1 hour.
The liquid should measure about 2 quarts (1.9L
or 1900g); if there is more, continue cooking
to reduce, and if there isn't enough, add more
water to make the proper amount.

5 Remove from the heat. Pour the stock through
a mesh strainer into a bowl or plastic container. Place the container of stock in an ice-water
bath, then cover with plastic wrap or a lid and
transfer to refrigerator to cool completely.

6 Skim fat off the top of the stock, if desired.

Homemade Vegetable Stock

I like to keep a plastic bag or other container in the freezer and add vegetable scraps to it over the course of a couple of weeks—the ends and peels from carrots, shallot roots, bits of celery, and other scraps tend to pile up while making other recipes. Stock is also a good way to use up vegetables that are fading fast in the crisper drawer. When the bag is full, I roast the vegetables and then make stock. If you need to make a stock right away, using whole fresh vegetables is always an option. Leeks are a great addition, but they are quite pungent, so use them judiciously to avoid overwhelming the stock. This stock is perfect for our Curried Winter Vegetable Pie (p. 268), for soups, and as a replacement for water when cooking rice.

Ingredients

Makes about 2 quarts (948L or 960g)

2 cups	**celery scraps**	240g		1 head	**garlic, halved horizontally across its equator**	50g
2 cups	**carrot scraps and peels**	256g		2 Tablespoons	**olive oil**	28g
2 cups	**onion scraps or 1 whole onion, roughly chopped**	300g		1 Tablespoon	**tomato paste**	15g
1 cup	**roughly chopped green leek tops and white root ends, thoroughly washed**	89g		1 teaspoon	**whole black peppercorns**	2.75g
				4 quarts (3.8L)	**water**	3520g
½ cup	**shallot scraps**	75g			**Kosher salt, to taste**	

Next page

HOMEMADE VEGETABLE STOCK

Continued

1   Preheat the oven to 350°F (180°C).

2   Combine all of the vegetables and the garlic in a roasting pan. Toss with the olive oil to prevent the vegetables from sticking to the pan. Roast for 50 to 60 minutes.

3   Transfer the roasted vegetables to a stockpot and add the tomato paste and peppercorns.

4   Add the water and bring to a boil, then reduce the heat to low and simmer until the liquid is reduced by roughly half, about 90 minutes. Season to taste with salt.

It is good for the vegetables to brown a little. The extra roasting step will add depth of flavor to the finished vegetable stock.

GOOD ADDITIONS TO STOCK

- Mushrooms and mushroom stems
- Thyme
- Parsley stems and leaves
- Tomatoes and tomato cores
- Fennel (use judiciously to avoid overwhelming the stock)
- Corn cobs
- Spicy peppers like jalapeño peppers
- Hearty greens like beet greens and chard
- Green beans
- Winter squash and squash skin

VEGETABLES TO AVOID FOR STOCK

- Turnips
- Cruciferous vegetables like cabbage and brussels sprouts
- Beets
- Artichokes
- Rutabagas
- Asparagus

SAUSAGES

Tell your butcher you are making sausage and need a mix

of pork shoulder and pork back fat in a 70/30 ratio. If you don't have a grinder, ask the butcher to grind the meat and fat for you. Avoid using packaged ground pork from the grocery store meat case, as it may contain a different fat ratio and is often ground too finely.

GOOD PRACTICES FOR GOOD SAUSAGE

Chill your mixer bowl and any attachments (paddle, grinder) in the freezer for at least one hour prior to using. Keeping the meat cold throughout the process is the first priority in sausage making.

Making sure your final mix of meat appears hairy and sticky (not smooth or shiny) will ensure the sausage holds together in a pleasant texture and is not dry or crumbly when cooking.

No stand mixer? Roll up your sleeves and prepare for an upper-body workout. Combine the ground pork, fat, salt, and seasonings in a chilled bowl and mix, folding and pressing constantly with gloved hands, for one minute. The seasonings should be evenly incorporated and the meat will be sticky. Add the liquid and mix vigorously with your hands for thirty seconds, or until the mixture looks almost hairy.

If you are grinding the meat at home: Chill the bowl, paddle, and grinder attachment of a stand mixer in the freezer for at least two hours. Combine the pork, fat, salt, and seasonings in another bowl and chill in the refrigerator for at least two hours, up to overnight. Or, you may freeze the seasoned meat for thirty minutes to one hour. Grind the pork and fat into the chilled bowl of the stand mixer and finish according to the recipe instructions.

Italian Sausage

Giardiniera, a staple Chicago condiment, is spicy mix of pickled peppers, fresh vegetables, and olive oil. We eat a lot of giardiniera—on everything. I had always put it on Italian sausages, but while working on our own recipe, it occurred to me to put it directly into the sausage. Brands such as Dell'Alpe and Mezzetta can be found at a variety of spice levels in your local supermarket (check the condiment aisle, near the olives or pickles). The relish version works best, but you can also buy the chunky variety and chop it up for the sausage. See p. 327 for more information on making sausage.

Ingredients

Makes 1 pound (454g)

1 Tablespoon	**fennel seeds**	5g	1½ teaspoons	**hot giardiniera relish**	6g
1½ teaspoons	**whole coriander seeds**	2g	1 teaspoon	**freshly ground black pepper**	2g
1 pound	**ground pork** (70% shoulder, 30% back fat)	454g	¾ teaspoon	**granulated sugar**	3g
2 teaspoons	**chopped fresh oregano**	3g	½ teaspoon	**red pepper flakes**	1g
2 teaspoons	**chopped fresh Italian parsley**	4g	1 clove	**garlic, minced**	5g
1½ teaspoons	**kosher salt**	3.5g	2 teaspoons	**red wine vinegar**	8g

Use within a few days or store frozen until ready to cook.

1 Chill the bowl and paddle attachment of a stand mixer in the refrigerator for at least 1 hour.

2 Place the fennel and coriander seeds in a cold, small, heavy skillet over medium heat.

3 Cook, shaking or stirring the seeds often to prevent burning, until the seeds are fragrant and starting to take on color, about 1 to 2 minutes. If the seeds start to smoke, remove them from the pan immediately. Transfer them to a bowl to cool.

4 Place the seeds in a coffee grinder and pulse until well ground.

5 Combine all of the ingredients except for the red wine vinegar in the chilled bowl of the stand mixer fitted with the chilled paddle attachment. Mix on Low for about 1 minute. The ingredients should be evenly incorporated and the meat will be sticky.

6 Add the vinegar and mix on Low for 1 more minute, or until the meat mixture looks almost hairy.

7 Sauté a small bit of the sausage in a small skillet. Taste and adjust seasonings as needed.

8 Wrap the raw sausage in parchment paper and then tightly in plastic wrap.

9 Chill overnight in the refrigerator.

Bratwurst

When my Grandma Jones's kitchen was bustling with

gossipy aunts, the kids weren't allowed underfoot. My cousins and I played near an upstairs vent so we could eavesdrop, but also so we could enjoy the scents of homemade German sausages wafting up. Every family makes its own special recipe. Inspired by my grandma, this is mine. While bratwurst is traditionally an encased sausage, we make ours loose so there's pork in every slice and every bite of our Oktoberfest Pie (p. 256). See p. 327 for more information on making sausage.

Ingredients

Makes 1 pound (454g)

1 pound	**ground pork (70% shoulder, 30% back fat)**	454g
1½ teaspoons	**kosher salt**	4.5g
2 teaspoons	**dried milk**	4g
½ teaspoon	**ground mace**	2g
½ teaspoon	**freshly ground white pepper**	2g
½ teaspoon	**ground ginger**	2g
½ teaspoon	**mustard powder**	2g
½ teaspoon	**ground cardamom**	2g
½ teaspoon	**ground nutmeg**	2g
3 Tablespoons (45mL)	**Oktoberfest beer, such as Spoetzel's Shiner Bock**	44g
1 Tablespoon	**heavy cream**	14g

1 Chill the bowl and paddle attachment of a stand mixer in the refrigerator for at least 1 hour.

2 Combine the ground pork and all the dry ingredients in the chilled bowl of the stand mixer fitted with the chilled paddle attachment. Mix on Low for about 1 minute, until the ingredients are evenly incorporated and the meat is sticky. Add the beer and cream and mix on Low for 1 more minute, or until the meat mixture looks almost hairy.

3 Sauté a small bit of the sausage in a small skillet. Taste and adjust seasonings as needed.

4 Wrap the raw sausage in parchment paper and then tightly in plastic wrap.

5 Chill overnight in the refrigerator.

Use within a few days or store frozen until ready to cook.

Mexican Chorizo

Traditional loose sausages, like Mexican chorizo, require
no casing, which makes them great for sausage-making beginners. A home cook can easily learn
basic techniques and play with unique flavor combinations before investing in tools like a grinder
and stuffer. See p. 327 for more information on making sausage.

Ingredients

Makes 1 pound (454g)

1 pound	**ground pork** **(70% shoulder, 30% back fat)**	454g
3 teaspoons	**sweet paprika**	9g
2 teaspoons	**finely chopped fresh oregano**	3g
1–1½ teaspoons	**cayenne pepper**	2–3g
1¼ teaspoons	**kosher salt**	4.5g
2	**garlic cloves, minced**	9g
½ teaspoon	**granulated sugar**	2g
½ teaspoon	**ground cumin**	1g
½ teaspoon	**freshly ground black pepper**	1g
¼ teaspoon	**ground nutmeg**	1g
1 Tablespoon	**red wine vinegar**	12g

1 Chill the bowl and paddle attachment of a stand mixer in the refrigerator for at least 1 hour.

2 Combine all of the ingredients except the red wine vinegar in the chilled bowl and mix on Low using the paddle attachment for about 1 minute. The seasonings should be evenly incorporated and the meat will be sticky.

3 Add the vinegar and mix on Low for 1 more minute, or until the meat mixture looks almost hairy.

4 Sauté a small bit of the chorizo in a small skillet. Adjust the seasonings if needed.

5 Wrap the sausage in parchment paper, then tightly in plastic wrap.

6 Chill overnight in the refrigerator.

Use within a few days, or store in the freezer for up to 1 month.

ACKNOWLEDGMENTS

This book was a lot of fun to write, and I need to thank some folks who helped to make it happen.

First of all I want to thank our farmers, because you can't make good pie without great produce.

To the whole Hoosier Mama crew, past and present: You signed on to my dream and did everything from painting the ceiling to baking pies at 3 a.m. to make it a reality. I know you never imagined a career in the kitchen meant peeling so many apples.

Special thanks to *Lindsay Zamora*, who cheerfully tested pies and kept the shop humming along so Allison and I could (mostly) meet our deadlines.

Thanks to our amazing customers. You sought us out and championed our tiny shop from the beginning. Occasionally, you even brought me dinner. Thank you so much! Of course, we couldn't be here without you.

To my dad—apparently love of pie is hereditary.

Finally, thanks to the fine folks at *Metropolis Coffee Company* for early encouragement, and for keeping us caffeinated enough to finish this!

—Paula

My husband Kris always insisted that we get a dishwasher. Halfway through the recipe-testing process, we finally did. I appreciate it (and him) every day.

My family has been unwavering in their support of my foray into food. My parents and sister have been instrumental throughout the writing process by reading drafts, calling with encouragement, and forgiving me for hunkering down to write during the holidays instead of flying home to visit. Thanks also to *the Kellys*, who have taken me under their wing in Chicago.

Thank you to my grandmothers, who taught me to cook, and to *my grandfathers*, who taught me to love eating.

Andrea Deibler, my go-to authority on butchery and a trusted friend since junior high school, provided her expertise in the meat department for savory pie recipes.

I appreciate the readers of drafts for their valuable comments and notes: *Abra Berens*, *Kelsey Coday*, and *Julie Lippmann*.

Thanks to recipe-and-taste-testers *Tom Hershewe* and *Brandon Parker*, for their helpful pulled pork feedback.

—Allison

REFERENCES

Boggiano, Angela. *Pie*, 48–49. London: Cassell Illustrated, 2006.

Bullard, Larcenia J. "SB 676—Official State Pie/Key Lime." *Florida House of Representatives*, June 20, 2006. http://www.myfloridahouse.gov/Sections/Bills/billsdetail.aspx?BillId=32043.

Canadian Minister of Health. "Healthy Living: Garlic-In-Oil." *It's Your Health*, February 18, 2009. http://www.hc-sc.gc.ca/hl-vs/iyh-vsv/food-aliment/garlic-ail-eng.php.

Caplow, Theodore, Louis Hicks, and Ben J. Wattenberg. *The First Measured Century: An Illustrated Guide to Trends in America, 1900-2000*, 13. Washington, D.C.: AEI, 2001.

Case Pie Company. *Chicago Loxias*, page 4. Advertisement. June 3, 1911.

Child, Julia. *Mastering the Art of French Cooking*, Volume 1. New York: Alfred A. Knopf, 1977.

Chu, Louisa. "The Truth About Pumpkin Pie." *Moveable Feast: Chicago*, WBEZ 91.5, November 11, 2011. http://www.wbez.org/blog/louisa-chu/2011-11-23/truth-about-pumpkin-pie-94245

Curtin, Kathleen, and Sandra L. Oliver. *Giving Thanks: Thanksgiving Recipes and History, from Pilgrims to Pumpkin Pie*. New York: Clarkson Potter/Publishers, 2005.

Edge, John T. "How the Microplane Grater Escaped the Garage." *The New York Times*, January 11, 2011.

Eicher, Lovina, and Kevin Williams. The Amish Cook at *Home: Simple Pleasures of Food, Family, and Faith*, 141. Kansas City, MO: Andrews McMeel Pub. LLC, 2008.

Fitch, Noel Riley. *Appetite for Life: The Biography of Julia Child*. Random House Digital, Inc., 2012.

Harrigan, Edward. "Chicago Eats Pie by the Acre; Would Roof County Building." *Chicago Daily Tribune*, February 14, 1909.

Hess, Karen. *Martha Washington's Booke of Cookery and Booke of Sweetmeats*. New York: Columbia University Press, 1996.

Highlands Today. "Key Lime Pie Purists Demand the Real Thing." *Highlands Today*, January 30, 2011. http://www2.highlandstoday.com/news/columns/2011/jan/30/key-lime-pie-purists-demand-real-thing-ar-307722/

Martin, Chuck. "Derby Pie was born 50 years ago." *The Cincinnati Inquirer,* April 28, 2004. Accessed December 13, 2012. http://www.enquirer.com/editions/2004/04/28/tem_pie28main.html

Mazurek, Tim. "Apple Cider Cream Pie." *Lottie + Doof.* Last modified October 26, 2011. http://www.lottieanddoof.com/2011/10/apple-cider-cream-pie/

McGee, Harold. "Basic Kitchen Resources: Water, the Pantry, and the Refrigerator." In *Keys to Good Cooking: A Guide to Making the Best of Foods and Recipes,* 17-41. New York: Penguin, 2010.

McGee, Harold. "Fruits and Vegetables, Herbs and Spices." In *On Food and Cooking: The Science and Lore of the Kitchen,* 221-25. First Collier Books Edition ed. New York: Collier, 1988.

McLagan, Jennifer. "Butter: Worth It." In *Fat: An Appreciation of a Misunderstood Ingredient, with Recipes,* 13-65. Berkeley, CA: Ten Speed, 2008.

Medrich, Alice. *Pure Dessert.* New York: Artisan, 2007.

Neil, Marion Harris. *The Story of Crisco.* Cincinnati: Procter & Gamble, 1914.

Nichols, Nell B., editor. *Farm Journal's Complete Pie Book.* New York: Doubleday & Company, Inc., 1965.

Nold, James, Jr. "Pie Fight Derby." Saveur, October 16, 2000. Accessed December 13, 2012. http://www.saveur.com/article/Kitchen/Pie-Fight-Derby

Perelman, Deb. "homemade wafers + icebox cupcakes." *Smitten Kitchen.* Last modified March 25, 2009. http://smittenkitchen.com/blog/2009/03/homemade-chocolate-wafers-icebox-cupcakes/

"Pumpkin | Archives | Aggie Horticulture." *Pumpkin | Archives | Aggie Horticulture.* Accessed November 6, 2012. http://aggie-horticulture.tamu.edu/archives/parsons/vegetables/pumpkin.html

Ramsey, MD, Drew, and Tyler Graham. "How Vegetable Oils Replaced Animal Fats in the American Diet." *The Atlantic,* April 26, 2012. Accessed June 20, 2012. http://www.theatlantic.com/health/archive/2012/04/how-vegetable-oils-replaced-animal-fats-in-the-american-diet/256155/.

Sanders, Lisa, M.D. "Diagnosis: A Red Scare." *The New York Times Magazine,* February 20, 2011. Accessed August 20, 2012. http://www.nytimes.com/2011/02/20/magazine/20fob-diagnosis-t.html?_r=2.

Schneider, Edward. "Warning: Measure Your Salt." *Diner's Journal Blog, The New York Times,* April 28, 2010. http://dinersjournal.blogs.nytimes.com/2010/04/28/warning-measure-your-salt/.

United States Department of Agriculture. "Shell Eggs from Farm to Table." Last modified April 20, 2011. http://www.fsis.usda.gov/Fact_Sheets/Focus_On_Shell_Eggs/index.asp#3.

United States Department of Health and Human Services. "Safe Minimum Cooking Temperatures." *FoodSafety.gov: Your Gateway to Federal Food Safety Information.* http://www.foodsafety.gov/keep/charts/mintemp.html.

RESOURCES

INGREDIENTS

BUTCHERS

Visit the Members page of the Butcher's Guild to find a quality butcher in your area. We visit the Butcher & Larder in Chicago.

www.thebutchersguild.org

CHOCOLATE

You can find any chocolate you need on Amazon. Try Callebaut, Cacao Barry, Guittard, Scharffen Berger, or Valrhona.

www.amazon.com

www.callebaut.com

www.cacao-barry.com

www.guittard.com

www.scharffenberger.com

www.valrhona-chocolate.com

COARSE-GRAINED SUGAR (DISCO SUGAR)

We use large (size AA) decorative sugar crystals.

www.amazon.com

www.preparedpantry.com

DRIED BEANS AND NEW MEXICAN RED CHILE POWDER

Rancho Gordo

www.ranchogordo.com

ESPRESSO BEANS

We use Metropolis Coffee Company's Redline Espresso in our Red Line Espresso Cream Pie (p. 136).

www.metropoliscoffee.com/shop

FARMERS' MARKETS AND RESOURCES FOR LOCAL, SUSTAINABLE FOOD

We visit Chicago's Green City Market, where we often pick up produce from Ellis Family Farms,

Leaning Shed Farm, and River Valley Ranch & Kitchens.

www.greencitymarket.org

www.ellisfamilyfarm.com

www.leaningshed.com

www.rivervalleykitchens.com

You can find farmers' markets and food local to your area using the links below.

search.ams.usda.gov/farmersmarkets

www.localharvest.org

FLOUR

www.heartlandmill.com

www.kingarthurflour.com

FRUIT PURÉES

Ravifruit

www.amazon.com

www.ravifruit.com/en/index.htm

GELATIN SHEETS, SILVER STRENGTH

www.modernistpantry.com

www.amazon.com

GOLDEN SYRUP

Lyle's

www.lylesgoldensyrup.com

www.worldmarket.com

MAPLE SYRUP

Burton's Maplewood Farm

www.burtonsmaplewoodfarm.com

PERSIMMON PULP

Tuttle Orchards

store.tuttleorchards.com

PORK BREAKFAST SAUSAGE (ILLINOIS AND INDIANA ONLY)

C&D Family Farms

http://cdfamilyfarms.com

SPICES, DRIED CHILIES, SPICE BLENDS, ROSEWATER, ALMOND EXTRACT

The Spice House

www.thespicehouse.com

TAPIOCA STARCH

www.amazon.com

www.kingarthurflour.com

VANILLA BEAN PASTE

Nielsen-Massey

www.amazon.com

www.nielsenmassey.com

www.surlatable.com

www.thespicehouse.com

WOOD CHIPS FOR SMOKERS

www.cabelas.com

EQUIPMENT

It doesn't take a lot of special equipment or high-tech gadgets to make good pie, but here are some tools we find useful.

CHERRY PITTER

For small jobs, any sturdy handheld pitter should do the trick. They are available at most kitchen supply stores, and even some grocery stores during cherry season. Cherry-pie fanatics will want the Leifheit Cherry Stoner, available at kitchen supply stores, Lehman's (lehmans.com), and on Amazon.

CRUST GUARDS

Crust guards (or shields) are helpful for getting an even, golden-brown crust without burning the crimp or edge of your pie—but finding the correct size is problematic. We don't recommend silicone shields, despite their sizing flexibility; they tend to fall off the pie during baking, and removing or moving them can be difficult without accidentally disturbing a smooth-topped custard or quiche. Your best option is a metal or aluminum crust guard used in conjunction with foil or a modified foil pan. We cut out the center of a foil pan and invert it over the pie, then put the guard over the top to cover the edge and weigh down the foil pan.

DIGITAL SCALE

We love Escali digital scales (escali.com)—we use the Alimento Pro, which has a stainless steel weighing surface that's removable for easy cleanup. It's a heavy-duty scale for frequent use. For home cooks, important features are weight capacity (up to 10 pounds), weight increments in grams and ounces, and a tare function. A good, basic kitchen scale should cost around $50 from Amazon or a kitchen supply store.

HAND-CRANK APPLE PEELER

If you make more than a couple of apple pies, you need a hand-crank apple peeler. Its 18th-century technology will save you hours of peeling and coring. The old-fashioned, cast-iron version with the new-fangled suction cup base attaches easily to any table or counter. The traditional clamp model lasts forever. We used them in the shop for years before upgrading to an industrial-size, but still hand-crank, peeler. It is available at kitchen supply stores and through many online retailers. Lehman's (lehmans.com) carries several wonderfully low-tech options.

HANDHELD CITRUS JUICER

Simple, inexpensive, and efficient, citrus juicers come in three different sizes for oranges, lemons, and limes. Choose the stainless steel or brightly colored enameled versions; avoid uncoated aluminum models that can react with acidic citrus juice. Available at kitchen supply stores, some grocery stores, and Amazon.

HEATPROOF SPATULA

A high-heat spatula or scraper, resistant up to 500°F (260°C), should be a staple in your pie-making kitchen. Rubbermaid (rubbermaid.com) and Le Creuset (lecreuset.com) make great spatulas that are flexible, but durable, and dishwasher safe.

MESH TEA BALL INFUSER

Basic tea infusers can be found in the kitchen sections of most major retailers, including Target and Walmart. Online retailers (like Amazon) and specialty stores will have more options. Our favorite, a 3-inch infuser, came from a tiny store in Chicago's Chinatown neighborhood.

MICROPLANE ZESTER

Invented in the '90s as a fine wood rasp, the Microplane zester was strictly a woodworking tool—until the frustrated wife of a Canadian hardware-store owner grabbed it one day to add orange zest to cake batter. Its row of tiny teeth removes the peel from all kinds of citrus and leaves the bitter pith behind. Use it to finely grate chocolate and nutmeg too. There are dozens of different versions and sizes, but the Classic Zester works for most recipes. Available at kitchen supply stores, the gadget aisle of upscale grocery stores, and at microplane.com.

ROLLING PIN

Choose a style to suit your preferences and needs. Standard pins have handles on either end, and those work fine. At the pie shop we use a column-style wooden pin that is uniform in circumference with no handles. These take some adjustment, since you roll using your palms rather than gripping small handles with your fingers. We feel like you have more control over the pressure you put on the dough, and without so many nooks and crannies, these pins are easy to keep clean. French pins are tapered and we sometimes use them for rolling out smaller rounds of dough. Vic Firth (vicfirth. com) makes quality rolling pins at a reasonable price.

PARCHMENT PAPER

Bakeries and professional kitchens use flat sheets of parchment because they fit the pan exactly, eliminating the need to cut from a roll—and saving the dishwasher a lot of work! Anyone who has dealt with the annoying ends of parchment curling up knows it is worth investing in a box of flat, pan-lining parchment paper. A reusable alternative, less expensive than silicone liners, is the Regency line of heat-resistant cookie sheet liners, which can be cut to fit your pans. You can find both flat parchment liners and the reusable Regency liners on Amazon.

TOMATO CORER

I've never used one of these to core a tomato—a paring knife works just fine—but I do use it to remove the core and stem from halved pears before I chop them. It's also great for removing any bits of apple core missed by the hand-crank peeler. Available at kitchen supply stores, grocery stores, and on Amazon. The inexpensive versions work best.

VEGETABLE PEELER

An everyday tool, the Kuhn Rikon Original Swiss Peeler is the best investment you can make for your kitchen—for less than $5. These peelers are durable, effective, and comfortable to use. Available at kitchen specialty stores and on Amazon.

INDEX

ABOUT THE AUTHORS

Paula Haney (right) founded Hoosier Mama Pie Company in 2005. An Indiana native, she was formerly the head pastry chef at Pili.Pili, One Sixtyblue, and Trio, where she worked with Grant Achatz, Shawn McClain, and Della Gossett. Haney and her husband live in Chicago, Illinois.

Allison Scott (left) works at Hoosier Mama Pie Company and develops their savory pies. She contributed to the *Soup & Bread Cookbook*, by Matha Bayne (Agate Publishing). She lives in Chicago, Illinois.